Jan Hedh

Photography by Ulf Widell

Translation by Stine Skarpnes Osttveit

SWEDISH COOKIES, TARTS, AND PIES

Skyhorse Publishing

All inquiries should be addressed to Skyhorse Publishing, 307 West 36th Street, 11th Floor, New York, NY 10018.
Skyhorse Publishing books may be purchased in bulk at special discounts for sales promotion, corporate gifts, fund-raising, or educational purposes.
Special editions can also be created to specifications.
For details, contact the Special Sales Department, Skyhorse Publishing, 307 West 36th Street, 11th Floor, New York, NY 10018 or
info@skyhorsepublishing.com.

Skyhorse® and Skyhorse Publishing® are registered trademarks of Skyhorse Publishing, Inc.®, a Delaware corporation.
Visit our website at www.skyhorsepublishing.com.

10 9 8 7 6 5 4 3 2 1
Library of Congress Cataloging-in-Publication Data is available on file.
ISBN: 978-1-61608-826-2

Printed in China

FOREWORD:
MY LOVE FOR THE PASTRY CHEF PROFESSION

I decided to create this book because I feel that so many of the classic Swedish pastries have become standardized and taste exactly the same everywhere. It seems important to preserve our culture of the fine pastries one could find in bakeries in previous times and that you can still find in finer bakeries today. In this book I share the recipes of many of my personal favorites. You might feel that some recipes are lacking, but my initial ambition was that most should be represented.

I have tried to remember all the cakes and pastries that I believe are part of our cultural heritage. This work became a journey through time for me, and it took me back to all of the places I've worked and all the people with whom I've worked or that in one way or another have meant a lot for my professional career.

At Olof Viktors Bageri in Glemminge you can find a selection of these classic pastries, and they are baked with care and real ingredients. Our best customer is Christer Alfredsson, who gladly treats himself to a delicious pastry with a glass of good wine. I am certain that many of these pastries will continue to be part of our selection for years to come.

Similarly, at the Chocolater Jan Hedh and Maria Escalante in Malmö, the quality of the chocolate and pastries is always excellent. All of the production is overseen by the chocolate specialist Maria Escalante, originally from Peru and raised with first-class chocolate and real pastries that her grandmother and mother would make in Lima. Her sons Jan Erik and Henry are in charge of the actual chocolate production; Jan Erik has been with me since he was fourteen years old.

When I first started as a pastry chef apprentice 46 years ago, I had already spent one summer working at the Kramers Conditori in Sweden and had practiced the profession at the Residens Schweizeri, where the chief pastry chef Carl Andersson reigned in an underground kingdom of pastries. At that time you could find pâtisseries and bakeries on every street corner in my hometown, Malmö. Brauns Konditori at Gustaf Adolf's Place was considered the very best of them all.

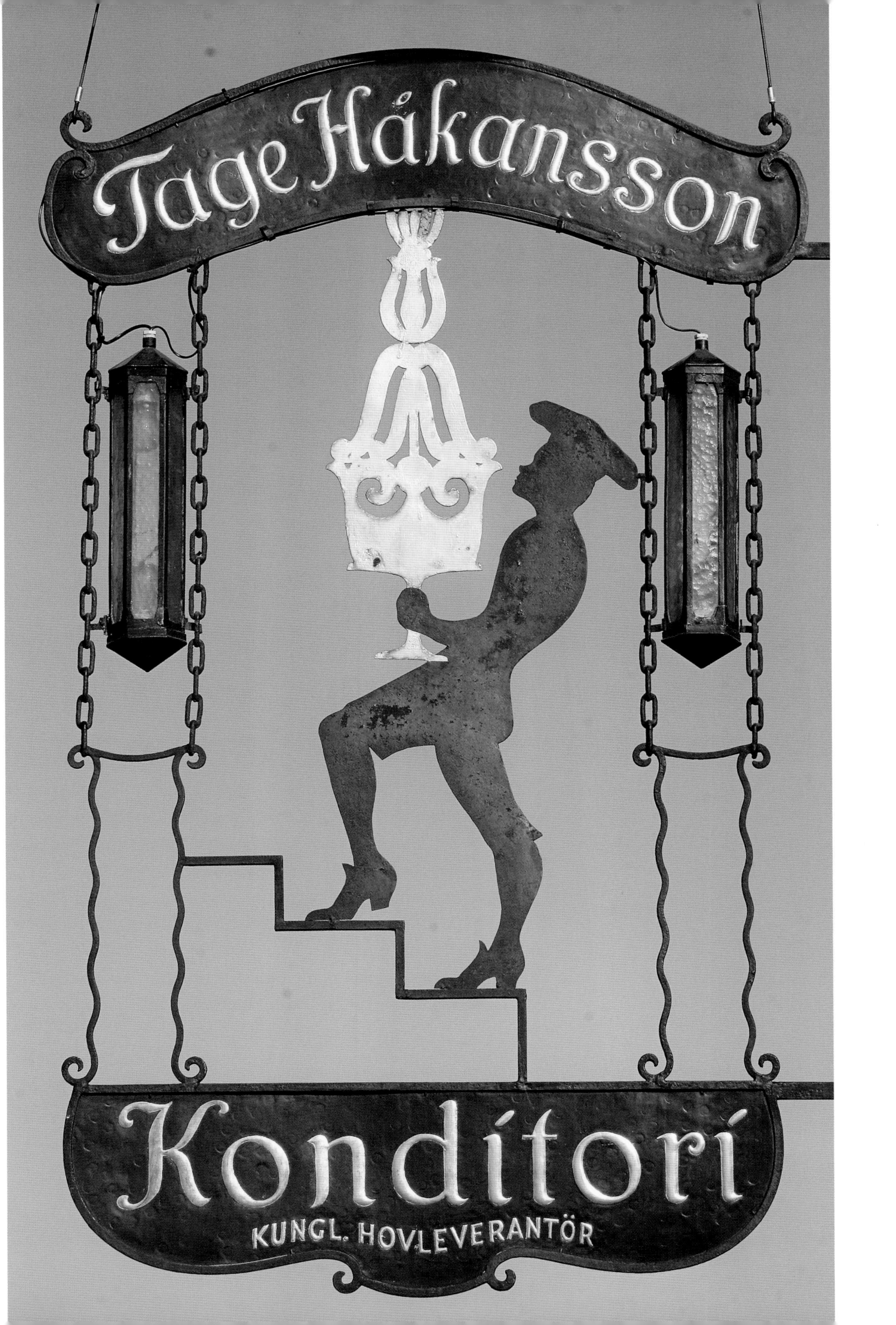

Tage Håkansson
Konditori
KUNGL. HOVLEVERANTÖR

I started as an apprentice at the Conditori Heidi in Limhamn. Filip Liljekvist was the main chef. Since Filip had previously worked in Denmark, we baked both classic Swedish and Danish pastries. I especially remember the kirsch buns that tasted amazing with real almond paste made with Spanish sweet almonds and a pinch of bitter almonds. The apprenticeship lasted for 5 years and earned me a journeyman's certificate.

My next learning experience was at Blekingborgs Conditori, where Curt Lindgren was the main chef. He taught me all the Swedish classics and was very meticulous with both the taste and look of every pastry. The pastry chef Jan Gunnar Malmberg owned the pâtisserie, and he was especially talented with butter-dough pastries. They both taught me the classic basic recipes, including breads, as both Kurt and Jan Gunnar had previously worked at Sundets Bageri in Malmö, which specialized in bread.

I completed my journeyman's exam at the pâtisserie trade school in Uppsala. The school was owned by the Swedish Pâtisserie Association and enrolled students from all over Scandinavia.

At the pâtisserie trade school one attended a three-month course and every fourteen days you would complete a partial exam, six exams altogether.

The tables would be prepared anonymously, and some pastry chefs from Uppsala would judge them. The principal of the school was the famous pastry chef Migg Sporndly with a background at the world famous pâtisserie Confeserie Sprungli at the Paradeplatz in Zurich. It was deemed one of the world's best pâtisseries with a long tradition and the absolute best selection of pastries. If you are ever in Switzerland, do not miss this place! Walter Hartfelder and Algot Svensson were the other teachers at the school.

Migg taught both theory and marzipan modeling, as well as how to make beautiful brittle and cornucopias. Walter taught classic pastries and introduced us to the exciting world of chocolate and pralines. Walter is the only teacher that's left; we still keep in touch by phone, and sometimes we meet and talk about the pastry chef profession that we both love so much.

Algot Svensson came from my hometown, Malmö, where he was a pastry chef at Brauns Conditori. All of his five brothers were pastry chefs in Malmö as well, so, needless to say, it was in his blood. Algot specialized in tart decoration and taught my favorite subject, caramel handling. I wish that such a fine education with such high quality teachers still existed in Sweden.

When I was young, my idols weren't soccer players, but talented pastry chefs. In Malmö, for instance, the pastry chef Gunnar Svensson was the very best at beautiful caramel work, which he would ornament the windows with. The pastry chef Calle Widell was the marzipan king, and I really admired his Christmas displays. At the Residens Schweizeri the pastry chef Curt Andersson would demonstrate his skill through beautiful cocoa paintings. At the Konditori Hollandia in Malmö, Rolf Augustsson took care of the classic Swedish pastry tradition.

In Stockholm, pastry chefs Helmut Rosenthal and Oscar Barregard represented two important role models for me as a professional. Eve Rundberg was the chief pastry chef at Filips, and I admired his chocolate sculptures. In Gothenburg, the pastry chef Birger Lundgren, a teacher at the school there, became a rolemodel with beautiful caramel work as his specialty.

At the Savoy Hotel in Malmö, the pastry master Yngve Malmqvist became my teacher of restaurant pâtisseries and fine pastries. Yngve was a talented professional; moreover, he was a specialist when it came to decorating and creating beautiful caramel works.

After the Savoy Hotel, I moved on to the Coba School in Basil, the Richemonte School in Lucerne, and the restaurant pâtisserie program at the Montana School in Lucerne. Afterward I worked at several different pâtisseries in Switzerland, such as Confiserie Hanold in Zurich and Confiserie Brandli in Basil and I interned at the Confiserie Sprungli in Zurich.

Here I will end the story of my background and the love of pastries that was conveyed to me by the best professionals of the time during my basic pastry chef education. I hope that I have managed to create a book that aptly shares some of the knowledge and experience I've had the pleasure of taking part of, developing, as well as passing on throughout a long professional life.

I wish to thank photographer Ulf Widell for his excellent photographs of my pasties, and a special thank you goes to the *chef garde manger* Sabina Ceazar, who helped bake during the summer of 2009.

I dedicate this book to my mother, who passed in 2006, and I thank her for teaching me to enjoy good pastries and well-made food, which has been so important to me.

Confectioner and Pastry Chef Jan Hedh

BEFORE YOU BEGIN

- Always use first-class ingredients for your pastries.

- Never substitute margarine for butter, and use fresh, good, unsalted butter.

- Make sure that you buy eggs from cage-free and happy hens, which will be reflected in the quality of the eggs.

- Never buy industrial butterdough or puff pastry that is made with margarine instead of butter; oddly enough it is still called a "butterdough."

- Use regular, white, all-purpose flour for cakes and pastries. For bread you need wheat flour with more gluten, while cakes will become chewy and hard if the wheat flour is too tough.

- Always use fine quality chocolate. Personally, I prefer to use Valrhona chocolate from France as I like that best; it has the finest quality with a high cocoa content. Valrhona chocolate costs a bit more that regular chocolate, but it tastes so much better.

- Replace salt with fleur de sel (sea salt from salt beds in France)—the finest and best salt there is.

Vanilla—the Most Important Spice for a Pastry Chef

Preferably use Tahitian vanilla or vanilla from Madagascar, for instance bourbon vanilla. Bourbon vanilla is the classic vanilla; Tahitian vanilla has a somewhat sweeter, rounder flavor. A high-quality vanilla bean should be long and sturdy with a strong aroma. White, needle-like crystals should occasionally appear on the bean. The black seeds are rather flavorless; it is the quality of the bean that determines the taste. Store vanilla beans in an airtight container; if they dry up, they lose their aroma.

Butter

Butter is one of the most important ingredients when you bake. In Sweden the selection of butter is quite narrow; for the regular consumer, you can really only choose among normally salted butter, extra salted butter, and unsalted butter. For professionals there is also the choice of concentrated butter (also called clarified butter), which is lactose-free. I mostly use unsalted butter for my baking.

CHOCOLATE TECHNIQUE

Valrhona Chocolate

Valrhona is considered the best quality of chocolate, and the highest varieties are called "Grands Crus de Chocolate." Today you may find Valrhona chocolate all over Sweden in chocolate specialty stores and from spice vendors. You may, of course, use another kind of chocolate as well, but I think Valrhona is the best.

Tempering

Not many achievements within gastronomy can be credited to England, but in 1847 the first chocolate cake was made in Bristol by the chemist Joseph Fry, so you may say that the issues concerning properly tempering chocolate were solved there. In other words, we needed a chemist to solve the problem of the crystals in cocoa butter.

In order to dip cakes and biscuits in chocolate, you have to learn to temper the chocolate, or rather, the cocoa butter in the chocolate. It is solely the cocoa butter that is affected by the temperature. If you do not temper chocolate properly, it becomes grey and flat, and it won't solidify the way it should.

Reasons to Temper Chocolate

The chocolate gets:
- Beautiful color
- Powerful crunchiness and hardness
- Soft, melting texture
- Ability to shrink, which allows it to let go of pans and cups

These desirable characteristics are dependent on the treatment of the cocoa butter. If tempered wrong, you may risk
- Grey chocolate
- Grainy and short texture
- Quick melting at touch
- Chocolate that doesn't shrink and thus sticks to pans and cups

Cakes and pastries to be dipped in chocolate should be kept at a temperature of about 68 °F (20 °C) in order to create a pretty and shiny surface.

Never dip anything cold in chocolate, because it will turn matte and grey as it stiffens from the inside and not the outside. Biscuits with buttercream should be cooled down and then be left in room temperature for about 30 minutes before you dip them.

Various kinds of chocolate needs to be tempered differently. White chocolate and milk chocolate have lower melting points than dark chocolate, and the tempering should be done at lower temperatures. They should not be heated past 118 °F (48 °C), as the milk protein casein "binds" at 129 °F (54 °C), and at that point the chocolate is ruined.

Equipment

When you temper chocolate you need to be in control of the various temperatures. You therefore need to use a thermometer that will show the temperature up to 122 °F (50 °C). A regular oven thermometer works fine. Furthermore, you need a small marble slab, a microwave, a putty knife, and a plastic, microwave-safe bowl to melt the chocolate in.

Melt the chocolate in the microwave, never directly on the stove, and watch it very carefully so that it doesn't burn. Stir often, and try not to use metal objects. You may also melt the chocolate in a double boiler as people used to do. In that case, avoid dampness and stir often as the water may quickly reach temperatures of 175–195 °F (80–90 °C).

Method 1—The Seed Method

This method is a good choice if you do not have a marble slab, but the shine will always turn out better if you do the classic tempering on a marble slab. The reason is that you mix in too much air during all of the stirring and the less air in the chocolate, the better the shine is.

1. Finely chop the chocolate.
2. Warm half to 118–122 °F (48–50 °F) for dark chocolate, 113 °F (45 °C) for milk chocolate, and 104 °F (40 °C) for white chocolate.
3. Stir in the rest of the chocolate.
4. Stir until the temperature reaches 80–82 °F (27–28 °C) for dark chocolate, 78–80 °F (26–27 °C) for milk chocolate, and 77–78 °F (25–26 °C) for white chocolate.
5. Then heat up to 88–90 °F (31–32 °C) for dark chocolate, 84–86 °F (29–30 °C) for milk chocolate, and 82–84 °F (28–29 °C) for white chocolate. The easiest and best way is to warm the chocolate in a microwave. Warm for 30 seconds at the time, control the temperature, and stir in between each time.

Method 2—Classic "Tabling"

This is the most common method among professionals.

1. Warm the chocolate to the right temperature according to the kind of chocolate you are using.
2. Pour three-fourths of the chocolate on a marble slab.
3. Stroke back and forth with a spatula until the chocolate starts to stiffen.

4. Scrape the chocolate off the plate, place back into the bowl with the remaining chocolate, and blend well.
5. Warm while stirring to the right temperature.

Dark Chocolate

Warm to 118–122 °F (48–50 °C), cool to 80–82 °F (27–28 °C), and later reheat to 88-90 °F (31–32 °C)

Milk Chocolate

Warm to 113 °F (45 °C), cool to 78–80 °F (26–27 °F), reheat to 84–86 °F (29–30 °C)

White Chocolate

Warm to 104 °F (40 °C), cool to 77–78 °F (25–26 °C), reheat to 82–84 °F (28–29 °C)

Time—Stirring—Temperature

It is very important that you are meticulous with these three things. If you are careless with this, the tempering is impossible.

There are three fat crystals in the cocoa butter: alpha, beta, and gamma. The goal of tempering is to make the crystals as small as possible. Only the beta shape is stable. The others are unstable and have lower melting points as well as a tendency to become stable crystals with time, which will create grey spots. It is therefore important to control the process so that only the stable beta crystals remain in the chocolate. This happens through tempering.

The shine depends solely on the position of the crystals – the flatter the crystals are situated against each other, the better the shine.

1/2 lb (245 g) dark chocolate, Valrhona Grand Cru Guanaja (When I specify Valrhona chocolate, this is because my experience is based in this chocolate. The taste sensation is controlled by the chocolate variety and the cocoa content and influences the texture of ganache for pastries. If you wish to use a different chocolate, see the diagram below.)

10.6 oz (300 g) heavy whipping cream
1.75 oz (50 g) glucose or honey

DAY 1
1. Finely chop the chocolate and place it in a plastic bowl.
2. Bring the cream to a boil with glucose or honey and empty it on top of the chocolate while still boiling.
3. Stir with a plastic spoon or hand mixer into a homogeneous and elastic ganache.
4. Pour into a bowl, cover with plastic wrap, and let it sit in room temperature overnight.

DAY 2
5. Fill a decorating bag with the ganache and add to various pastries. It is perfect to pipe on the second day.

BASIC RECIPES

Pâtisserie Ganache (also called truffle base)

Ganache for baking is an emulsion with a mayonnaise-like texture. It should be soft and smooth, easy to pipe, and easy to spread, but it should maintain its shape in various fillings for tea-breads and petits-fours.

Amount of chocolate depending on kind and cocoa content:

Araguani 8.3 oz (235 g)	Extra Amer 8.8 oz (250 g)
Guanaja 8.6 oz (245 g)	Caraque 10.6 oz (300 g)
Porcelana 8.6 oz (245 g)	Jivara Lactée milk chocolate 15.9
Pur Caribe 8.8 oz (250 g)	oz (450 g)
Manjari 9 oz (255 g)	Ivoire, white chocolate 20.3 oz
Extra bitter 9.5 oz (270 g)	(575 g)

Glazing Ganache

7 oz (200 g) dark chocolate, preferably Valrhona Grand Cru
   Guanaja 70%
2.6 oz (75 g) milk 3%
1.2 oz (35 g) heavy whipping cream 40%
0.9 oz (25 g) sugar
0.9 oz (25 g) honey
0.9 oz (25 g) butter

1. Finely chop the chocolate and place it in a plastic
   bowl. Melt it in the microwave to a temperature of
   about 95–104 °F (35–40 °C).
2. Bring milk, cream, sugar, and honey to a boil and
   empty it over the chocolate while boiling.
3. Mix the ganache smooth with a hand mixer.
4. Lastly mix in the butter and cover the ganache with
   plastic wrap until use.

Vanilla Cream

Crème pâtisserie is the French term for vanilla cream. In
Sweden we call it pastry cream. The cream was first
mentioned in pâtisserie literature during the 1600s in the
book *La Cusine La Pâtisserie Varenne*, but it was not flavored
with vanilla then. The vanilla cream is one of the most
important creams for chefs and pastry chefs, and I practiced
a lot during my apprenticeship. Every afternoon we would
boil another batch for the next morning.

Cold-whipped cream with vanillin instead of real vanilla
bean is a sad cheat that is unfortunately served in many
bakeries. Fresh baked vanilla hearts or butterdough puffs with
a generous amount of vanilla cream are fantastically delicious.

17.6 oz (500 g) milk 3% (2 ½ cups)
1 vanilla bean
4.2 oz (120 g) egg yolk (approx. 6)
4.5 oz (125 g) sugar
1.4 oz (40 g) cornstarch
0.9 oz (25 g) unsalted butter

1. Pour the milk into a saucepan with a thick bottom.
2. Cut the vanilla bean lengthwise. Scrape the seeds into the milk. Add the bean.
3. Bring the milk to a boil. Remove the saucepan from the stove; let it sit and stew for 10–15 minutes. Remove the vanilla bean.
4. Whisk yolks, sugar, and cornstarch until light and airy in a bowl.
5. Pour the milk in the egg mixture while whisking. Whisk until smooth.
6. Pour the blend back into the saucepan. Warm while carefully stirring until the cream has come to a proper boil.
7. Add the butter. Remove the cream from the stove and whisk until smooth.
8. Pass the freshly boiled cream through a sieve into a low pan.
9. Cool the cream as quickly as possible, preferably in an ice-cold water bath. The quicker the cooling is, the longer the cream will keep. Cover the pan with plastic wrap.

Storage:
The cream will keep in the fridge for 1–2 days. You may freeze leftover vanilla cream if you do it quickly. Bring it to a boil once more in a microwave when you need to use it, so that it binds again.

GOOD TO KNOW
If the vanilla cream "lets go" and has a loose texture, it means that the cornstarch hasn't cooked properly and the starch has not gelatinized enough. You can use all-purpose flour instead of cornstarch if you wish.

The protein of the yolk also contributes to the thickening/coagulating of the cream.

Real Vanilla Sugar
Never use vanillin sugar for your pastries or mine; make your own vanilla sugar or buy something that you are certain is the real deal.

2 vanilla beans
8.8 oz (250 g) granulated sugar

1. Cut the vanilla beans lengthwise and scrape the seeds out with a knife.
2. Mix the sugar with the beans and the seeds in a food processor or mixer until it looks like powdered sugar with black dots.
3. Sift through a sieve.

If you wish to make vanilla sugar with vanilla beans you've already used, which I always do, clean and dry the vanilla beans, and mix 3.5 oz (100 g) dried vanilla beans with 2 lb (900 g) sugar into powder and sift through a sieve.

Store the vanilla sugar in an airtight container with a lid.

Fondant
Fondant means melting in French. Through tempering the sugar crystals become smaller, which provides a melting feel. The glucose makes the sugar bind, obtain a smooth texture, and form smaller crystals.

Some chefs also add cream of tartar, which inverts the fondant (makes it softer) and makes it runny in pralines.

Fondant has a nice shine, more so than a so-called water glaze, which consists of water and powdered sugar; but if you overheat it, the shine will be lost. For glazing pastries, such as mazarin, petits-fours, and Swiss tea-breads, you warm the fondant to 86–104 °F (30–40 °C).

It is important to first brush the pastries you wish to glaze with apricot icing (see p.17). If you don't, the pastry will absorb the water from the fondant and the glaze "dies" and it will lose its shine.

7 oz (200 g) water
17.6 oz (500 g) sugar
3.5 oz (100 g) glucose (corn syrup)

1. Pour the water in a saucepan. Add the sugar while whisking.
2. Place the saucepan on the stove and warm on low heat so that the sugar dissolves properly. Remove any foam with a tea strainer.
3. Add the glucose.
4. Boil on the highest setting. Continuously brush the sugar crystals from the inside of the saucepan with a brush dipped in cold water. Placing a lid on top, slightly ajar, will have the same effect.
5. As soon as the syrup reaches 244 °F (118 °C), empty it onto a water resistant surface, preferably a marble slab or a well-cleaned countertop.
6. Sprinkle cold water on the syrup so that it doesn't form a crust.
7. After about 5 minutes, when the syrup has cooled, you may work it with a spatula until the glaze whitens.

Storage:

Place the glaze in a glass jar and spray water on the surface. Cover with an airtight lid and keep in the fridge. It will keep for weeks.

If you are using the fondant for glazing, warm it carefully to 86–104 °F (30–40 °C) and add syrup if it is too thick, see below. Never make it thinner with solely water; if you do the glaze will lose its shine.

Apricot Icing

Used as a base for glazed pastries and to brush on butter-dough pastries with fruit.

3.5 oz (100 g) apricot jam, strained without fruit bits (see, for instance, apricot jam in my book *The Jam and Marmalade Bible*)
0.9 oz (25 g) lemon juice
0.9 oz (25 g) sugar
0.9 oz (25 g) water

1. Bring all of the ingredients to a boil. Then simmer on low heat until the mass forms a thick jelly.
2. Perform a jelly-test by slipping a drop on a plate. Feel it after 1 minute; it should be firm and not feel sticky.

French Buttercream

Unfortunately, buttercream has gotten a bad reputation, because many bakeries use margarine instead of butter. People may think it's unethical to call something butter-cream when it doesn't even contain butter. The butterdough has suffered the same problem, which can also be made with margarine in less meticulous bakeries and the industry. When buttercream is made right, it is a delicacy and not a bore, that I promise.

This delicious buttercream is lean and porous as a result of the yolks that contain lecithin and fat.

The cream should be light and airy as whipped cream if it is made right.

Stir the cream slowly so that the air bubbles do not collapse. This goes for Italian buttercream as well.

5.6 oz (160 g) egg yokes, about 8
8.8 oz (250 g) sugar
4.5 oz (125 g) water
½ vanilla bean, preferably Tahitian
17.6 oz (500 g) unsalted butter

Italian Buttercream

Italian buttercream is somewhat firmer and more neutral. It is therefore easier to flavor, if you want a clean chocolate flavor.

5.3 oz (150 g) egg whites, about 5
1 tsp (5 g) lemon juice
12.3 oz (350 g) sugar
½ vanilla bean, preferably Tahitian
0.9 oz (25 g) honey or glucose (corn syrup)
17.6 oz (500 g) unsalted butter

Preparation of buttercream (for both recipes):
1. Whisk the yolks until light and airy. For the Italian variety, whisk the egg whites with the lemon juice.
2. Cut the vanilla bean lengthwise and scrape the seeds into a small saucepan.
3. Add water and sugar. Bring to a boil and brush the inside of the saucepan with a brush dipped in water. Boil until the thermometer reaches 242 °F (117 °C) for the French buttercream and empty it over the yolks while constantly whisking. For the Italian buttercream, boil the sugar to 251 °F (122 °C) and empty it over the egg whites while constantly stirring.
4. Whisk the mass cold with alternate speeds.
5. Add the butter at room temperature; if you have a food processor use the blade and stir the cream on low setting until it is foamy and light.

Base Syrup

A batch of base syrup weighs 22.6 oz (640 g), half a batch weighs 11.3 oz (320 g). If you measure with an aerometer, a so-called sugar weight, this syrup is 32 Baume.

8.8 oz (250 g) water
12 oz (340 g) sugar
2.1 oz (60 g) glucose (corn syrup)

1. Bring water and sugar to a boil in a saucepan; dip a brush in cold water and brush the crystals off of the walls of the saucepan. You achieve the same effect if you cover the saucepan with a lid, slightly ajar. Remove foam with a tea strainer.
2. Add the glucose and bring to a boil. Pour into a well-rinsed glass jar and cover with a lid.

Apple Jam

I can still remember how the apple jam would splash in our faces when we boiled it in fall. We always used Swedish apples from Kivik.

When I received the award "The Golden Apple" from Apple's House in Kivik for my contribution to Swedish apples, I thought of exactly this: how the apple jam would splash in my face when it was strained and close to done.

This jam has a firm texture and works well with pastries where the jam should be firm and not run out during baking. Feel free to use *transparente blanche* apples, which are great for apple mash.

4 ½ lb (2 kg) tart apples
2.2 lb (1 kg) water (4 cups)
Juice of 1 lemon
17.6 oz (500 g) sugar for each 2.2 lb (kg) of purée .

1. Clean the apples and cut them down the middle. Place them in a pot with the water and lemon juice. Bring to a boil.
2. Boil under a lid until the apples are completely soft, 20–30 minutes.
3. Remove the apples and pass them through a sieve.
4. Weigh the purée and add the correct amount of sugar. Boil in the pot while constantly stirring with a long ladle. Be careful, strained jam burns easily and splashes.
5. Brush the inside of the pot now and then with a brush dipped in cold water to prevent sugar crystals in the finished jam.
6. At 220 °F (105 °C), the jam is ready. If you do not have a thermometer, perform a jam-test, see below.
7. Pour the jam directly into sterilized jars and cover with the lids right away. Turn the jars upside down a couple of times.

Storage:
Unopened jars may be stored at room temperature; keep opened jars in the fridge.

Place a spoon of the jam on a cold plate. After a minute, pull the spoon shaft through the jam. If it doesn't float back together it is ready.

Swedish Apple Compote for Baking

This is how we did it at my first workplace when we were boiling compote for pastries, which was my next task after boiling the vanilla cream for the following day. We always used cox oranges, which have a nice flavor. This is how the recipe is written in my recipe book that I started writing as a fifteen-year-old.

1. Peel and core the apples, and slice them in small wedges.
2. Measure them with a measuring cup.
3. For each 13 cups (3 liters) of apple wedges take the juice of 1 lemon and 17.6 oz (500 g) sugar.
4. The apples are boiled with the sugar and the lemon juice on high heat until you can easily crush the apples against the walls of the pot with the ladle. Add a cinnamon stick and let it boil.
5. Continue boiling on high heat until all the liquid evaporates.
6. Empty into a bowl and cover with plastic wrap.
7. Let it cool and keep the compote in the fridge until use. It will keep for about 5 days.

Raspberry Jam for Pastries and Bites

For this jam I first purée the berries so that the jam doesn't contain any whole berries. While mixing I also release the pectin from the berries, which will help the jam thicken nicely.

If you wish to make the jam less sweet, use only 17.6 oz (500 g) sugar per 2.2 lb (1 kg) of berries, but if so you have to store the jam in the fridge. You can only store jam in room temperature if it holds 65% sugar or more.

The sweeter jam is often called bake firm, which means that it keeps stable during baking and does not seep out.

2.2 lb (1 kg) raspberries
1.7 lb (800 g) sugar
2.6 oz (75 g) lemon juice

DAY 1
Blend the raspberries with the sugar and the lemon juice. Mix in the food processor for 5 minutes. Cover with plastic wrap and let it sit in the fridge overnight.

DAY 2
1. Pour the berries in a pot and bring to a boil.
2. Keep stirring during boiling and brush the inside of the pot with a brush dipped in cold water to prevent sugar crystals. Now and then, remove the foam with a spoon so that the jam turns out clear.

3. Boil to 222–224 °F (106–107 °C). At this point the surface of the jam is usually wrinkly and the raspberries transparent, which is an indicator that the jam is ready. Or perform a jam test, see p.18.
4. Pour the jam directly onto sterilized jars and cover with the lids right away. Turn the jars upside down a couple of times.

Makes about 3.3 lb (1500 g) jam.

Strawberry Jam

2.2 lb (1000 g) frozen strawberries
1.7 lb (800 g) sugar
2.6 oz (75 g) lemon juice

1. Purée all of the ingredients.
2. Boil the purée while stirring sporadically to 222–224 °F (106–107 °C), or perform a jam test on a cold plate.
3. Pour into warm clean jars and turn the jars upside down a couple of times.

Express-Preserved Orange Peel or Lemon Peel

2.2 lb (1 kg) oranges or lemons
2.2 lb (1 kg) water (5 cups)
2.2 lb (1 kg) sugar
1 vanilla bean

1. Thoroughly clean the fruit with a brush under running water.
2. Cut the peel in 4 pieces and peel it off the fruit. Squeeze the juice from the fruit, freeze it, and use it for something else, such as sorbet.
3. Boil the peels in water in a covered pan for about 30 minutes or until they are completely soft. Hold under cold running water and let them drain in a sieve.
4. Bring 4 1/4 cups (1 liter) of water to a boil with 8.8 oz (250 g) sugar and 1 vanilla bean.
5. Add the peels and bring to a boil once more. Let the syrup simmer at about 194 °F (90 °C) for 15 minutes. Add another 8.8 oz (250 g) sugar and simmer for another 15 minutes.
6. Repeat the process two more times with 8.8 oz (250 g) sugar each time.
7. Pour into sterilized jars and simmer in a water bath for 20 minutes in an oven at 175 °F (80 °C).

Store the jars in the fridge.

Preserved Pineapple

Use one 20 oz (560 g) can of Del Monte pineapple in juice and prepare the pineapple slices the same way you did the orange peels, see above. This is used to decorate almond bread and bites, and for plum cakes.

Citrus Concentrate

This great fruit concentrate is perfect for flavoring dough and creams and to enhance lemon or orange flavors.

Equal parts citrus fruits and sugar.

1. Weigh the citrus fruit.
2. Clean it thoroughly with a brush under running water so that you remove all of the preservatives.
3. Slice the fruit and place it in a mixer/food processor. Add the equal amount of sugar in ounces/grams.
4. Purée the fruit and sugar for about 10 minutes.
5. Pass the fruit mass though a sieve; use a spoon to squeeze it through.
6. Pour into well-cleaned jars and store in the fridge.

The citrus concentrate will keep for weeks.

Almond

The almond tree stems from southwestern Asia and Northern Africa and is now cultivated in all the Mediterranean countries and in California. The tree can grow up to 26 feet (8 meters) tall. The fruits are so-called stone fruits and have a chewy, rubbery meat and a deep rough peel, within which you will find one, or sometimes two, seed we call almond. If the peel is thin and a grainy matte, the seeds are called soft-shelled almond.

There are two varieties of almond: sweet almond and bitter almond. They are very similar, as they contain the same nutrients, about 45–55% fat oil (almond oil), egg white

protein, and sugar. The difference lies in the fact that the bitter almond also contains glycoside, amygdalin, which is very poisonous as it breaks down into benzaldehyde, glucose, and prussic acid when in contact with water. Real bitter almond oil is free of the prussic acid; never use anything else.

The most important growing regions are Italy, especially Palma and Girgenti. Bari almonds are recognized as the best in the world, while Spain cultivates Valencia almonds, Corona, and Longuettes Alicante. In California they cultivate Nonpareil, Peerless, and Jordano. In France cultivation of almonds happens in Provence.

Italian and Spanish almonds are recognized as the best as they are spicier and have a sweet almond aroma. Californian almonds are large and pretty, but lack the full almond aroma. In contrast to Spain and Italy, though, you can't find bitter almonds on California trees.

Almond Paste

In Sweden, Zell almond paste is best as it is made the old-fashioned way; unfortunately, the common consumer can't buy this. I therefore recommend that you make your own almond paste; it is not hard if you have a food processor with blades. The so-called almond paste you can buy at the store today is usually packed with preservatives and corn syrup and multiple months old. No, make your own almond paste instead—that will turn out the best.

In one of my favorite books, *Den praktiske konditorn,* from 1915, Edv. Ehrstrom writes the following. The section concerns almond paste:

"If more housewives would work together so that about 10 kg almond paste could be prepared at once, one could have it ground with a motor-run machine for 10 ore pennies per kilo at the following companies: Chokladjabriken Sture, Fridhemsgatan, Kungsholmen and Lindqvists karamellaffiir, Sibyllegatan 26, Stockholm. It is simple math to grind more than one kilo at a time, for the mass can be saved in an air-tight container and be dissolved with water or egg white as needed."

Most pâtisseries buy industrially manufactured almond paste these days, which is either prepared in an almond milling machine or in large mixers, so-called Stephan machines, with sharp knives in them.

Almond paste is one of the main ingredients within the pastry chef profession. It is the basic pillar of many pastries. The skill of making a good almond paste was one of the most important steps as an apprentice. I was allowed to do everything except spin the rolls on the milling machines when the mass was to be milled smooth. If the almonds were milled too hard, the oil of the mass could burst out and ruin the entire paste.

The first time I milled almond paste it oiled and I was prepared to be reprimanded, but the chef said:

"We will make it into a bun filling, and nobody will notice." And then he pointed out once more that making almond paste was one of the most important skills as a real pastry chef, "and later I will teach you how to make roasted marzipan, which is much harder."

What is Almond Paste?

Almond paste is a finely ground mass of equal parts scalded almond and sugar that is made in a milling machine or mixed in a mixer, which is most common today. Milled almond paste has a nicer texture. The mass should have a water content of about 10–11%; if it gets too dry it oils while you work on it.

My first almond paste consisted of
21 lb (9500 g) Spanish sweet almond (Corona)
17.6 oz (500 g) bitter almond

The almonds were emptied into boiling water and were blanched under water for about 1 minute until the shells fall off. They should not remain in the water for too long; if they do, the chewy layer under the shell loosens and makes it hard to peel the almonds. Rinse them in cold water and pull the shells off by hand. Luckily, we had a milling machine; one can only imagine how it was in earlier days when the almonds were shelled by hand and the mass was crushed in stone mortars; one could only take on 6 ½ lb (3 kg) at a time before one got too tired.

The shelled almonds were then spooled with cold water and placed in a sieve to drain, covered with a moist cloth. We would let it sit overnight.

Afterwards we added 22 lb (10 kg) granulated sugar and first placed a small test batch in the mill to make sure that it didn't get oily, if it did we would add more water to the mass, as it was supposed to feel moist. It was milled in three rounds and the mill would be tightened between each time so that the mass ended up as smooth as possible.

At home the easiest way to make almond paste is by following this recipe (makes about 4 ½ lb [2100 g] finished paste)

2 lb (950 g) sweet almond, preferably Spanish or Italian
1.7 oz (50 g) bitter almond (never use bitter almond oil in almond paste)
2.2 lb (1 kg) sugar

1. Scald the almonds in a generous amount of boiling water for a couple of minutes until the shells start to let go of the nut. Hold them under cold running water.
2. Empty them in a sieve and let them drain. Peel the shells off.
3. Mix almonds and sugar for a few minutes in a food processor/mixer until you have a smooth mass.
4. Wrap the mass in plastic wrap and let it sit overnight.

If you prefer not to use bitter almonds, you may replace it for sweet almonds. However, a mass with bitter almonds gets a more intense almond flavor, and in this book we are baking the right way.

Tant Pour Tant

Tant pour tant (TPT) means equal amounts of both. For the almond paste the relationship is 50% nuts and 50% sugar. The 50/50 base is a good founding rule when it comes to recipes. TPT works for all kinds of nuts, like hazelnuts, walnuts, macadamia nuts, pine nuts, brazil nuts, pecans, pistachios, or coconut flakes.

Almond Flour

Most professionals buy almond flour, since it is practical and just as good as homemade. If you rather wish to make it yourself, you scald and dry the almonds and grind them into a fine powder that you later pass through a fine sieve.

Roasted Almond Flakes

Preheat the oven to 390 °F (200 °C). Place the almonds on a baking sheet and roast them until golden brown while stirring now and then.

Unpeeled almonds are roasted at the same temperature, but for a much longer time, until you can smell the roasted almonds.

You may roast hazelnuts the exact same way. When the shell starts to let go of the nuts and they are golden brown, they are ready.

Storage:

Keep all roasted nuts in a jar or can with a lid.

Roll-Out Marzipan

The word marzipan may stem from the Italian marzapane. It is needed for certain cakes, like Swedish *dammsugare*, or "vacuum cleaner," and potato pastries.

Today, most bakeries buy their rollout marzipan from the food-industry, which results in the same tastes in each bakery and the loss of distinctive flavor. When I was an apprentice we followed this recipe:

8.8 oz (250 g) powdered sugar
17.6 oz (500 g) almond paste 50/50
3.5–5.3 oz (100–150 g) glucose (corn syrup)
Optional coloring, preferably natural

1. Sift the powdered sugar and warm the almond paste in a microwave to about 86 °F (30 °C) (Clearly there were no microwaves back then, but they make it easier as they prevent that the oil seeping out).
2. Blend everything smooth in a food processor and add color if wanted.
3. Roll the mass in plastic wrap and let it rest for a couple of hours.
4. Roll it out with the help of powdered sugar, according to what you will be using it for (never use wheat flour when you roll out marzipan as it may start rising).

Storage:

Keep leftovers in the fridge, but always let marzipan reach room temperature before you use it; if not, it will crack when you roll it out. If the marzipan turns out too dry, you may carefully soften it with some syrup, see base syrup on p.17.

Mazarin Paste

Mazarin paste is one of the basic pastes within Swedish baking, and mazarins are a national pastry in Sweden. The cake and filling received thier names from the French Cardinal Mazarin, but the pastry does not exist under the same name in France. The French mazarin paste is called *crème d'amande* and consists of almond flour, powdered sugar, butter, eggs, and 50% vanilla cream, which is added at the end. This filling is very tasty as well.

Correctly prepared mazarins—baked with good, fresh almond paste based on Spanish almonds, good butter, and fresh eggs—are an important delicacy that we need to preserve in a time when most people buy their pastries in grocery stores and gas stations, where the pastries are industrially prepared with cheap margarine and added salt to make the dough cheaper with less fat.

When you see foil cups or marks from foil cups on a mazarin you know that it's not made the right way, and that it's rather a mediocre product, which in the worst cases doesn't even contain almonds but apricot cores.

The mazarin is a good way to establish a bakery's stance when it comes to quality. If they line their short-crust pastry with good classic short-crust dough and fill them with the right filling, you will most often be able to eat other pastries as well with confidence.

Roll-Out Marzipan

A few important things to remember when making mazarin paste:
- Always use ingredients at room temperature; cold butter and almond paste will squeeze the water from the eggs and will make the mass divide (If this still happens, let it sit in room temperature and stir it back together again).
- Do not stir too much air in the mass during blending as it will seep over during baking.
- If you have mazarin paste in the fridge, then allow it to reach room temperature before you stir it together and add it to your pastries.

Mazarin Paste

Here follow three varieties of mazarin paste. In my opinion, the first recipe is the perfect recipe for classic mazarins. The second is somewhat more fluffy since it contains more egg and therefore works well for so-called capsules that are cut out of mazarin paste. Sometimes people also add 1.7 oz (50 g) wheat flour to make it easier to cut the pieces. We always used the third, luxurious mazarin paste, as marzipan triangles, which is a classic Swedish cake. This mazarin paste is somewhat softer and with a more filling and creamy texture because of the yolks.

All of the mazarin recipes are prepared the same way.

1.

17.6 oz (500 g) almond paste 50/50
8.8 oz (250 g) butter
8.8 oz (250 g) eggs (approx. 5)

2.

17.6 oz (500 g) almond paste 50/50
8.8 oz (250 g) butter
13 oz (375 g) eggs (approx. 7 large eggs)

3.

10.5 oz (300 g) almond paste 50/50
8.8 oz (250 g) butter
1.7 oz (50 g) egg (approx. 1)
2.1 oz (60 g) egg yolks (approx. 3)

1. Blend the almond paste at room temperature with one third of the butter, also at room temperature. Blend into a smooth mass with the help of a blade if you have a food processor, if not, by hand.
2. Add an additional third of the butter and lastly the remaining butter and blend until there are no lumps.
3. Add the eggs at room temperature one at the time. Just blend enough so that every ingredient is blended together.

Nut Paste

Try to find hazelnuts from Italy; the best ones are from Piedmont.

7 oz (200 g) roasted and shelled hazelnuts.

Mix the nuts in a food processor/mixer with jagged knifes until you have a liquid cream with a temperature of 158 °F (70 °C).

Make the almond paste the same way with roasted, shelled almonds, preferably Spanish corona almonds.

Keep the paste in a can with a lid in the fridge. It will keep for multiple weeks.

Pistachio Paste

Try to find pistachio nuts from Italy.

7 oz (200 g) pistachio nuts

Prepare the same way as the hazelnut paste, but do not roast the pistachio nuts.

Prepare walnut paste the same way.

Pistachio Nuts · Bitter Almond · Walnuts · Sweet Almond · Roasted Hazelnuts · Hazelnuts · Shelled Hazelnuts · Shelled Almond

Lemon Curd

My mother would always serve this curd with her tasty graham crackers with tea or coffee. Sometimes we would get some of her delicious green tomato marmalade as well.

This is a classic pastry cream, almost as classic as the vanilla cream.

If you wish to make passion fruit curd instead, substitute the lemon juice with 1.7 oz (50 g) passion fruit purée and 0.9 oz (25 g) orange juice instead, but keep the lemon zest for the right tartness in the cream.

1 gelatin sheet
5.3 oz (150 g) eggs (approx. 3)
5.3 oz (150 g) sugar
2.6 oz (75 g) lemon juice
1 ½ yellow, ripe lemons
3.5 oz (100 g) unsalted butter

1. Soak the gelatin in a generous amount of cold water.
2. Whisk eggs and sugar until fluffy.
3. Bring lemon juice and grated lemon zest of 1 ½ yellow, ripe lemons with the butter to a boil.
4. Pour the lemon blend over the whisked egg and sugar foam. Blend well with a whisk.
5. Carefully warm under constant whisking until the cream comes to a boil.
6. Remove the saucepan from the stove and whisk the cream smooth.
7. Lift the gelatin sheet from the water and let the water drain off.
8. Place the gelatin in the warm cream and stir until it's melted.
9. Strain through a sieve.
10. Let cool and keep it covered with plastic wrap in the fridge.

Storage:
The lemon curd will keep for up to a week in the fridge. If you don't need it right away, it is best to freeze it.

Short-Crust Dough

Short-crust dough should be tender and melt in your mouth. This tender, crumbly dough is quite different from butterdough, which is crispy with multiple crunchy layers.

The French method of blending short-crust dough at the table is the best method to avoid overworking the dough. Naturally, you may also use a mixer, but in that case you need to be careful so that you do not work the dough too much. When I worked in Switzerland we would blend all of the pastry dough by hand when we baked Swiss tea-bread.

- Added dough in short-crust dough makes it easier to roll out.
- Yolks make the dough shorter and crispier.
- Powdered sugar makes the dough harder and lengthens its shelf life, as well as creates a more sandy texture.
- Granulated sugar makes the dough crunchier.

TIPS!

Remember to bake the short-crust dough till it obtains a golden color and the sugar and butter have partly caramelized. Poorly baked short-crust dough will feel mealy in your mouth. Always place freshly baked short-crust pastries directly onto a cooling rack to cool, especially if the filling is soft.

Classic Short-Crust Dough

In Sweden it is most common to use a "1-2-3 dough." This kind of dough is fine for lining mazarin cups, but if a form has straight walls it will sink down. In these cases, different dough will be better.

1 1/3 lb (600 g) wheat flour
14 oz (400 g) butter
7 oz (200 g) sugar
3.5 oz (100 g) eggs (approx. 2)

1. Sift the wheat flour onto the baking table. Shape into a ring.
2. Place the butter, at room temperature, and sugar in the middle.
3. Pinch together into a crumbly mass and add the eggs. Work into dough with your hands.

4. Roll the dough in plastic wrap and keep it in the fridge for at least one hour.

Almond Short-Crust Dough

There are many different types of short-crust dough. This is very tasty and works with almost anything.

10.5 oz (300 g) wheat flour
4.2 oz (120 g) almond paste 50/50
1/2 lb (240 g) butter
1.7 oz (50 g) egg (approx. 1)
3.8 oz (110 g) powdered sugar
0.3 oz (10 g) real vanilla sugar
1 tsp (5g) salt, preferably fleur de sel (1 tsp)
1.7 oz (50 g) ground, unpeeled almond

1. Sift the wheat flour onto the baking table. Shape into a ring.
2. Stir the almond paste, at room temperature, smooth on the table with one-third of the butter and continue to add the remainder of the butter until all lumps are gone.
3. Stir in the eggs and pinch the dough together. Blend together, but do not overwork. Lastly, add the sugar, salt, and ground almond. Roll in plastic wrap and let it rest in the fridge for at least one hour.

If you wish to make a so-called French almond short-crust dough, take 8.8 oz (250 g) almond paste, 8.8 oz (250 g) butter, 8.8 oz (250 g) wheat flour, and blend to a dough. You will then have a nice short-crust dough, but completely white. Both are just as tasty.

Hazelnut Short-Crust Dough

5.3 oz (150 g) butter
5.3 oz (150 g) finely ground roasted hazelnuts
5.3 oz (150 g) powdered sugar
0.1 oz (4 g) salt, preferably fleur de sel (approx. 1 tsp)
0.3 oz (10 g) real vanilla sugar
3.5 oz (100 g) eggs (approx. 2)
8.8 oz (250 g) wheat flour

Blend as a classic short-crust dough, see p.26.

Short-Crust Dough for Wiener Confectionary and Swiss Tea-Bread

5.3 oz (150 g) almond paste 50/50
1.7 oz (50 g) egg (approx. 1)
1.7 oz (50 g) powdered sugar
4.5 oz (125 g) butter
8.8 oz (250 g) wheat flour

1. Work the almond paste, room temperature, in with the egg.
2. Sift and work in the powdered sugar.
3. Carefully work in the butter (at room temperature) and wheat flour. Work into dough.
4. Wrap the dough in plastic wrap and let it chill in the fridge for about 2 hours.

Classic Butterdough – Pâte Feuilletée

The French are rightly known for their lightly crispy butterdough pastries, and a pâtisserie without freshly baked napoleon pastries is non-existent in France. And when they are baked the right way they are quite the delicacy. The Frenchman Claude Gellée, also known as Claude Lorrin (1600–1682), created the butterdough. He started as a pastry chef, but later became a famous artist, whose paintings may be found at the Louvre in Paris.

There are good butterdoughs available for sale, but not if you've ever tasted freshly baked butterdough made with butter. Industry butterdough is prepared with margarine, but it is still called butterdough. Let's hope our legislators at some point get around to sorting this out and protecting the butterdough name.

2.2 lb (1 kg) wheat flour special
2.2 lb (1 kg) unsalted butter
14 oz (400 g) cold water (approx. 2 cups)
2.8 oz (80 g) yolk (approx. 4)
0.7 oz (20 g) freshly squeezed lemon juice or white wine vinegar
0.7 oz (20 g) salt, preferably fleur de sel

1. Sift the wheat flour onto the baking table. Shape into a ring.
2. Melt 5.3 oz (150 g) of the butter and pour into the middle of the ring. Work in with the flour.
3. Pour in the cold water, yolks, lemon juice or white

wine vinegar, and salt.
4. Work the dough by hand until smooth, but not for so long that it turns elastic.
5. Roll the dough together into a bun.
6. Wrap the dough in plastic wrap and let it rest for two hours in the fridge.

7. Pound the remaining cold butter with a rolling pin on the buttered paper 8 x 8 inches (20 x 20 cm). You should end up with a sheet that is about 1 inch (2 cm) tall and the same size as the paper sheet.

8. Cut a cross on the dough bun. Fold and roll the flaps out. Place the butter in the middle (see p.28)

9. Fold the dough flaps over the butter sheet. Press the dough out so that it completely covers the butter (see p.28).

10. Roll the dough out a little and wrap it in plastic wrap. Let it rest for 30–60 minutes in the fridge.

11. Roll the dough out on a surface covered with flour, preferably a marble slab. Roll it out to 28 x 16 inches (70 x 40 cm)—measure with a ruler.

12. Brush any surplus flour off the dough. Fold it together in 3 parts, a "treslag" or tri-fold (see p.28).

13. Repeat the rolling out and do another tri-fold. Wrap it in plastic wrap and let the dough rest for one hour in the fridge.

14. Repeat with another two roll outs and folding three ways.

15. Wrap it in plastic wrap once more and let it rest for an hour in the fridge.

16. Repeat the procedure one last time, and you now have a classic butterdough with six "turns"/tri-folds.

Swedish pâtisseries will often do two three-way foldings ("treslag") and two four-way foldings ("fyrslag") instead, but the dough doesn't turn out as light and airy as with six three-way folds. The millefeuille dough received its name because it shows over a thousand layers through the repetition of folding. The first round it forms 7 layers, the second 19, third 55, fourth 163, fifth 487 and the sixth 1459 layers. In total you now have 729 layers of butter and 730 layers of dough.

GOOD TO KNOW
- Lemon juice or vinegar and the cold water help slow the development of gluten, and you avoid elastic dough.
- Steam will form between the layers of butter and dough during baking. The steam melts the butter, which in turn prevents the layers from sticking together. Furthermore, the protein (gluten) coagulates and the starch stiffens. The encapsulated steam that forms also forces the dough to expand and rise.
- Always allow butterdough to rest for at least half-an-hour on the baking sheets before you bake it. This prevents the dough from pulling together and changing the shape of the pastry. You may also splash water on the parchment paper to avoid the dough pulling together.
- Always bake at high temperatures, 440°F (225°C).
- Always bake the butterdough properly so that it is really crunchy and crisp.

Storage:
Wrapped in plastic wrap, the dough may be stored in the fridge for a couple of days without significant damage. The dough can be stored in the freezer for a couple of weeks. The dough should then thaw in the fridge, and it is important to roll it out carefully so that you do not damage any of the layers.

Express Butterdough (Blixt Butterdough)

Sometimes called American butterdough or pie dough. Pâtisseries usually use this dough to line baking pans and as bottoms for napoleon pastries and thousand leaf tarts. The advantage is that it doesn't shrink as much as regular butterdough.

17.6 oz (500 g) wheat flour special
0.3 oz (10 g) salt, preferably fleur de sel (2 tsp)
17.6 oz (500 g) unsalted butter
1.4 oz (40 g) egg yolks (approx. 2)
7 oz (200 g) water (approx. 2 dl)
0.3 oz (10 g) pressed lemon juice or white wine vinegar (2 tsp)

1. Sift the wheat flour and salt onto the baking table. Shape a ring out of the flour (or pour it in a food processor).

2. Dice the cold butter in bits the size of sugar cubes and place them in the middle.

3. Blend butter, flour, and salt with your finger tips or in a food processor until the butter starts to crumble. Add the yolks, water, and lemon juice or vinegar.

4. Working the blend together, you should still have lumps of butter left in the blend.

5. Wrap the dough in plastic wrap and let it rest for at least 30 minutes in the fridge.

6. Roll out three three-way folds (treslag), see classic butterdough p. 28–30. Let the dough rest for 30 minutes in the fridge.

7. Roll out three additional three-way folds and let the dough rest for at least 30 minutes in the fridge.

Bake and store as the classic butterdough.

Petit-Four Wrap

1.7 oz (50 g) butter
13 oz (375 g) almond paste 50/50
5.3 oz (150 g) eggs (approx. 3)
1/2 lb (240 g) yolks (approx. 12)
3.5 oz (100 g) wheat flour

1. Preheat the oven to 446°F (230°C).

2. Melt the butter in a saucepan and set aside.

3. Dissolve the almond paste, room temperature, with the eggs so that you get a smooth mass without lumps.

4. Whisk until light and airy with a hand beater for about 10 minutes.

5. Sift in the wheat flour and stir with a silicone spatula.

6. Take one large spoonful of the mass and stir it in with the butter. Add this to the dough as well.

7. Spread the mass out on 2 baking sheets lined with parchment paper.

8. Bake the bottoms until golden brown, for 8–10 minutes.

9. Let them cool completely. Place them in the freezer for 2 hours.

10. Turn the bottoms out on a piece of parchment paper with sugar and pull the parchment paper off.

ALMOND PASTRIES

CROQUEMBOUCHE

Croquembouche is a kind of almond pastry; the classic cornucopia is the queen and the crown is the princess. It used to be mandatory to bake this for your journeyman's certificate, but nowadays you will only have to do it for a master's exam.

Baked the right way, not too dark, they are not only decorative but also work well with all kinds of ice cream desserts. At every single one of my workplaces, we've made croquembouche; at Conditori Lundagard in Lund we would make several of these pastries a week, which would go to weddings and various bed & breakfast establishments. The pastry chef Thure Collbring was a real pastry chef and very skilled at making croquembouche.

The pastry is made with fine almond paste and egg whites. The dough is dissolved with enough egg whites that it becomes smooth and can easily be rolled without cracking. It used to be common to make the templates on brown paper, but now we use parchment paper. You can either arrange the dough with a decorating bag or, as I do, roll the mass out finger thick and shape it directly on the paper.

Let the gates and squiggles dry in room temperature for 24 hours. Bake them golden brown in a 390 °F (200 °C) oven for about 5 minutes. If the baking time is too short, they won't harden sufficiently and the pastry will fall apart, if you bake them for too long, they won't taste good. Squeeze out thin lines of airy icing while the pastry is still warm and it will dry quickly.

Shape the rings that the bottom will rest on with a diameter of about 2 inches (5 cm). The bottoms, which the parts will stand on, are rolled out to 1/16 inch (2.5 mm) thickness and poked all over with a fork. Bake them till they are hard enough that they will hold. Take them right out of the oven and roll them even.

Glaze thinly with the icing, see recipe p.180, and set to dry in the oven. Fill the rings, which the plates rest on, with red caramel. This will make them more stable. Build the whole thing using caramel as glue.

Caramel:
17.6 oz (500 g) sugar
8.8 oz (250 g) glucose (corn syrup)
7 oz (200 g) water

Boil to 240 °F (115 °C) while constantly brushing the inside of the pot with a brush dipped in water.

Color one-fourth of the caramel with 1 drop of red food coloring, preferably natural, and pour it in the holes of the rings.

The cornucopia at page 31 is in Swedish style, the way we did them at Conditori Lundagard in Lund. Many would also make them lying down. This dough also consists of almond paste 50/50, softened with egg whites so that it is easily shapeable. Roll the rings to the horn and shape them around a cone. Also roll a batch of ¼-rings, and about ten equally sized rings that the plate with the horn will stand on. Roll out squiggles as pictured and roll out a plate as for the croquembouche. Let the almond paste dry overnight and bake it on parchment paper in 390 °F (200 °C) for 3–5 minutes. Decorate with icing right away. Let the croquembouche cool and arrange them like the large croquembouche rings, filled with red caramel, on a plate.

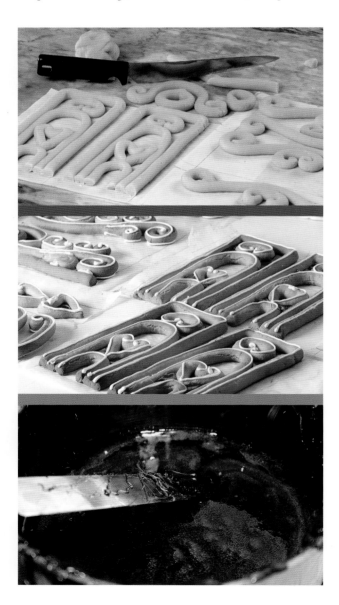

Cornucopias used to be very popular for weddings, birthdays, and tributes, and we would make them in three different sizes.

You could also get the croquembouche in different sizes, from 1 level with a top to 3 levels with a top. They were made squared, pentagonal, and hexagonal with the equal amount of squiggles and gates.

Most pâtisseries had their own models.

LUNDAGARD'S FROZEN PUDDING

We would often make croquembouche crowns for weddings. They would be filled with Lundagard's frozen pudding and garnished with spun sugar.

5 CUPS (1 LITER)

2 oranges, juice and zest
2.6 oz (75 g) sugar
17.6 oz (500 g) whipped cream
0.7 oz (20 g) lemon juice
6 macaroons
6 candied red cherries
2 slices preserved pineapple, see recipe p.20
1 preserved green pear, see my book *The Jam and Marmalade Bible* (or a ring of pineapple)
1.7 oz (½ dl) classic orange juice, see my book *The Jam and Marmalade Bible*

1. Clean and grate the outer zest of the oranges with a grater.
2. Massage it with the sugar until it starts to drain off.
3. Blend the cream with the orange zest, orange juice, and lemon juice.
4. Layer the cream with the chopped macaroons and fruit in a 5 cup (1 liter) pan.
5. Freeze overnight.
6. Dip the pan in lukewarm water and take the pudding out. Garnish with spun sugar and place it in the croquembouche crown.

CLASSIC MAZARINS

My father, Fritz, loved mazarins, but he wanted them without the icing. All pâtisseries used to have mazarins without the glazing and with just the sugar on top. Personally, I loved Parisian waffles with arrak buttercream and my mother most often wanted apple strudel or "nutkongress."

When you glaze mazarins it is important that you first brush the surface with apricot icing, so-called apricoting, to prevent the pastry from absorbing all the water in the glaze. If not, the surface will look dull and in professional jargon, we say that the glaze dies. The fondant should not be heated over 104 °F (40 °C). Anything over that and it turns dull; dilute it with some fresh lemon juice and the glaze will have a fresh taste.

Dry the glaze in the oven with the oven door slightly ajar and it will stiffen and contain the water. It will shine for multiple days and doesn't stick if you place all of the mazarins in a bag.

30 MAZARINS (traditionally they should weigh 2.5 oz [70 g] with the filling)

30 thin mazarin cups
1 batch classic short-crust dough 1-2-3, see p.27
1 batch mazarin paste number 1, see p.25
0.3 oz (10 g) sugar to sprinkle on top
1 batch apricot icing, see p.17
1 batch fondant, see p.16

1. Preheat the oven to 370 °F (190 °C).
2. Set the cleaned mazarin cups out on the baking table.
3. Work the cold short-crust dough even and smooth by hand.
4. Roll it out to 1/8 of an inch (3 mm) with the help of a rolling pin and wheat flour.
5. Roll the dough onto the rolling pin and roll it out over the cups. Powder flour on top and push the cups together a little.
6. Take a piece of dough and pound the dough onto the cups. Roll over them with the rolling pen so that that the dough lets go of the cups.
7. Set the cups on a baking sheet and fill them with mazarin paste with the help of a decorating bag. Use tip no. 12 or cut a small hole in the bottom.
8. Bake the mazarins golden brown, about 8 minutes.
9. Sprinkle sugar on top and cover with a piece of parchment paper; place an edged baking pan on top (without the edge, the mazarins will easily slip off when you turn it.) Turn everything upside down so that the tops of the cakes are even.
10. Let cool in the cups.
11. When the mazarins have cooled, brush a thin layer of apricot icing on top of the baked surface.

12. Warm the fondant to about 95 °F (35 °C), dilute it with some lemon juice, and dip the apricot icing covered side in the fondant. Scrape off the surplus icing with a small straight spatula. When all of the mazarins are glazed, set them in the oven for 1 minute with the oven door slightly ajar, so that the glaze dries and obtains a nice shine.

STORAGE:
The mazarins will keep in room temperature for 3–5 days. You can freeze them both baked and raw, but not glazed.

36

CARAC CAKES

This classic cake is quite new in Sweden, but it has existed in Europe for a very long time. This is because pastry chefs, and chefs, were an itinerant people and there were many Swiss, French, and German pastry chefs that brought their national pastries to the Swedish culture.

I made many of these delicious cakes when I was working at the Confiserie Honold in Zurich, where they could be found in any pâtisserie.

20 CAKES

20 mazarin cups
1 batch sugar dough, see lemon cake
1 batch pâtisserie ganache with Valrhona Grand Cru Pur
    Caribe 66%, see p.14
7 oz (200 g) fondant, see p.16
1 drop of green food coloring, preferably natural
optional: some syrup to dilute the fondant, see p.17
2.8 oz (80 g) chocolate, preferably Valrhona Manjari

1. Bake the cups the same way as for lemon cake.
2. Pour the freshly boiled ganache in a decorating bag. Use tip no. 12 or cut a small hole in the bottom.
3. Fill the cups with the ganache and level them off with a straight spatula.
4. Place them in the fridge to stiffen somewhat, about 1 hour.
5. Warm the fondant to 95 °F (35 °C) and lightly color it with green natural food color. Control the texture; if it is too thick then dilute with syrup.
6. Dip the cakes with the chocolate ganache-filled side facing down in the fondant and remove any surplus icing with a straight spatula. Place them on a piece of parchment paper.
7. Temper the chocolate, see p.13.
8. Pour the chocolate in a small cone made of paper and cut a small hole in front.
9. Squeeze out a medium sized dot at the middle of the cake, as pictured.

STORAGE:
The cakes may be kept in the fridge for 1–2 days, after which the glaze dulls.

LEMON CAKES

A crunchy short-crust dough with creamy lemon filling, covered with a thin elegant lemon fondant with a tart flavor and the word Lemon written with chocolate. This tasty classic cake used to be baked in many bakeries. At the esteemed Fahlmans you could always find this cake, and also at Konditori Intim in Malmö.

I still remember how, in the afternoons after I had finished the dishes, I would stand and practice cake script for at least 2 hours in order to be able to write beautifully on the cakes.

When you bake this kind of pastry you should use dough that keeps its form better than the regular short-crust dough; make a sugar dough instead and the dough won't sink down but rather become a beautiful shell.

20 CAKES

20 mazarin cups

Sugar dough:
8.8 oz (250 g) wheat flour
3.5 oz (100 g) butter
3.5 oz (100 g) powdered sugar
0.1 oz (3 g) salt
3.5 oz (100 g) eggs (approx. 2)

1 batch lemon curd, see p.26
½ batch French butter cream, see p.17
1 lemon
7 oz (200 g) fondant, see p.16
1 drop of yellow food color, preferably natural
2.8 oz (80 g) dark chocolate, preferably Valrhona
    Grand Cru Guanaja 70%

1. Make the sugar dough by following the steps for classic short-crust dough, see p.27
2. Work the cold dough smooth with your hands.
3. Roll it out and line the cups the same way as for the mazarins, see p.36.
4. Poke the bottoms of the cups with a fork and set them in the fridge for 30 minutes to stiffen.
5. Warm the oven to 390 °F (200 °C).
6. Bake the cups golden brown for about 12 minutes. Release them from the cups as soon as they have cooled.
7. Whisk the cold lemon curd with the buttercream into a light cream.
8. Fill the cream in a decorating bag. Use tip no. 12 or cut a small hole in the bottom.
9. Fill the cups all the way to the edge and stroke them

even with a straight spatula.

10. Place them in the fridge for 1 hour to stiffen.
11. Squeeze the lemon and blend the juice in with the fondant and the yellow color. Warm to 95°F (35°C).
12. Dip the top of the cold cake in the fondant and scrape off any surplus icing with a straight spatula.
13. Temper the chocolate, see tempering on page 13.
14. Place the chocolate in a small paper cone and cut a small hole in the bottom. Write Lemon on the cake as nicely as you can.

STORAGE:

They will keep in the fridge for 1–2 days, after which the glaze will dull.

MAZARIN TART

1 tart dish, 8 inch (20 cm) diameter, ½ inch (1 cm) tall
1 batch short-crust dough, see p. 27
¼ batch mazarin paste number 1, see p.25
0.3 oz (10 g) sugar to sprinkle on top
1 batch of apricot icing, see p.17
0.9 oz (25 g) dark chocolate
1 tsp (5g) butter
3.5 oz (100 g) fondant, see p.16
Optional, syrup to dilute the fondant, see p.17
Optional, 0.3 oz (10 g) chopped pistachio nuts

1. Preheat the oven to 370°F (190°C).
2. Roll out the short-crust dough 1/8 of an inch (3 mm) thick with the help of a rolling pin and some wheat flour; roll it out somewhat larger than the size of the pan. Sprinkle flour on top of it and roll it onto the rolling pin.
3. Roll the dough over the dish and place the lined dish on a baking sheet.
4. Fill the dish three-quarters with mazarin paste.
5. Set the dish in the oven. Lower the temperature to 340°F (170°C) after 10 minutes. Bake it golden brown for 35–40 minutes.
6. Sprinkle some sugar over the cake, turn it out on a piece of parchment paper and remove the dish.
7. When the cake has cooled, turn it back around and brush the surface with apricot icing.
8. Melt chocolate and butter and lightly whisk it together.
9. Pour the mix in a small paper cone and cut a small hole in the bottom.
10. Warm the fondant to 95°F (35°C). Make sure that the texture is okay, if not add some syrup (never add water, that will dull the glaze).
11. Glaze the tart with a straight spatula and squeeze a beautiful spiral of chocolate on top of the glaze. Start at the middle and work your way outwards with a sharp knife to create a spindle pattern and decorate with some chopped pistachio nuts if desired.

Lemon Cakes

38

Mazarin Tart

Carac Cakes

Mazarins

Up until the 1980s, pâtisseries would often display their pastries on mirrors.

TOSCA CAKES

These cakes are unbelievably tasty if they are made the right way with wonderful almonds and nuts that, because of the caramelizing in the oven, look delicious. As a 16-year-old I became a specialist on this pastry, and if any stuck to the pan, they were a great snack for a teenage pastry chef.

At the NK Pâtisserie, they also make a delicious Tosca cake that they call Walewska after the famous Polish countess who was Napoleon Bonaparte's lover. She was also made memorable through the dish Dover sole Walewska.

At NK they brush kirschwasser-buttercream on the mazarin bottom, and top it off with a Tosca lid, which also tastes fantastically good.

30 CAKES

30 tosca cups, also called tartlet cups, about 3 inches (80 mm) diameter and ½ inch (1 cm) tall.
1 batch classic short-crust dough, see p.27
½ batch mazarin paste number 1, see p.25

Tosca topping:
3.5 oz (100 g) unsalted butter
3.5 oz (100 g) sugar
3.5 oz (100 g) whipped cream 40%
3.5 oz (100 g) honey
3.5 oz (100 g) sliced almonds

1. Line the cups the same way you lined the mazarin cups, see p.36.
2. Arrange the cups on two baking sheets. Squeeze about 0.9 oz (25 g) mazarin paste in each cup with the help of a decorating bag. Use tip no. 12 or cut a small hole in the tip.
3. Preheat the oven to 370 °F (190 °C).
4. Bake the cakes, but only until they are almost done and quite light as they will be baked again. It takes about 12 minutes.
5. Boil all of the ingredients for the Tosca topping to 240 °F (115 °C) while constantly stirring. When the Tosca mix starts to let go of the walls of the saucepan it is ready. (If you wish a variation by adding hazelnuts or pecans, you boil the Tosca batter to 244 °F (118 °C). The whole nuts do not bind the Tosca batter the same way flaked almonds do.) Or perform a marble-test:

Dip your fingers in cold water and get a hold of some of the batter. If you can roll it into a small marble between your thumb and index finger, it is perfect.
6. Stir in the flaked almonds.
7. Spread a layer of Tosca topping on each cake with the help of a spatula.
8. Preheat the oven to 445 °F (230 °C), and bake the cakes golden brown for about 5 minutes; watch them closely as they burn easily, which would be a shame.
9. Loosen them from the cups as soon as they have cooled down by knocking them against the table. Use a knife as help if some of them are stuck.

Tosca cakes with hazelnuts, walnuts, pecans, and almond flakes, as well as Tosca tart.

dough stiffens.

5. Preheat the oven to 370 °F (190 °C) degrees.
6. Spread a thin layer of raspberry jam over the bottom with a straight spatula.
7. Fill the dish with the mazarin paste three-quarters full and spread it out with a straight spatula.
8. Set the tart in the oven and lower the temperature to 340 °F (170 °C) after 10 minutes, bake it for 30–40 minutes altogether. Make sure that it is ready with a testing stick.
9. Sprinkle some sugar over the cake and turn it out on a cooling rack to cool. Preheat the oven to 445 °F (230 °C).
10. Spread a thin layer of tosca topping with flaked almonds on top and place the tart on a baking sheet lined with parchment paper. Bake it golden brown, about 5 minutes.

Empty the cake out of the dish as soon as it's cold.

STORAGE:
Preferably in room temperature; it will easily get moist in the fridge and lose its quality.

TOSCA TART

SERVES ABOUT 6 PEOPLE

1 tart dish, about 8 inches (20 cm) diameter and 1 cm tall.
1 batch classic butterdough 1-2-3, see p.27
1.7 oz (50 g) raspberry jam, see p.19
¼ batch mazarin paste number 1, see p.25
0.3 oz (10 g) granulated sugar to sprinkle on top
½ batch tosca topping, see p.40

1. Work the short-crust dough smooth with your hands and roll it out to about 1/8 of an inch (3 mm) thickness, somewhat larger than the dish in size, with the help of a rolling pin and wheat flour.
2. Lightly powder the dough and roll it onto the rolling pin. Roll it over the dish.
3. Press the dough down into the dish and roll it over so that it doesn't stick to the dough.
4. Set the dish in the fridge for 30 minutes so that the short-crust

STRAWBERRY MAZARINS

I used to bake these delicious strawberry mazarins in summertime, and they were always popular among the customers. We were sold-out when we closed almost every day, and if there were any left, we would have them for breakfast the next day.

In reality you can fill these with all kinds of berries, and they are great all year long as we have access to fresh berries during all seasons nowadays. You can also make them in a tart dish the same way as the mazarin tart; it is both beautiful and tasty.

ABOUT 10

10 tosca cups, also called tartlet cups, about 3 inch (80 mm)
    diameter and ½ inch (1 cm) tall
½ batch white linzerdough, see vanilla hearts on p.80
¼ batch mazarin paste number 1, see p.25

Tea-bread filling:
8.8 oz (250 g) almond paste
0.9 oz (25 g) sugar
1 oz (30 g) egg white (approx. 1)

17.6 oz (500 g) fresh strawberries
5.3 oz (150 g) red currant jelly (see my book *The Jam and
    Marmalade Bible* or use your own)
0.9 oz (25 g) pistachio nuts for decorating

1. Line the cups with the linzerdough the same way you would for classic mazarins, see p.36.
2. Fill mazarin paste in each cup with a decorating bag. Use tip no. 12 or cut a small hole in the tip.
3. Bake the cups for about 12 minutes; they are going back into the oven later on to finish baking.
4. Dissolve the almond paste, at room temperature, at the baking table with the sugar and the egg white, a little at a time, until you have a completely smooth paste. It should be squeezable and not too loose. Add more egg whites if it is too firm.
5. Fill the tea-bread filling in a plastic decorating bag with curly tip number 12. Knock the cakes out of the cups and arrange them on a baking sheet.
6. Squeeze a garland around the cakes with the filling. Let it sit and dry for an hour; this way the contours will look better when you bake them.
7. Preheat the oven to 480 °F (250 °C).
8. Bake the cakes quickly in the oven so that the filling gets a nice color. Remove them and let them cool down.
9. Fill the hole with rinsed strawberries.
10. Warm the red currant jelly to the boiling point and brush the jelly on the strawberries. Sprinkle some pistachio nuts on top.

STORAGE:
The cakes lasts for a day in room temperature, if you place them in the fridge the short-crust dough will go soft.

BIENSTICK BITES

This is how they did them at the old Brauns Hovkonditori in Malmö.

40–50 BITES

1 batch of classic short-crust dough, see p.27

Filling:
2.2 lb (1 kg) almond paste 50/50
9.3 oz (265 g) unsalted butter
7 oz (200 g) eggs (approx. 4)

Prepare the same way as for the mazarin paste number 1, see p.25.

1 batch tosca topping, see tosca cakes on p.40
14 oz (400 g) dark chocolate, preferably Valrhona Grand Cru Guanaja 70%

Do as described for tosca bites on p.87, but without the raspberry jam on the bottom.

STORAGE:
Keep in the fridge for about 1 week.

FRENCH SOFTIES

This too is a delicious almond cake from the esteemed Brauns Conditori in Malmö.

40–50 BITES

1 batch of classic short-crust dough, see p.27

Filling:
2.2 lb (1 kg) almond paste 50/50
5.3 oz (150 g) eggs (approx. 3)
1.7 oz (50 g) chopped, preserved orange peels, see p.20

Flaked hazelnuts or flaked almond
14 oz (400 g) dark chocolate, preferably Valrhona Grand Cru Guanaja 70 %
Powdered sugar

1. Dissolve the almond paste at room temperature by adding one egg at a time until it is a lump-free mass.
2. Carefully work in the orange peel and blend well.
3. Bake the short-crust dough like described for tosca bites on page 87.
4. Let the baked short-crust dough cool down and spread the filling evenly on top with the help of a straight spatula.
5. Sprinkle flaked hazelnuts or almonds on top.
6. Bake for about 45 minutes in 355 °F (180 °C) until the cake is golden brown.
7. Take it out and carefully release it from the edges with the help of a knife.
8. Place a piece of parchment paper on a baking sheet and place the whole capsule on top.
9. Cut in pieces of 2 x ¾ inches (55 x 20 mm) with the help of a ruler and a sharp jagged knife.
10. Turn the pieces and powder them with powdered sugar.

TRONDHEIMARE

I've never seen these cakes in Trond-
heim, but they are moist and tasty. When
you melt the butter the filling becomes
creamier. It's all about the fresh almond
paste here.

20 CAKES

20 mazarin cups
1 batch almond short-crust dough, see fursten
on page 47

Filling:
5.3 oz (150 g) butter
1 lemon, yellow and ripe
16 oz (450 g) almond paste 50/50
1.7 oz (50 g) sugar
0.7 oz (20 g) real vanilla sugar
5.3 oz (150 g) eggs (approx. 3)

1 oz (30 g) flaked almond for decorating
1 batch apricot icing, see p.17

1. Line the cups the way described for
   mazarins, see p.36.
2. Preheat the oven to 370 °F (190 °C).
3. Melt the butter in a small saucepan and
   boil it for 5 minutes, then set it aside to
   cool.
4. Clean and finely grate the lemon.
5. Dissolve the almond paste, at room temperature, with the sugar, lemon zest, and
   eggs one at a time into a lump-free mass.
6. Lastly work in the melted butter.
7. Fill the cups three-fourths full by using a
   decorating bag. Cut a hole in the tip or
   use tip no. 12.
8. Sprinkle flaked almonds on top.
9. Bake the cakes golden brown, about
   20 minutes.
10. Let the cakes cool in the form before you
    knock them out.
11. Boil the apricot icing and brush it over
    the cakes to give them a nice shine.

STORAGE:
Will keep for about 3 days in the fridge, and
you can also freeze these.

Fürsten

Trondheimare

Rhubarb Mazarins

Truffle Mazarins

TRUFFLE MAZARINS

This is a favorite mazarin of the chocolate lover and is fantastically tasty with its intense chocolate flavor from the Guanaja chocolate. Enjoy the cakes at room temperature, as that is when they taste the best. These are great with a cup of coffee and grappa. I hope you agree when you try them that way! Do not get tempted to use a cheaper chocolate, as it won't taste the same.

30 CAKES

1 batch classic mazarins (without the apricot icing and fondant) see p.35
1 batch pâtisserie ganache with Valrhona Grand Cru Guanaja 70%, see p.14
cocoa powder, preferably Valrhona red-brown cocoa

DAY 1
1. Bake the mazarins
2. Make the ganache

DAY 2
3. Release the mazarins from the cups and arrange them on a baking sheet.
4. Fill the ganache in a decorating bag and cut a hole in the bottom.
5. Squeeze out a ball of ganache on every mazarin.
6. Spread and shape the ganache unevenly with a spoon, see picture on p.45.
7. Powder the cocoa powder on top.

STORAGE:
In the fridge for 2–3 days. Truffle mazarins may also be frozen without the cocoa.

RHUBARB MAZARINS

Terribly delicious mazarins, which are not only good in spring, but may be varied with other fruits and berries dependent on the season. These taste wonderful with raspberries as well. Or why not blueberries? Yes, try whatever you wish; this way the baking is more fun as well. My good friend Ingar Nilsson knows everything there is to know about rhubarb and then some; she would love these cakes.

30 CAKES

30 mazarin cups

Rhubarb compote:
½ vanilla bean
26.4 oz (750 g) rhubarb
8.8 oz (250 g) sugar
4.5 oz (125 g) water

1 batch classic short-crust dough, see p.27
½ batch mazarin paste number 1, see p.25
0.3 oz (10 g) roughly ground cardamom

Topping:
3.5 oz (100 g) unsalted butter
3.5 oz (100 g) wheat flour
3.5 oz (100 g) sugar
3.5 oz (100 g) almond flour
Stir the cold butter in with the other ingredients to a crumbly sprinkle, pass through a potato ricer, and set in the freezer to stiffen.

Powdered sugar

1. Peel the rhubarb and dice.
2. Cut the vanilla bean lengthwise and scrape the seeds out with a knife. Bring sugar and water to a boil with the vanilla bean and add the rhubarb.
3. Simmer the rhubarb for 1 minute, and later let it cool in the sauce.
4. Preheat the oven to 370 °F (190 °C).
5. Line the cups as described in the recipe for classic mazarins, see p.36.
6. Flavor the mazarin paste with cardamom.
7. Place the paste in a decorating bag and fill the cups half full.
8. Place about 1 tbsp drained rhubarb compote in each form.
9. Remove the topping from the freezer and add a tbsp of topping on each cake.
10. Bake the cakes golden brown for about 25–30 minutes.
11. Let them cool down and take them out of the cups. Dust some powdered sugar on top.

STORAGE:
The cakes keep for 1–2 days in room temperature.

FURSTEN

This cake, with its piquant flavoring, is both tasty and easy to bake. You never grow tired of the fresh taste of lemon and cardamom.

20 CAKES

20 oval almond mussel cups

Almond short-crust dough:
1 lemon, yellow and ripe
13.6 oz (385 g) wheat flour
8.8 oz (250 g) finely grated almond
8.8 oz (250 g) butter
7.9 oz (225 g) powdered sugar
0.9 oz (25 g) real vanilla sugar
0.3 oz (10 g) roughly ground cardamom
1.7 oz (50 g) egg (approx. 1)
1 oz (30 g) egg white (approx. 1)

Filling:
1 lemon, yellow and ripe
14 oz (400 g) almond paste 50/50
5.3 oz (150 g) butter
1.7 oz (50 g) egg (approx. 1)
1.4 oz (40 g) yolks (approx. 2)
0.3 oz (10 g) real vanilla sugar
0.2 oz (5 g) roughly ground cardamom

Egg wash:
1 egg
1 yolk
1 pinch of salt
Whisk everything together.

Short-crust dough:
1. Clean and finely grate the lemon.
2. Place the flour and the almonds in a ring on the baking table.
3. Place the butter, at room temperature, with the sifted powdered sugar, vanilla sugar, and cardamom in the middle.
4. Add the eggs, egg whites, and grated lemon zest.
5. Quickly work the dough together.
6. Wrap in plastic wrap and place in the fridge for 1 hour.
7. Work the dough smooth and line the cups, see lining short-crust cups of mazarins, p.36.

Filling:
8. Rinse and finely grate the lemon.
9. Stir the almond paste (room temperature) with 1/3 of the butter into a mass without lumps; add the remaining butter a little at a time.
10. First add the eggs and later the yolks. Flavor with lemon zest, vanilla sugar, and cardamom.
11. Fill the cups three-fourths full with the help of a plastic decorating bag. Cut a hole in the bottom or use tip no. 12.
12. Spread the almond filling in the cups with a spatula for an even surface.
13. Roll out the remaining short-crust dough about 1/16 inch (2 mm) thick and cut out finger thick lengths with the help of a pastry cutter or a knife.
14. Add the short-crust dough as a cross.
15. Preheat the oven to 370 °F (190 °C).
16. Place the cakes on a baking sheet. Brush them with the egg wash.
17. Bake them golden brown, about 20 minutes.
18. Let the cakes cool in the cups before you knock them out.

STORAGE:
These good cakes will keep for about 3 days. You may freeze them both baked and raw.

POLYNEE TART

These delicious, dry tarts have an amazing taste—chewy and crispy. My friend Ulla Rosander, a nutritionist, almost ate the entire cake on her own when we visited her in Kivik last summer. So there goes that diet.

6 BITES

1 tart dish, 8 inch (20 cm) diameter and about ½ inch (1 cm) tall
1 batch sort-crust dough, see p.27
1.7 oz (50 g) raspberry jam, see p.19
½ batch macaroon filling, see p.49

1. Roll the short-crust dough out to about 1/8 of an inch (3 mm) thickness, somewhat larger than the dish. Lightly powder with flour and roll it onto the rolling pin.
2. Roll the dough out over the dish and lightly powder flour on top.
3. Press the dough down in the dish with the help of a piece of dough.
4. Roll over the dough and loosen around the edges.
5. Place the dish in the fridge for 30 minutes to stiffen.
6. Preheat the oven to 320 °F (160 °C).
7. Pipe raspberry jam in the dish and fill it about three-fourths full with the macaroon filling.
8. Roll out short-crust dough to about 1/16 (2 mm) thickness and cut out 3/16 inch (5 mm) long lengths. Place in a cross, see picture on p.48–49.
9. Bake golden brown, about 45 minutes.
10. Let it cool in the dish and then carefully lift it up without breaking it.

POLYNEER

When baking polyneer, it is very important that you bake them right away so that the filling doesn't develop a crust; if so, it will crackle roughly instead of evenly and beautifully. The texture of the filling is also important for it to crackle beautifully.

I would know, because God help me if one of the polyneer didn't crackle beautifully when Kurt Lundgren at Blekingborg's Pâtisserie in Malmö checked the pastries before they were brought up in the store. He would simply say "Jan, just grind these up and make 'vacuum cleaners' of them. Make new ones this instant!" That was the way one learned to become a pastry chef back then.

30 CAKES

30 small mazarin cups
1 batch classic short-crust dough, see p.27
5.3 oz (150 g) raspberry jam. See p.19

Macaroon filling (It should be a bit looser than the one used for macaroons)
17.6 oz (500 g) almond paste 50/50
8.8 oz (250 g) sugar
5.3 oz (150 g) egg whites (approx. 5)

1. Preheat the oven to 340 °F (170 °C).
2. Line the cups the way described for mazarins, see p.36. Skip the cross on top.
3. Squeeze out a small top of raspberry jam 1 tsp (5g) in each cup, with the help of a small paper cone.
4. Dissolve the almond paste (room temperature) with the sugar and one-third of the egg whites. Blend into a mixture free of lumps. Add the remaining egg whites a little at a time.
5. Fill the cups about three-fourths full with the mixture.
6. Roll out some of the short-crust dough to about 1/16 (2 mm) thickness with the help of some wheat flour and cut lengths of about 3/16 inch (5 mm).
7. Place a cross of short-crust dough on top of the cups and pinch off any surplus dough with your fingers. Bake them right away for about 25 minutes until they are golden brown and beautifully crackled.
8. Lift the cakes from the cups right away and let them cool on a cooling rack.

STORAGE:
Polyneer will stay fresh for about 3 days in room temperature, but you may also freeze them.

Variation:
Follow the above recipe but instead of adding the cross, squeeze some raspberry jam (or other jam) on top of the cakes instead of the bottom and sprinkle some almond flakes on top, see the picture.

ALEXANDER CAKES

I would make these tasty cakes often as a young boy, and I wondered how people could eat them because they seemed so sweet. The tart and cakes received a thin layer of apricot icing, then one would roll out green marzipan, about 1/16 (2 mm) thick, and cut out 3/16 inch (5 mm) wide lengths that were arranged in a crisscross pattern on the cakes. The holes were filled with all kinds of jam, then they were glazed with jelly.

In the picture I've made them as a tart, cakes, and as petits-fours. I have modernized them a little bit since I love the filling. This is how I want them to look in the twenty-first century!

30 CAKES

30 mazarin cups
1 batch of short-crust dough, see p.27
5.3 oz (150 g) raspberry jam, see recipe p.19

Alexander filling:
17.6 oz (500 g) almond paste 50/50
8.8 oz (250 g) eggs (approx. 5)

1 batch of apricot icing, see p.17
Fresh fruits and berries for decorating
Powdered sugar

1. Work the almond paste (room temperature) smooth with the eggs one at a time, avoid lumps. If there are lumps, pass through a sieve.
2. Work the cold short-crust dough smooth with your hands.
3. Line the cups as described for mazarins, but squeeze out a small circle of 1 tsp (5g) raspberry jam in the bottom and then fill them with alexander filling to about three-fourths full. Bake the cakes the same way, and let them cool, see p.36.
4. Bring the apricot icing to a boil and brush the top of the cakes.
5. Decorate with berries and fruit as pictured and dust powdered sugar on top.

ALEXANDER TART

6 BITES

1 tart dish, 8 inch (20 cm) diameter and about ½ inch (1 cm) thi
1 batch classic short-crust dough, see p.27
1.7 oz (50 g) raspberry jam, see p.19
½ batch alexander filling, see alexander cakes
0.3 oz (10 g) sugar to sprinkle on top
1 batch apricot icing, see p.17
Fresh fruits
Powdered sugar

1. Roll out the short-crust dough to a thickness of about 1/8 of an inch (3 mm), somewhat larger than the dish.
2. Lightly powder flour on top and roll the dough onto the rolling pin.
3. Roll the dough over the dish and press it down with a piece of dough.
4. Set the dish in the fridge for 30 minutes so that it stiffens.
5. Preheat the oven to 370 °F (190 °C).
6. Spread raspberry jam on the bottom, with a straight spatula.
7. Scoop the alexander filling in the dish so that it is about three-fourths full.
8. Bake it for 10 minutes and then lower the temperature to 340 °F (170 °C).
9. Bake the cake golden brown, about 35–40 minutes; make sure that it is baked all the way through by testing with a toothpick.
10. Sprinkle sugar on top and turn the cake out on parchment paper. Remove the dish and let the tart cool down.
11. Turn it back around and spread boiling apricot icing over the surface with a brush.
12. Decorate with fresh fruits as pictured, and dust some powdered sugar on top.

AMBROSIA CAKE

Very few cakes have suffered a fate more tragic than the ambrosia tart, which is manufactured by the industry in packaging that will keep for months and is full of preservatives.

At Blekinborgs Pâtisserie we would bake them the proper way, and the customers would buy them right out of the oven.

Traditionally, the glaze is covered only with some sprinkles of preserved orange zest, but Kurt at Blekingborgs Pâtisserie wanted us to add some pistachio nuts as well. Back then we would color white almonds with green food coloring to make it look like pistachio nuts, because it was so hard to get a hold of them then. Pistachios were only used for pralines.

30 CAKES

30 mazarin cups
1 batch classic short-crust dough, see p.27
1 batch fondant, see p.16
1 batch apricot icing, see p.17
1 drop green food color, preferably natural
5.3 oz (150 g) chopped, preserved orange peels, see p.20
1.7 oz (50 g) pistachio nuts

Ambrosia filling:
17.6 oz (500 g) almond paste 50/50
7 oz (200 g) butter
3.5 oz (100 g) yolks (approx. 5)
7 oz (200 g) eggs (approx. 4)
1.7 oz (50 g) wheat flour

1. Work the cold short-crust dough smooth by hand.
2. Line the cups as described for mazarins, see p.36.
3. Make the ambrosia mass as described for mazarin paste, see p.25.
4. Fill and bake the cups as described for mazarins.
5. Brush the cold cakes with boiling apricot icing.
6. Warm the fondant to 86 °F (35 °C). Color with 1 drop of green food color.
7. Dip the cakes in the icing and scrape off surplus fondant with a straight spatula.
8. Sprinkle a blend of chopped orange peel and pistachio nuts on top.

If you want to make a tart instead, follow the same process but use with ½ recipe.

STORAGE:
It will keep in the fridge for 2–3 days. If you are going to freeze them, do not glaze them.

LINZER EYES

Linzer Eyes are an international pastry classic. They used to be prepared as small petits-fours as well. Wiener waffles are just as good. Two sheets of brown linzer dough are glued together with raspberry jam. A pattern of glaze is added on top, and then they are left overnight before they are cut into squares, 2x2 inches (4x4 cm).

20 PASTRIES

Special short-crust dough:
8.8 oz (250 g) almond paste 50/50
1.7 oz (50 g) egg (approx. 1)
0.7 oz (20 g) egg yolk (approx. 1)
8.8 oz (250 g) butter
3.5 oz (100 g) powdered sugar
0.9 oz (25 g) real vanilla sugar
12.3 oz (350 g) wheat flour

14 oz (400 g) raspberry jam, see p.19
Powdered sugar for decorating

1. Work the almond paste (room temperature) smooth and add egg and egg yolk to form a dough without lumps. Stir in the butter (room temperature).
2. Sift powdered sugar and vanilla sugar on top and work that in with the rest. Fold in the wheat flour and knead into a dough, but do not overwork it.
3. Wrap in plastic wrap and let it sit in the fridge for at least 2 hours.
4. Work the cold dough smooth by hand and roll out half of it with some wheat flour, about 1/8 of an inch (3mm) thick.

5. Cut out about 20 circles with a scalloped cookie cutter, 3 inches (80 mm) in diameter, and place them on a baking sheet lined with parchment paper.
6. Cut the same amount of circles from the other half of dough, but make the dough a little thicker, about 1/8 of an inch (4 mm), so they will not easily break when there are holes in them. Cut three holes on each one of the thicker circles with a ¾ inch (20 mm) cookie cutter.
7. Preheat the oven to 390 °F (200 °C).
8. Bake the circles golden brown, about 10–12 minutes; do not leave the oven unattended, because they burn quickly.
9. Let the circles cool. Spread a thin layer of raspberry jam on the thin circles with a straight spatula.
10. Place the circles with holes in them on top and lightly press down.
11. Dust powdered sugar on top.

STORAGE:
The pastries will keep for 5 days at room temperature.

RASPBERRY SQUARES

This simple pastry was among the first I ever learned to bake as an apprentice, and they are just as good today as they were then. It does however need a good short-crust dough and a high-quality raspberry jam.

ABOUT 40

1 batch white linzer dough, see p.80
12.3 oz (350 g) raspberry jam, see recipe p.19
Egg wash, see p.47
1.7 oz (50 g) almond flakes

1. Preheat the oven to 355 °F (180 °C).
2. Roll out half of the linzer dough into a square, about 1/8 of an inch (3 mm) thick.
3. Roll it onto the rolling pin and roll it over a baking sheet lined with parchment paper.
4. Cut the dough edges evenly and poke the bottom with a fork.
5. Half-bake it in the oven for about 10 minutes and let it cool.
6. Spread a good layer of thick raspberry jam on top, about 3/16 inch (5 mm) thick.
7. Roll out the remaining dough about 1/8 of an inch (3 mm) thick with the help of some wheat flour.
8. Cut out finger-wide lengths with a rippled pastry cutter.
9. Place them in a woven pattern with about ½ inch (1 cm) space in between over the plate.
10. Brush the dough strips with egg wash.
11. Bake the plate golden brown on 355 °F (180 °C) for about 15 minutes. Let it cool.
12. Cut 2x2 inch (4x4 cm) squares with a sharp knife.

STORAGE:
Store in a dry place so that the squares do not soften.

RASPBERRY LINZER

This good cake originated in the city Linz in Austria, which is quite the land of pâtisseries and has many pastry specialties. The dough and pastry have spread all over the world just like their famous Sachertorte. This is also done as a tart and is shipped all over the world in cartons. The quality of the cake is dependent on a good raspberry jam and a fine dough with a distinct almond and cinnamon flavor. Serve with whipped cream like they do in Austria.

20 TARTS

20 classic mazarin cups

Brown linzerdough:
1/2 lb (240 g) wheat flour
5.3 oz (150 g) unsalted butter
5.3 oz (150 g) brown sugar
1 tsp (5g) salt, preferably fleur de sel
1 tsp (5g) ground cinnamon
1.7 oz (50 g) egg (approx. 1)
1 oz (30 g) egg white (approx. 1)
5.3 oz (150 g) ground unpeeled almonds

About 17.6 oz (500 g) raspberry jam, see recipe on p.19
Powdered sugar to sift on top

1. Place the flour in a ring and place the butter, at room temperature, in the middle.
2. Sprinkle brown sugar, salt, and cinnamon on top of the butter.
3. Pinch the butter in with the cinnamon sugar so that you get a crumbly mass.
4. Add egg, egg white, and almonds, and work into a short-crust dough. (Do not overwork the dough, it will become chewy and hard and will pull together in the cups.)
5. Roll the dough in plastic wrap and let it rest in the fridge for at least 2 hours. Preheat the oven to 370 °F (190 °C).
6. Line the cups as described for the classic mazarins, see p.36.
7. Fill the cups about three-fourths full of raspberry jam with the help of a decorating bag. Cut a hole in the bottom.
8. Roll out the remaining short-crust dough to about 1/16 (2 mm) thickness. Cut out finger-wide strips and place a cross of dough on top of the jam.
9. Bake the linzer tarts golden brown, about 20 minutes.
10. Let them cool down in the cups. Then knock them out and sift powdered sugar on top.

STORAGE:
Will keep for 3 days in the fridge. May also freeze.

LINZER DOMES

Sinfully good. I remember that the pastry chef Thure Collbring at the Conditori Lundagard was absolutely in love with these. They are very fragile and they should be eaten freshly baked.

ABOUT 30 DOMES

1 batch white linzer dough, see p.80
17.6 oz (500 g) almond paste 50/50
¼ batch vanilla cream, see p.15
Egg wash, see p.47
1.7 oz (50 g) almond flakes

1. Make a filling out of almond paste, at room temperature, that you work smooth with the vanilla cream; do not add all the vanilla cream at once as the filling will then get lumps.
2. Work the cold linzerdough smooth by hand.
3. Roll out half of the dough 1/8 of an inch (3 mm) thick with the help of a rolling pin and wheat flour.
4. Cut out 30 bottoms with a round cookie cutter, about 2 2/3 inch (70 mm) in diameter.
5. Place them on a baking sheet lined with parchment paper.
6. Scoop the mass into a decorating bag and cut a small hole in the bottom. Squeeze out small circle of filling, about 0.7 oz (20 g) on each bottom.
7. Brush the edges with the egg wash.
8. Preheat the oven to 370 °F (190 °C).
9. Roll out the rest of the dough and cut out circles with a cookie cutter, of about 3 inch (80 mm) diameter.
10. Place them on top of the domes and pinch them into place so that the dough sticks to the egg wash.
11. Brush the top with egg wash as well and sprinkle some almond flakes on top.
12. Bake the domes golden brown, about 15–20 minutes.
13. Let them cool on the plate, as they are very fragile.

STORAGE:
Keep at room temperature 1–2 days.

Raspberry Linzer

Linzer Domes

Lingonberry Purses

57

LINGON PURSES

I've baked this good pastry with lingonberries at multiple bakeries, and when they are fresh out of the oven they are quite the delicacy. In Northern Germany you often find them at the bakeries, where they call them Preisselbertaschen. When I visited Konditorei Stecker in Bremen, where my friend and colleague Hans Eichmuller learned the pastry chef profession, I saw them as part of their selection as well. Within this profession there's always been a constant influx of recipes from the rest of the continent.

ABOUT 30 PURSES

1 batch white linzerdough, see p.80
8.8 oz (250 g) almond paste
2.8 oz (80 g) yolks (approx. 4)

Topping:
3.5 oz (100 g) unsalted butter
3.5 oz (100 g) wheat flour
3.5 oz (100 g) sugar
3.5 oz (100 g) almond flour

Egg wash, see p.47
10.5 oz (300 g) classic lingonberry jam, see my book *The Jam and Marmalade Bible* or use your own (it is important that has a firm and jelly-like texture)

3.5 oz (100 g) powdered sugar
0.9 oz (25 g) real vanilla sugar

1. Work the cold butter in with the other ingredients for the wash.
2. Squeeze the dough through a potato ricer onto a plate. Place it in the freezer.
3. Mix the almond paste (room temperature) with the egg yolks, a little at a time, into a pipeable mass; if needed take an additional yolk.
4. Roll out the linzerdough about 1/8 of an inch (3 mm) thick with the help of a rolling pin and some wheat flour.
5. Cut out 3 circles with a cookie cutter, which has a 5 inches (11.5 cm) diameter.
6. Place them on a baking sheet lined with parchment paper and brush the edges with the egg wash.
7. Pipe a string of the paste in the middle of the circles, about 0.3 oz (10 g) on each.
8. Pipe the lingonberry jam the same way, about 0.3 oz (10 g) as well.
9. Fold the dough over the fill and close it along the edges with a fork.
10. Brush the purses well with the egg wash.
11. Take the topping out of the freezer and arrange about 0.4 oz (12 g) topping on each cake.
12. Preheat the oven to 390 °F (200 °C).
13. Bake them golden brown, about 15 minutes.
14. Dust sugar blended with vanilla sugar on top, and then they're ready to serve.

STORAGE:
In the fridge 1–2 days.

APRICOT CAKES

We would always bake these delicious cakes at Konditori Hollandia in Malmö and the recipe came from Konditori Desirée at the Hotel d'Angleterre at Kongens Nytorv.

30 CAKES

30 mazarin cups

1 vanilla bean, preferably Tahitian vanilla
2.2 lb (1 kg) water
17.6 oz (500 g) dried apricots

1 batch of classic short-crust dough, see p.27.

Cream filling:
14 oz (400 g) almond paste 50/50
7 oz (200 g) vanilla cream, see p.15

1 batch apricot icing, see p.17
7 oz (200 g) fondant, see p.16
0.3 oz (10 g) dark rum
1 drop of red food color, preferably natural

30 roasted hazelnuts for decorating

DAY I

1. Cut the vanilla bean lengthwise and place it in a saucepan with 2.2 lb (1 kg) boiling water. Remove the saucepan from the stove.
2. Add the dried apricots and cover with a lid. Let them soak overnight.

DAY 2

3. Bring the apricots to a boil and let them cool completely.
4. Work the cold short-crust dough smooth by hand.
5. Line the cups as described for mazarins, see p.36.
6. Put the cups close together.
7. Dissolve the almond paste with the vanilla cream, a little at a time, until you have a pipeable paste.
8. Scoop the paste into a decorating bag. Use tip no. 12 or cut a hole in the bottom.
9. Pipe about ½ oz (18 g) of filling on each form.
10. Add two drained apricots.
11. Roll out the dough about 1/8 of an inch (3 mm) thick and cut it into 2 inch (5 mm) wide strips, powder flour over the dough, and roll it onto the rolling pin. Roll

the dough over the cups. Remove surplus dough from the cups and place them on a baking sheet.
12. Preheat the oven to 390 °F (200 °C).
13. Bake the cakes golden brown for about 25 minutes.
14. Let them cool completely and then carefully knock the cakes out of the cups.
15. Brush the cakes with boiling apricot icing.
16. Warm the fondant to 95 °F (35 °C) degrees. Add rum and some red food color, if needed then adjust the texture with some syrup, see p.17.
17. Dip the apricot brushed side of the cake in the fondant, scrape off any surplus fondant with your finger, and let them stiffen on a baking sheet.
18. Place a shelled roasted hazelnut on each cake.
19. Set the plate back in the oven, which should still be lukewarm, for a couple of minutes so that the icing stiffens and obtains a nice shine.

STORAGE:
Keep in the fridge 1–2 days, or you may freeze them without the icing.

PRUNE CAKES

Herman Martensson was a talented professional whom I worked with at the Savoy Hotel in Malmö and at the Hotel Kramer. He often baked these tasty cakes. Herman is Danish, and he was educated in desserts at the Hotel d'Angleterre in Copenhagen under the great pastry chef Gosta Wennberg.

30 CAKES

30 elongated almond mussel cups

1 vanilla bean from Tahiti
2.2 lb (1 kg) water
17.6 oz (500 g) dried Katrin plums, preferably French from Pays d'Auge.

1 batch classic short-crust dough, see p.27.

Cream filling:
14 oz (400 g) almond paste 50/50
7 oz (200 g) vanilla cream, see p.15

1 batch apricot icing, see p.17
7 oz (200 g) fondant, see p.16
1 drop of green food coloring, preferably natural
1.7 oz (50 g) pistachio nuts

DAY I

1. Cut the vanilla bean lengthwise and place it in 2 1/5 lb (1 kg) boiling water. Add the plums and let them come to a boil.

2. Remove from the stove, cover with a lid, and let them soak overnight.

DAY 2

3. Work the cold short-crust dough smooth by hand.
4. Line the cups with short-crust dough as described for mazarins, see p.36.
5. Place the cups close together at the baking table.
6. Dissolve the almond paste with the vanilla cream, a little at a time, into a smooth filling.
7. Scoop it into a decorating bag. Use tip no. 12 or cut a small hole in the bottom.
8. Squeeze about ½ oz (18 g) of cream filling at the bottom of each cup.
9. Let the liquid drain from the plum and place two plums in each cup.
10. Roll out the remaining short-crust dough 1/8 of an inch (3 mm) thick and somewhat larger than the cups. Cut out strips from the dough of about 3/16 inch (5 mm) width. Powder with flour over the dough and roll it onto the rolling pin. Roll the dough over the cups.
11. Remove the dough from the sides of the cups and place them on a baking sheet lined with parchment paper.
12. Preheat the oven to 390 °F (200 °C)
13. Bake the cakes golden brown for about 25 minutes.
14. Let them cool and carefully knock them out of the cups.

15. Brush the surface with boiling apricot icing.
16. Warm the fondant to 95 °F (35 °C). Color with green food coloring and if needed adjust the texture with syrup if it is too thick, see recipe p.17.
17. Dip the top of the cakes in the fondant and remove extra icing with your finger.
18. Sprinkle some chopped pistachio nuts on top of the cakes.
19. Place them in the oven, which should still be lukewarm, to solidify the icing and obtain a nice shine.

STORAGE:
Keep in the fridge for 1–2 days, or in the freezer without the glaze.

APPLE DELICACIES

These apple-flavored cakes are guaranteed favorites in fall when the apples are at their best.

When you use a lot of yolks, just freeze the egg whites for another time. They freeze very well.

30 CAKES

30 mazarin cups, preferably elongated
1 batch classic short-crust dough, see p.27
½ batch apple compote, see p.19
1 lemon, yellow and ripe
17.6 oz (500 g) almond paste
4.2 oz (120 g) yolk (approx. 6)
30 whole almonds with the shell
1 batch apricot icing, see p.17

1. Work the cold short-crust dough soft by hand and line the cups as described for mazarins, see p.36.
2. Fill the cups about three-fourths full with the apple compote and bake them golden brown for 25 minutes in 355 °F (180 °C).
3. Let them cool completely.
4. Grate the outer zest of the lemon finely.
5. Dissolve the almond paste (room temperature) with the yolks, a little at a time, into a smooth filling without lumps. It should be just pipeable—absolutely not loose. If it is too hard, just add another yolk. Add the lemon zest.
6. Scoop the filling into a decorating bag with tip no. 12 and pipe a zigzag pattern on the cakes. Place an almond on top.
7. Let them sit and dry for 1 hour.
8. Preheat the oven to 480 °F (250 °C).
9. Bake them until they are golden brown as pictured, but do not leave the oven unattended—these burn easily.
10. Let the cakes cool completely and carefully knock them out of the cups.
11. Bring the apricot icing to a boil and brush the cakes with the jam.

STORAGE:
These will keep in the fridge for about 2–3 days.

Prune Cakes

Apricot Cakes

Apple Delicacies

ROLF'S APPLE LINZER

Rolf Augustsson was the owner of Konditori Hollandia in Malmö, and he loves pastries with apples. As soon as his wife Ingrid had some spare time she would peel apples for all kinds of pastries. Kivik's apples had a store at Storgatan in Malmö, so it was a short walk to go buy fresh apples.

30 PASTRIES

30 mazarin cups, round
1 batch linzerdough, see p.80
½ batch apriot compote, see p.19
½ batch vanilla cream, see p.15
Cinnamon sugar, see apple mazarins
1 batch apricot icing, p.17

1. Preheat the oven to 370 °F (190 °C)
2. Line the cups as described for classic mazarins, but with linzerdough instead, see p.36.
3. Fill 0.7 oz (20 g) apple compote in each cup with a decorating bag.
4. Sprinkle cinnamon sugar on the apple compote and fill the cups three-fourths full with vanilla cream. Use a decorating bag with a hole in the bottom.
5. Place the cups close together. Roll out the remaining dough 1/8 of an inch (3 mm) thick, powder flour over the dough, and roll it onto the rolling pin. Roll it over the cups.
6. Loosen the cups from the dough and poke them on top with a fork.
7. Sprinkle cinnamon sugar on top.
8. Bake the cakes golden brown for bout 25 minutes.
9. Remove the cups and brush them with apricot icing to obtain a nice shine.

STORAGE:
Keep 1 day at room temperature and 1–2 days in the fridge.

APPLE MAZARINS

These simple mazarins always turn out well as long as you use fresh apple and cinnamon sugar. In summertime you may vary this recipe with apricots or blue prune plums that taste great as well.

30 MAZARINS

30 mazarin cups

1 batch classic short-crust dough, see p.27
1 batch mazarin paste number 1, see p.25
4 green, fresh apples, preferable Swedish Gravensteiner,
    Cox Orange, Ingrid Marie, or Belle de Boskoop
1 batch apricot icing, see p.17

Cinnamon sugar:
0.3 oz (10 g) ground cinnamon
3.5 oz (100 g) granulated sugar
Blend cinnamon and sugar by hand.

1. Follow the instructions for regular classic mazarins, see p.36, up until step 7.
2. Place an apple wedge on top of the filling in each cup.
3. Sprinkle some cinnamon sugar on top.
4. Bake the apple mazarins the same way you would for regular mazarins, about 18 minutes.
5. Let the cakes cool and remove the cups.
6. Brush them with boiling apricot icing.

STORAGE:
These will keep in the fridge for 2–3 days.

APPLE CUPS

These simple pastries with an apple filling and short-crust dough are a traditional part of Swedish pâtisseries, and they always taste delicious as long as they're fresh. You may vary these by using a topping instead of dough strips (see recipe p.58) and then powder vanilla sugar on top, which tastes amazing as well.

Serve with a good vanilla sauce.

30 CAKES

30 mazarin cups
1 batch white linzer dough, see p.80

Alexander mass:
7 oz (200 g) almond paste 50/50
3.5 oz (100 g) egg (2)

1 batch apple compote, see p.19
Egg wash, see p.47
1 oz (30 g) almond flakes for decorating
1 batch apricot icing, see p.17

1. Work the cold linzerdough smooth and roll it out to about 1/8 of an inch (3 mm) thickness. Powder some wheat flour on top and roll it onto the rolling pin, roll the dough over the cups, powder some flour over the dough, and gather the cups a little bit.
2. Take a piece of dough and press the dough into the cups.
3. Roll over them and place them on a baking sheet.
4. Dissolve the almond paste (room temperature) with egg, a little at a time, so that all the lumps are gone. If there are lumps, then pass it through a sieve.
5. Pipe 0.3 oz (10 g) alexander filling in the bottom of each cup with the help of a decorating bag. Use tip no. 10 or cut a small hole in the bottom.

6. Fill the cups with 0.8–1 oz (25–30 g) apple compote.
7. Roll out linzer dough about 1/16 (2 mm) thick and cut about 3/16 inch (5 mm) long lengths. Place them over the cakes in a cross.
8. Brush the dough strips with the egg wash and sprinkle some almond flakes in the middle.
9. Preheat the oven to 390 °F (200 °C).
10. Bake the cakes golden brown, about 20 minutes.
11. Remove them from the oven and let them cool, knock them out of the cups, and place them on a cooling rack.
12. Bring apricot icing to a boil and brush the pastry with it.

STORAGE:
Keep in the fridge for 2 days.

APPLE DOMES

These beauties served ice cold with vanilla sauce and a glass of madeira make a great dessert, but you may also serve them with afternoon coffee or tea.

The bisquit I pipe in the bottom of the cups prevents the apple filling from moistening the short-crust dough so that it stays fresh all day.

If you don't want to make 20 domes, no problem. Just decrease the recipe accordingly.

20 DOMES

20 tosca cups or tartlet cups, pretty flat, about 3 inch (80 mm) diameter
1 batch white linzerdough, see p.80

Bisquit:
2.1 oz (60 g) yolks (approx. 3)
3 oz (90 g) sugar
3 oz (90 g) egg whites (approx. 3)
3 oz (90 g) wheat flour

Apple Filling:
2.1 oz (60 g) California raisins
1.7 oz (50 g) dark rum
1 lemon, yellow and ripe
17.6 oz (500 g) apple, preferably Gravenstein or belle de Boskoop
3.5 oz (100 g) butter
3.5 oz (100 g) brown raw can sugar
0.9 oz (25 g) real vanilla sugar
1 tsp (5 g) ground cinnamon
3.5 oz (100 g) bread crumbs
2.8 oz (80 g) crushed walnuts

For topping:
14 oz (400 g) almond paste 50/50
3.5 oz (100 g) yolks (approx. 5)

1 batch apricot icing, see p.17
10 walnuts for decorating

1. Marinate the raisins in dark rum for at least 30 minutes.
2. Work the cold linzerdough by hand.
3. Line the cups as described for apple tartlets, see below.
4. Preheat the oven to 390 °F (200 °C).
5. Whisk the yolk and half of the sugar, about 1.5 oz (45 g), to a firm foam.
6. Whisk the egg whites to a firm meringue with 1.5 oz (45 g) sugar and fold in the yolks with the help of a spatula. Sift in the wheat flour as well.
7. Scoop the bisquit dough in a decorating bag. Use tip no. 12 or cut a hole in the bottom.
8. Cover the bottom of the lined cups with dough.
9. Bake them golden brown, about 15 minutes.
10. Clean the lemon and grate the zest, but only the outer yellow peel; if you grate too much, you will get a bitter taste. Squeeze the juice from the lemon.
11. Peel and core the apples and dice them.
12. Add the butter to a large frying pan with the brown sugar and vanilla sugar. Add the apples, lemon zest, and lemon juice and let it brown lightly and become firm.
13. Remove the pan from the stove, add the marinated raisins, cinnamon, bread crumbs, and the crushed walnuts. Stir well.
14. Let the apple filling cool completely.
15. Scoop the blend into a decorating bag and cut a rather large hole in the bottom. Dispense the apple fill in all of the 20 cups.
16. Preheat the oven to 480 °F (250 °C)
17. Dissolve the almond paste with the yolks so that it is just pipeable; scoop it into a decorating bag with curly tip no. 12.

18. Squeeze out a cross over the apple filling.
19. Bake the pastry for a maximum of 5 minutes in the oven until the almond paste has attained a nice color.
20. Let it cool and then carefully brush them with boiling apricot icing. Garnish with half a beautiful walnut, preferably French.

STORAGE:
Keep in the fridge 1–2 days.

APPLE TARTLETS

I remember that Ingeborg Larsson's pâtisserie by the railroad in Tomelilla had these as part of their selection, and they were very popular at my grandma's in fall. I also remember that we loved her butterdough apple tart.

20 TARTLETS

20 tosca cups or tartlet cups, quite flat, about 3 inch (80 mm) diameter
1 batch white linzerdough, see p.80
10 small apples, not too ripe, preferably Gravenstein, Ingrid Marie, or Cox Orange
½ lemon
10.5 oz (300 g) almond paste
2.8 oz (80 g) yolks (4)
0.5 oz (15 g) rum
0.9 oz (25 g) dark rum
0.9 oz (25 g) real vanilla sugar
Cinnamon sugar, see p.62
1 oz (30 g) almond flakes
1 batch apricot icing, see p.17

1. Work the cold dough smooth by hand and roll it out to 1/8 of an inch (3 mm) thickness.
2. Set the cups out on the work surface.
3. Sprinkle flour over the dough and, rolling it onto the rolling pin, roll it over the cups.
4. Bring the cups closer together, sprinkle flour over them, and push the dough into the cups with the help of a piece of dough.
5. Roll over the cups and place the lined cups on a baking sheet.
6. Peel and core the apples. Rub them with half a lemon so that they do not brown.
7. Cut the apples down the middle, place the halves in a wooden spoon, and cut slits in them with a knife, like you would for hasselback potatoes.
8. Dissolve the almond paste (room temperature) with the yolks, rum, and vanilla sugar to a soft and pipeable filling; add an additional yolk if it is too hard.
9. Pipe 0.7 oz (20 g) filling in each cup with the help of a decorating bag. Use tip no. 12 or cut a small hole in the bottom.
10. Add the slotted apple and sprinkle cinnamon sugar and almond flakes on top.
11. Preheat the oven to 390 °F (200 °C).
12. Bake the tartlets golden brown, about 25 minutes, make sure that the apples are soft with a toothpick.
13. Let them cool in the cups. Lift them out and place them on a cooling rack.
14. Boil the apricot icing and brush the tartlets for a beautiful shine.

STORAGE:
Keep in the fridge for about 2 days.

ORANGE MOONS

ABOUT 45 PASTRIES

1 batch mazarin paste number 1, but sift in 1.7 oz (50 g) wheat flour at the end and fold in with a spatula, see p.25.
2 oranges
0.9 oz (25 g) sugar
0.7 oz (2 cl) Grand Marnier, red
1 batch pâtisserie ganache with Valrhona Grand Cru Manjari 64%, see p.14
14 oz (400 g) dark chocolate, preferably Valrhona Grand Cru Manjari 64 % as a topping
3.5 oz (100 g) roasted almonds with the shell

DAY 1
1. Bake the mazarin filling the same way as for the mint truffle, see p.66.
2. Rinse and grate the outer zest of the oranges.

3. Rub the zest with the granulated sugar with the help of a straight spatula, until it starts draining.
4. Whisk the orange zest and liqueur into the ganache and mix with a hand mixer.
5. Let it sit in room temperature covered with plastic wrap overnight.

DAY 2
6. Cut out half-moon shaped bites with a sharp cookie cutter with a diameter of about 2 inches (50 mm). Dip the cookie cutter in warm water to make it easier. Place them on a piece of parchment paper.
7. Temper the chocolate, see p.13, and dip the whole cake in the chocolate with the help of a fork. Scrape off surplus chocolate.
8. Place the cakes on parchment paper to harden.
9. Scoop the orange ganache in a decorating bag with curly tip no.8 and pipe a small spiral, like pictured.
10. Decorate with roasted almonds.

STORAGE:
Keep the Orange Moons in the fridge and they will keep for about 1 week. These may also be frozen.

Orange Moons to the left, Mint Truffles to the right.

MINT TRUFFLE

This delicious, classic chocolate delicacy was the first chocolate pastry I ever baked as a 15-year-old apprentice at Konditori Heidi in Limhamn. Moist mazarin pastry dipped in fine dark chocolate with chocolate truffle on top and a fresh peppermint fondant in the middle just can't go wrong. The chef was Philip Linqvist, who later became one of Skane's last cake oven builders.

ABOUT 50 TRUFFLES

1 batch mazarin paste number 2, but sift in 1.7 oz (50 g) wheat flour at the end and fold it in with a spatula, see p.35.
0.3 oz (10 g) sugar to sprinkle on top
14 oz (400 g) dark chocolate, preferably Valrhona Grand Cru Pur Caribe 66 % for dipping
1 batch pâtisserie ganache with dark chocolate, preferably Grand Cru Pur Caribe 66%, see p.14
1 batch fondant, see p.16
1 drop peppermint oil

DAY 1
1. Preheat the oven to 355 °F (180 °C)
2. Line an edged baking sheet with parchment paper.
3. Spread the mazarin paste evenly on the plate with a straight spatula.
4. Bake until golden brown for about 35–40 minutes. Make sure that it is baked all the way through by poking it with a toothpick.
5. Let the cake cool and place it in the fridge overnight, covered with plastic wrap.

DAY 2
6. Sprinkle some sugar on top of the baked surface and loosen the cake from the sheet with a small, sharp knife.
7. Lift onto a piece of parchment paper.
8. Cut out round cakes with a thin cookie cutter, about 1.5 inch (40 mm) in diameter.
9. Temper the chocolate, see p.13, and dip the cakes in the chocolate with the help of a fork.
10. Scrape off any surplus chocolate and let them dry on parchment paper.
11. Squeeze a garland of pâtisserie ganache with curly tip no.8.
12. Warm the fondant to 85 °F (30 °C) (do not exceed this temperature) in a water bath and flavor sparingly with the peppermint oil (be careful, the flavor will easily become too intense). Let it cool to 77 °F (25 °C) before you use it; if not the chocolate will melt.
13. Pour the fondant into a paper cone and cut a hole in the bottom.
14. Fill the hole in the truffles with mint fondant and let it cool.

STORAGE:
Keep the truffles in the fridge. They will keep for about 1 week, but you may also freeze them.

ALMOND ARCHES

Decorative almond arches are always a great side with desserts. Serve them with ice cream or old-fashioned lemon fromage, see my book *Passion for Desserts* and you'll find the recipe for a proper lemon fromage. You used to be able to order almond arches on Saturdays for desserts or parties, and many restaurants ordered these from pâtisseries.

The waterfall in the picture was a typical decoration for almond arches at the Savoy Hotel in Malmö when I was a boy.

ABOUT 20 ARCHES

1 sheet of wafer paper/rice paper, A4-size
8.8 oz (250 g) almond paste 50/50
1.4 oz (40 g) egg whites (approx. 1 ½)
1.7 oz (50 g) powdered sugar
1 batch apricot icing, see p.17
3.5 oz (100 g) chopped, preserved orange peels, see p.20
3.5 oz (100 g) roasted almond flakes
7 oz (200 g) fondant, see p.16
0.7 oz (2 cl) dark rum

1. Cut the wafer paper with a sharp knife in two lengths, 3 ½ inches (8 cm) wide.
2. Dissolve the almond paste (room temperature) with a third of the egg whites for a smooth mass. Add powdered sugar and the remaining egg whites. Work smooth, it should not be too loose.
3. Divide the almond paste between the two wafer lengths. Spread it out evenly on the lengths, about 2/16 of an inch (4 mm) thick.
4. Cut 1 inch (2 cm) wide strips of the mass and wafer. Use a knife blade as a ruler and cut with a small, sharp knife (I use a flat blade).
5. Preheat the oven to 390 °F (200 °C).
6. Warm a curved wooden pan or a rolling pin in the oven and brush it with some food oil so that the almond arches don't stick.
7. Place the almond arches on the wooden pan, and the wafer will bend like the curve because of the heat.
8. Bake them golden brown for 7–8 minutes and let them cool down in the pan.
9. Bring the apricot icing to a boil and brush it on top of the almond arches.
10. Blend orange peels and flaked almonds on a plate.
11. Warm the fondant to 95 °F (35 °C)
12. Dilute it with the liquor and brush the almond arches lightly with the icing. Then dip them in the almond and orange peel blend.

STORAGE:
Almond arches should be eaten fresh and should not be frozen.

PISTACHIO BITES

This tasty chocolate topped cake has a lovely aroma of real pistachio nuts and not the synthetic pistachio paste used in many places. The elegant chocolate Pur Caribe balances the almond flavor, and the contrast of some orange flower water and Kirschwasser or rum makes the cake a unique food experience. Make sure that you do not bake the bottom for too long; it should be soft and moist with a wonderful pistachio aroma.

ABOUT 50 CAKES

Pistachio mixture:
5.3 oz (150 g) pistachio nuts
3.5 oz (100 g) shelled sweet almonds
8.8 oz (250 g) granulated sugar
8.8 oz (250 g) butter
8.8 oz (250 g) eggs (approx. 5)
1.7 oz (50 g) wheat flour
3 drops orange flower water (may be found in specialty stores)
0.7 oz (2 cl) Kirschwasser or dark rum
1 drop green food coloring, preferably natural

0.3 oz (10 g) sugar to sprinkle on top
14 oz (400 g) dark chocolate, preferably Valrhona Grand Cru Pur
    Caribe 66%, for dipping
1.7 oz (50 g) chopped pistachio nuts for decorating

DAY 1
1. Make a so called tant pour tant with equal parts almonds and sugar by mixing it in a food processor with a jagged knife blade till you have a nice powder.
2. Blend a smooth dough out of the butter (room temperature) and the powder.
3. Add the eggs, one at the time. Eggs should be at room temperature as well.
4. Sift in the wheat flour and fold it in with a spatula. Add the orange flower water, liquor, and a drop of green food color.
5. Preheat the oven to 355 °F (180 °C).
6. Line a baking sheet with parchment paper. Spread the pistachio dough as evenly as possible on the sheet with the help of a straight spatula.
7. Bake the bottom golden brown for 35–40 minutes. Test that it's done with a toothpick.
8. Let it cool down and cover with plastic wrap. Leave in the fridge overnight.

DAY 2
9. Sprinkle sugar over the baked surface and cut it loose from the sheet with a small knife.
10. Place a baking sheet lined with baking paper on top, turn the cake over, and remove the baking sheet.
11. Cut the plate in 1 inch (1 ½ cm) wide and 2 inch (5 cm) long pieces with the help of a ruler and a sharp knife dipped in warm water.
12. Temper the chocolate, see p.13.
13. Dip the whole cut pieces in the chocolate with the help of a fork.
14. Remove any superfluous chocolate from the edges and place them on a piece of parchment paper. Sprinkle some chopped pistachio nuts on top and let the chocolate harden.

STORAGE:
Keep the pistachio bites in the fridge. They will keep for about 13 days, but you may also freeze them.

GREEN CORKS

I remember that Gunnar's Pâtisserie in Malmö used to have these tasty petits-fours as part of their selection. At Blekingborg's pâtisserie they served the same ones, except they had mandarin jelly as a filling in theirs, and we used ganache. I thought ours were better, but you can decide for yourself.

32 CAKES

17.6 oz (500 g) almond paste 50/50
1.4 oz (40 g) egg whites (approx. 1 ½)
Wheat flour for the rolling out
1 drop green food coloring, preferably natural
Egg wash, see p.47

Mazarin Paste:
3.5 oz (100 g) almond paste 50/50
1.7 oz (50 g) butter
1.7 oz (50 g) egg (1)
0.3 oz (10 g) wheat flour

½ batch pâtisserie ganache with Valrhona Grand Cru Guanaja 70%
7 oz (200 g) dark chocolate Valrhona Grand Cru Guanaja 70% for dipping
Optional gold leaf, alternatively candied violets, as decorations

DAY 1
1. Dissolve the almond paste (room temperature) with egg white, a little at a time, into a smooth paste that is easily rolled out. Color with the green food coloring.
2. Work the mass smooth and roll it out to a rectangle with the help of some wheat flour, 12 ½ inches x 10 inches (320 x 250 mm) and 1/8 of an inch (3 mm) thick.
3. Cut with a pastry cutter into 4 parts; the side that is 12 ½ inches (320 mm) is divided into 8 parts.
4. Brush some egg wash along the sides of the lengths.
5. Roll them as pipes around a small rolling stick, 5 inches (122 mm) in diameter. Pinch the joint together with the help of the egg wash and place them straight on a baking sheet lined with parchment paper.
6. Let them dry overnight.
DAY 2
7. Preheat the oven to 445 °F (230 °C).
8. Dissolve the almond paste (room temperature) with one-third of the butter. Blend into a smooth mass. Work in the rest of the butter and the egg (also room temperature) and sift in the wheat flour through a sieve. Blend with a spatula.
9. Scoop the mass into a decorating bag, cut a small hole in the bottom and squeeze a small top in each pipe.
10. Bake them in the oven until they have a little color on top and some on the sides.
11. Let the batter pipes cool. Fill them with ganache with the help of a decorating bag and decorate with some gold leaf that you attach with the tip of a knife, if wanted. Or you may decorate with candied violets; we used to decorate

them this way. You can usually buy candied violets in spice markets.
12. Place the cakes in the fridge for 30 minutes so that the ganache stiffens.
13. Temper the chocolate, see p.13, and dip the bottom in the chocolate, as pictured. Remove superfluous chocolate. If the chocolate thickens during the dipping than carefully reheat it without exceeding 90 °F (32 °C). In that case you will need to temper it again.

STORAGE:
The corks will keep in the fridge for 1 week, but you may also freeze them. Thaw for 30 minutes and they are as good as new.

PISTACHIO AND RASPBERRY BITES

ABOUT 50 BITES

1 batch pistachio filling as for pistachio bites, see p.68
0.3 oz (10 g) sugar to sprinkle on top
5.3 oz (150 g) raspberry jam, see recipe on p.19
17.6 oz (500 g) milk chocolate, preferably Valrhona Grand Cru Jivara Lactée 40%
3.5 oz (100 g) dark chocolate, preferably Valrhona Grand Cru Guanaja 70%

DAY 1
1. Spread the pistachio mass out on two baking sheets with edges; they should be lined with parchment paper.
2. Preheat the oven to 410 °F (210 °C).
3. Bake the base golden brown, about 5 minutes.
4. Let them cool. Wrap them in plastic wrap and let them sit in the fridge overnight.
DAY 2
5. Sprinkle sugar on the top and turn both of the pans out on parchment paper.
6. Spread a thin layer of raspberry jam on one of the pieces and place the other on top.
7. Cover with parchment paper and push the two pieces together.
8. Cut the sheet in squares, 2 1/3 inch x 2 1/3 inch (60 x 60 mm) in diameter, by using a ruler and a small sharp knife dipped in warm water.
9. Temper the milk chocolate, see p.13.
10. Dip the squares in the milk chocolate with the help of a fork and scrape off any superfluous chocolate on the sides of the bowl.
11. Place them on parchment paper to cool down.
12. Temper the dark chocolate the same way, and fill it in a small paper cone. Cut a hole in the bottom.
13. Squeeze out thin lines over the cakes and let them stiffen.
14. Cut the cakes diagonally into triangles with a knife dipped in warm water; dry it off between each cut.

STORAGE:
These cakes will keep in the fridge for about a week. You may also freeze them.

HAZELNUT CLUSTERS

You don't commonly see this classic pastry today, but at the master pâtisserie Bernachon in Lyon they still keep them as part of their selection. With the chef Paul Bocuse they are always offered as petits-fours with coffee since Bernachon delivers to them. This might just be one of the finest petits-fours there is, moist and tasty and works well with a glass of sweet wine. Maurice Bernachon is, by the way, married to Paul Bocuse's daughter.

ABOUT 30 PASTRIES

17.6 oz (500 g) almond paste 50/50
1.4 oz (40 g) egg whites (approx. 1 ½)
1 drop green food coloring, preferably natural
Granulated sugar for rolling out
14 oz (400 g) hazelnuts, roasted and peeled
½ cup (100 g) base syrup, see recipe on p.17
7 oz (200 g) dark chocolate to dip the bottoms in, preferably Valrhona Grand Cru Guanaja 70%

1. Dissolve the almond paste with some of the egg white, a little at a time. You should have a smooth, rather than sticky, paste, soft and easy to roll out.
2. Color with green food coloring.
3. Roll out the almond paste about 1/8 inch (3 mm) thick in granulated sugar.
4. Cut 1–1 ½ inch (2–3 cm) wide lengths with a wavy cutter.
5. Brush the lengths ever so lightly with water.
6. Place 2 lightly roasted hazelnuts in the one end of the jagged lengths, roll them once with the paste, cut off, and press down at the middle of the roll. Continue to roll the nuts.
7. Attach three rolls to each other and arrange them as a hazelnut cluster. Let the clusters dry for 1 hour on a baking sheet lined with parchment paper.
8. Preheat the oven to 480 °F (250 °C) and bake the clusters until golden brown.
9. Brush them with the syrup right out of the oven. Let them cool.
10. Temper the chocolate, see p.13.
11. Dip the foot of the cakes in the chocolate and scrape off superfluous chocolate against the edge of the bowl.
12. Place them on parchment paper so that they may stiffen.

STORAGE:
The hazelnut clusters will keep for about 2–3 days in the fridge and may also be frozen.

Orange mirrors

Hazelnut Clusters

Green Corks

ORANGE MIRRORS

Many call these Seville Orange Garlands, but "Mirrors" is the most common name. This mirror cake with orange and almond, dipped in first-class chocolate, can't help but turn out delicious. At Conditori Lundagard in Lund we baked these beauties fresh every day.

At the various cruise ships I've worked at we made these as petits-fours to be served with the coffee, and they were always very much appreciated by the passengers. Feel free to freeze them down if they start to feel dry on the surface; in that case you just need to pack them in an airtight box. They will seem almost like fresh when you thaw them for 30 minutes.

ABOUT 45 CAKES

8.8 oz (250 g) almond paste 50/50
1 oz (30 g) egg white (1)

Filling for the rings:
1 orange
8.8 oz (250 g) almond paste
3 oz (90 g) butter
2.8 oz (80 g) yolks (approx. 4)
0.9 oz (25 g) wheat flour

1 batch apricot icing, see p.17

Orange glaze:
5.3 oz (150 g) powdered sugar
1.7 oz (50 g) juice from freshly squeezed orange
0.9 oz (25 g) glucose or honey
1 drop orange food coloring, preferably natural
Strips of preserved orange peels as décor, see p.20
10.5 oz (300 g) dark chocolate, Valrhona Grand Cru Guanaja 70%, for dipping

1. Carefully dissolve the almond paste (room temperature) with the egg white so that you get a smooth mass without lumps.
2. Mark rings on a piece of parchment paper, 2 ½ inch (65 mm) diameter, with the help of a pencil and a cookie cutter.
3. Fill the paste in a decorating bag with tip no. 12.
4. Squeeze out rings by tracing the drawings.
5. Clean and finely grate the orange, only use the outer zest.
6. Blend the almond paste with the orange zest and one third of the butter so that you get a mass without lumps.
7. Work in the remaining butter to a smooth filling, and stir in the yolks on at a time.
8. Sift in the wheat flour and fold in with a spatula.
9. Put the filling in a decorating bag and cut a hole in the bottom.
10. Fill the rings three-fourths full with the mass.
11. Preheat the oven to 370 °F (190 °C).
12. Bake the cakes golden brown, about 10 minutes.
13. Remove the sheet from the oven and brush the cakes with apricot icing right away.
14. Blend the glaze in a saucepan and warm to 95 °F (35 °C)
15. Brush the cakes with the glaze and decorate with a strip of preserved orange peel.
16. Place the cakes in the fridge and let them sit for 30 minutes.
17. Temper the chocolate, see p.13.
18. Dip the bottoms of the cakes in the chocolate with the help of a fork and scrape off any superfluous chocolate against the edge of the bowl. Place them on parchment paper and allow them to harden.

STORAGE:
These will keep in the fridge for about 3 days, then the glaze will dull down. May be frozen.

KING'S PEAKS WITH PISTACHIOS

This almond cake with the juicy marinated cherry in the middle is a real delicacy.

Buy the cherries in a gourmet store, or look in my books *Chocolate Passion* or *Chocolate—More of the Good*, where I describe how to preserve cherries in alcohol. Do not fall for the temptation of buying preserved cherries, they're not the same thing.

ABOUT 20 CAKES OF 1 OZ (30 G)

20 small muffin cups
1.7 oz (50 g) butter for the cups
1 oz (30 g) almond flakes for the cups

1.7 oz (50 g) peeled sweet almonds, preferably Spanish
2.6 oz (75 g) pistachio nuts
4.5 oz (125 g) powdered sugar
4.5 oz (125 g) unsalted butter
3.5 oz (100 g) yolks (approx. 5)
1.7 oz (50 g) egg (approx. 1)
0.9 oz (25 g) wheat flour

20 cherries in alcohol
0.3 oz (10 g) sugar for sprinkling
2.8 oz (80 g) dark chocolate, preferably Valrhona Grand Cru Guanaja 70%
About 1.7 oz (50 g) whole pistachio nuts for decorating

1. Grease the cups with softened butter by using a brush. Sprinkle almond flakes in the cups and shake out the ones that don't stick.
2. Place them on a baking sheet lined with parchment paper.
3. Preheat the oven to 370 °F (190 °C).
4. Mix almonds and pistachio nuts with the powdered sugar in a food processor in a so-called TPT (equal parts).
5. Stir the almond sugar in with the butter (room temperature) so that you get a dough with no lumps.
6. Stir in the yolks and egg. Lastly sift in the wheat flour and blend everything with a spatula.
7. Fill the dough in a decorating bag. Use tip no. 12 or cut a hole in the bottom.
8. Fill the cups half-full and add the drained cherries.
9. Add another layer of dough until the cups are filled to three-fourths full.
10. Bake the cakes golden brown, about 15 minutes.
11. Let them sit on the sheet for 5 minutes before you sprinkle some sugar on top so that they won't stick to the cooling rack.
12. Turn over onto a cooling rack and pull the cups off. Let them cool completely.
13. Temper the chocolate, see p.13, fill it in a paper cone, and cut a hole in the bottom. Squeeze out a small dot on each cake and garnish with a pistachio.

STORAGE:
Will keep for 3 days in the fridge and may also be frozen both baked and raw.

JOSEFINER

This cake is a clear favorite that you will never tire of. Moist and tasty with a lovely almond aroma, creamy texture from the yolks, and chewiness that is so characteristic of almond cakes. The contrast of the preserved orange peel makes it especially good.

20 CAKES OF 1 OZ (30 G)

20 small muffin cups
1.7 oz (50 g) butter for the cups
About 1 oz (30 g) almond flakes for the cups

9 oz (260 g) almond paste 50/50
3.5 oz (100 g) unsalted butter
2.1 oz (60 g) sugar

3.5 oz (100 g) eggs (approx. 2)
3.5 oz (100 g) yolks (approx. 5)
0.9 oz (25 g) wheat flour
1.7 oz (50 g) chopped preserved orange peel
0.3 oz (10 g) sugar for sprinkling on top

1. Preheat the oven to 370 °F (190 °C).
2. Grease the cups with the softened butter by using a brush.

3. Sprinkle with almond flakes and shake out any that don't stick.
4. Place them on a baking sheet lined with parchment paper.
5. Blend the almond paste (room temperature) with one third of the butter and the sugar so that you get a smooth mass without lumps. Add the remaining butter a little at a time.
6. Add the eggs and yolks a little at a time.
7. Sift in wheat flour and stir with a spatula.
8. Fold in the finely chopped orange peel.
9. Fill the mixture in a decorating bag. Cut a hole in the bottom or use tip no. 12.
10. Fill the cups three-fourths full with the dough.
11. Bake the cakes golden brown, about 15 minutes.
12. Let them rest on the sheet for 5 minutes.
13. Sprinkle some sugar over the cakes to prevent them from sticking to the cooling rack.
14. Turn the cakes out on the cooling rack and pull the cups off.

STORAGE:
Will keep in the fridge for three days and may also be frozen.

ALMOND AND COCONUT RINGS

These rings are moist and tasty, and they will last for days. A good pastry for the afternoon coffee or as a side with fresh pineapple.

ABOUT 20 CAKES OF 1 OZ (30 G)

20 small savarin molds (ring molds)
1.7 oz (50 g) butter in room temperature for the molds
1.7 oz (50 g) grated coconut for the molds

10.5 oz (300 g) almond paste 50/50
3.5 oz (100 g) butter
0.9 oz (25 g) cornstarch
2.8 oz (80 g) egg yolks (approx. 4)
1.7 oz (50 g) egg (approx. 1)
1.7 oz (50 g) grated coconut
0.7 oz (2 cl) dark rum
0.3 oz (10 g) sugar for sprinkling

White chocolate ganache with rum:
4.2 oz (120 g) white chocolate, preferably Valrhona Ivoire
2.8 oz (80 g) heavy whipping cream 40%
0.3 oz (10 g) honey
0.3 oz (1 cl) dark rum
0.3 oz (10 g) unsalted butter
Shredded coconut for decorating

King's Peaks with Pistachios   *Josefiner*

74

Kirsch Buns   Ephemeral Wreaths   Almond and Coconut Rings   Pain de Gênes

1. Preheat the oven to 390 °F (190 °C).
2. Grease the molds with the softened butter and pour in the grated coconut. Pour out the coconut that doesn't stick.
3. Place the molds on a baking sheet lined with parchment paper.
4. Stir the almond paste (room temperature) with one third of the softened butter. Add the remaining butter a little at a time and stir into a completely smooth paste (do not overwork the mixture, as it will run over the molds during baking).
5. Sift the cornstarch in the bowl.
6. Add the yolks and the egg a little at a time, then add the grated coconut and rum.
7. Fill the molds about three-fourths full with the paste by using a decorating bag. Cut a hole in the bottom or use tip no. 12.
8. Bake them golden brown for about 12–15 minutes.
9. Remove them from the oven and let them rest for 5 minutes.
10. Sprinkle sugar on them and turn them over on a cooling rack to cool.
11. Finely chop the chocolate for the ganache and place it in a bowl.
12. Bring heavy whipping cream and honey to a boil, and empty it over the white chocolate while still boiling. Stir until the chocolate is melted.
13. Add the alcohol and the butter and mix with a hand-held mixer.
14. Scoop the ganache in a paper cone and cut a hole in the bottom. Squeeze out a small spoonful of ganache in the indents of the rings. Sprinkle some grated coconut on top.
15. Place them in the fridge and let them stiffen.

STORAGE:
Will keep for 3 days in the fridge, but may just as well be frozen.

KIRSCH BUNS

Nut-tasting Kirschwasser enhances the almond aroma in this delicious almond cake. But don't let this become an obstacle—if you can't find Kirschwasser, use dark rum instead. It is just as good. And buy a couple of bottles of Kirschwasser the next time you are abroad, as it is great for pastries, desserts, and pralines.
These good cakes also disappeared unexpectedly from the pâtisseries during the 1970s.

30 CAKES

30 round dome molds or small red flexipan cups
1.7 oz (50 g) butter for the molds
1.7 oz (50 g) almond flakes for the cups

(390 g) almond paste 50/50
4.2 oz (120 g) granulated sugar
1.4 oz (40 g) real vanilla sugar
10 oz (280 g) butter
4.2 oz (120 g) corn starch
3.5 oz (100 g) eggs (approx. 2)
3.5 oz (100 g) yolks (approx. 5)

Kirsch syrup:
3.5 oz (100 g) base syrup, see p.17
3.5 oz (100 g) Kirschwasser or rum
3.5 oz (100 g) fondant, see p.16
0.3 oz (10 g) Kirschwasser or rum
1 drop red food coloring, preferably organic

1. Preheat the oven to 370 °F (190 °C).
2. Brush the round molds with softened butter and sprinkle almond flakes in them. Shake off the flakes that don't stick.
3. Stir the almond paste (room temperature) until soft and blend with the sugars and one third of the butter. Add the remaining butter, a little at a time, until you have a mass free of lumps.
4. Sift in the cornstarch and work in the egg and yolks one at a time (do not overwork the dough as it will rise too much).
5. Scoop the dough in a decorating bag. Use tip no. 12 or cut a hole in the bottom. Fill the molds about three-fourths full.
6. Bake them golden brown, about 15 minutes.
7. Sprinkle sugar on top and turn them over on a cooling rack.
8. Brush the buns with the Kirsch syrup right away and continue until the pastry has absorbed all of it.
9. Warm the fondant to 95 °F (35 °C). Color it with a drop of red food coloring.
10. Let it cool down to room temperature, scoop it into a cone and cut a hole in the bottom.
11. Pipe a beautiful marble on every cake without allowing the fondant to run down, see picture on p.74–75.

STORAGE:
These good pastries will keep for about 3 days in the fridge, but they may also be frozen.

EFEMÄRKRANSAR, "EPHEMERAL WREATHS"

This old fine pâtisserie specialty, with its unique crumbly texture and discreet nuttiness, is definitely a favorite of mine. The pastry chef and baker Birger Lundgren would always use this exact recipe at the Pâtisserie University in Gothenburg.

TIP!

Do not stir the batter until it is fluffy; if you do it will rise above
the cups and seep over.

About 30 cakes of 1 oz (30 g)

30 small savarin molds
1.7 oz (50 g) butter for the molds
3.5 oz (100 g) roasted, peeled, finely ground hazelnuts for the molds

10.5 oz (300 g) butter
5.3 oz (150 g) sugar
2.8 oz (80 g) yolks (approx. 4)
5.3 oz (150 g) whipping cream
8.8 oz (250 g) wheat flour
0.3 oz (10 g) sugar for sprinkling
¼ batch pâtisserie ganache with Valrhona Grand Cru Manjari 64%
3.5 oz (100 g) roasted peeled hazelnuts for decorating.

1. Grease the molds with softened butter and sprinkle the finely ground hazelnuts on top.
2. Preheat the oven to 355 °F (180 °C).
3. Stir the softened butter light and airy with the sugar. Add the yolks and the cream (room temperature) a little at the time.
4. Sift the wheat flour in the bowl and fold it in with a spatula.
5. Scoop the batter in a decorating bag. Cut a hole in the bottom or use tip no. 12.
6. Fill the molds three-fourths full.
7. Bake the wreaths golden brown, about 15 minutes.
8. Remove them from the oven and let them rest for 5 minutes.
9. Sprinkle some granulated sugar on top and turn the molds upside down on a piece of parchment paper. Let them cool.
10. Fill the freshly made ganache in a paper cone. Pipe a small spoonful in each wreath and top it off with a hazelnut.

STORAGE:
The wreaths will keep in the fridge for 2 days, but may also be frozen down.

PAIN DE GÊNES

You could find this tasty cake from France in most pâtisseries when I was an apprentice forty-five years ago. In the bottom of the buttered cup one would always place a note that said Pain de Gênes. Then the batter was piped on top and the cake was baked in the oven. Afterward, the baking note was left on, and sometimes it even had the name of the pâtisserie on it. But it is just as traditional and tastes better to sprinkle flaked almonds on top.

Bake them in small cups, because they are quite filling. They are also great as a crust for pies or as part of a dessert.

20 CAKES OF 0.7 OZ (20 G)

20 low small cups
1.7 oz (50 g) butter for the cups
1.7 oz (50 g) almond flakes for the cups
8.8 oz (250 g) almond paste 50/50
6 oz (175 g) butter
2.8 oz (80 g) yolks (approx. 4)
1.7 oz (50 g) egg (approx. 1)
0.9 oz (25 g) wheat flour
0.9 oz (2.5 cl) dark rum
0.3 oz (10 g) sugar for sprinkling

1. Brush the cups with the softened butter and sprinkle almond flakes on top. Shake out the bits that do not stick.
2. Preheat the oven to 355 °F (180 °C).
3. Place the cups on a baking sheet lined with parchment paper.
4. Stir the almond paste in with one third of the softened butter. Blend into a smooth batter without lumps. Add the remaining butter a little at a time until you have an even batter.
5. Add the yolks (room temperature) one at a time while stirring and later the entire egg.
6. Sift in the wheat flour and carefully fold it in with a spatula. Lastly add the liquor. Do not overwork the batter, as it will seep over in the cups.
7. Fill the cups three-fourths full with a decorating bag. Cut a hole in the bottom or use tip no. 12.
8. Bake them golden brown for about 15 minutes.
9. Sprinkle some sugar on top of the baked surface, and turn the cups over on a cooling rack. Remove the cups.

STORAGE:
Will keep in the fridge for 3 days, may also be frozen.

FRENCH MAZARINS

Wonderfully moist cake with a powerful almond aroma thanks to the unpeeled almonds. Try to find Spanish or Italian almonds for the absolute best flavor.

TIP!

Begin by making the ganache. This kind of ganache doesn't dry on the surface and is therefore ideal for decorating certain cakes.

20 CAKES OF ABOUT 1.7 OZ (50 G)

20 flat mazarin cups, ¼ cup
1.7 oz (50 g) butter for the cups
1.7 oz (50 g) almond flakes for the cups

Butter ganache:
1.7 oz (50 g) dark chocolate, preferably Valrhona
    Grand Cru Pur Caribe 66%
1.7 oz (50 g) butter

8.8 oz (250 g) unpeeled finely ground almonds
8.8 oz (250 g) powdered sugar
8.8 oz (250 g) butter
7 oz (200 g) eggs (approx. 4)
2.8 oz (80 g) yolks (approx. 4)
2.1 oz (60 g) flour
0.3 oz (10 g) sugar to sprinkle on top
Unpeeled almonds for decorating

1. Brush the cups with the softened butter. Sprinkle the almond flakes in the cups and shake out the bits that don't stick.
2. Place the cups on a baking sheet lined with parchment paper.
3. Preheat the oven to 370 °F (190 °C).
4. Finely chop the chocolate.
5. Bring the butter to a boil and pour it over the chocolate. Stir until the chocolate has melted.
6. Mix it with a handheld mixer. Pour the ganache on a plate so that it stiffens.
7. Make a so-called TPT (equal measures) with the almonds and butter by mixing it to a powder in a food processor/mixer.
8. Stir the almond sugar in with the softened butter and add the eggs and yolks (room temperature).
9. Sift in the wheat flour and carefully blend with the other ingredients.
10. Fill the cups three-fourths full with the help of a plastic decorating bag. Cut a hole in the bottom or use tip no. 12.
11. Bake the cakes golden brown for about 15 minutes.
12. Remove the sheet from the oven. Sprinkle some sugar on the cakes and let them rest for 5 minutes.
13. Turn the cakes over on a cooling rack and remove the cups. Let them cool.
14. Fill the ganache in a small decorating bag with small curly tip no.8 and pipe a rosette on each cake. Decorate with unpeeled almond.

STORAGE:
Will keep for 3 days in the fridge and may also be frozen.

NUT MAZARINS

This good recipe is from Zander Kellerman's fine pâtisserie that was situated in Ystad. The pastry chef Jan Gunnar Malmber, whom I worked with as a boy, had worked with the legendary Zander and he always baked these tasty mazarins and told us of his experiences working at Kellerman's in Ystad. Back then, Ystad was a pâtisserie town.

25 CAKES OF ABOUT 1.7 OZ (50 G)

25 small round mazarin cups, ¼ cup
1.7 oz (50 g) butter for the cups
3.5 oz (100 g) roasted finely grated
    hazelnuts for the cups
14 oz (400 g) almond paste 50/50
10.5 oz (300 g) butter

7 oz (200 g) eggs (approx. 4)
1.7 oz (50 g) wheat flour
7 oz (200 g) finely grated hazelnuts
0.3 oz (10 g) sugar to sprinkle on top
2.8 oz (80 g) dark chocolate, preferably Valrhona
    Grand Cru Pur Caribe 66 %
3.5 oz (100 g) roasted whole hazelnuts for decorating

French Mazarins

Nut Mazarins

1. Brush the cups with the softened butter.
2. Sprinkle the hazelnuts in the cups and shake out the bits that don't stick.
3. Preheat the oven to 370 °F (190 °C)
4. Stir the almond paste (room temperature) with one third of the butter. Blend into a smooth batter without lumps. Add the remaining butter a little at a time for an even batter.
5. Work the eggs in, one at a time.
6. Sift the wheat flour and hazelnuts in the bowl and fold it in with a spatula.
7. Fill the cups three-fourths full with a decorating bag. Cut a hole in the bottom or use tip no. 12.
8. Bake the cakes golden brown for about 15 minutes.
9. Take them out of the oven and let them rest for 5 minutes.
10. Sprinkle sugar on top and turn them out on a grid to cool down.
11. Lift the cups off.
12. Temper the chocolate, see p.13.
13. Scoop the chocolate in a small paper cone and decorate the cakes with a chocolate dot.
14. Decorate with a peeled and roasted hazelnut.

STORAGE:
Will keep for 3 days in the fridge and may also be frozen.

VANILLA HEARTS

This amazingly good cake with its melting dough and creamy filling will make most cake lovers wax poetic. In stores, you will often find vanilla hearts in foil molds with margarine dough and some sort of artificial filling that is supposed to be reminiscent of vanilla cream. No! If we are going to bake, we're going to bake the proper way; if not, we might as well just give up.

If you don't have or can't get a hold of heart shaped molds you may do as our Norwegian and Danish neighbors do: In both Norway and Denmark th ey bake rounds, so-called linzers. I ate these at the famous Halvorsens Pâtisserie in Oslo a few years back, which is one of the best pâtisseries in Oslo.

30 CAKES

30 heart-shaped molds

White linzer dough:
17 oz (480 g) wheat flour
14 oz (400 g) unsalted butter
3.5 oz (100 g) powdered sugar
0.3 oz (10 g) real vanilla sugar
A pinch (2 g) fleur de sel
1.4 oz (40 g) yolk (approx. 2)

1 batch vanilla cream, see p. 15
Powdered sugar for decorating

1. Sift the wheat flour onto the baking table. Shape into a ring.
2. Place the softened butter, powdered sugar, vanilla sugar, and salt in the middle.
3. Pinch everything together with your fingertips into a crumbly mass.
4. Add the yolks.
5. Work into dough by hand. Do not work it more than you have to.
6. Wrap the dough in plastic wrap and let it rest for at least 1 hour in the fridge.
7. Preheat the oven to 370 °F (190 °C)
8. Place the molds close to one another on the baking table. Roll out half of the dough to about 1/8 of an inch (3 mm) thickness with the help of a little flour and a rolling pin.
9. Roll the dough onto the rolling pin and roll it out over the molds.
10. Lightly sprinkle flour over the molds, take a piece of dough and press the dough into the molds.
11. Roll over the molds so that surplus dough will be cut off. Place them as close to one another as possible.
12. Scoop the vanilla cream in a decorating bag and cut a hole in the bottom.
13. Fill the molds three-fourths full with the vanilla cream.
14. Roll out the rest of the dough the same way and cover the molds with the sheet of dough.
15. Release the dough from the molds and place them on a baking sheet.
16. Poke the cakes on top with a fork to prevent cracking during the baking.
17. Bake them golden brown for about 25 minutes.
18. Turn the cakes out on a piece of parchment paper right away and remove the molds as soon as they are out of the oven.
19. Dust powdered sugar on top when they have cooled.

STORAGE:
The hearts will keep in room temperature for 1 day or in the fridge for 2 days.

RASPBERRY GROTTOES

These popular cakes may be varied with blueberry jam and apple jam. Children love the chewy jam in the middle. Why not give in to temptation and bake them for the kids—they're likely to get snatched up by some adults as well.

ABOUT 22 GROTTOES

12.3 oz (350 g) wheat flour
3.5 oz (100 g) corn starch
0.9 oz (25 g) real vanilla sugar
2.6 oz (75 g) powdered sugar
1/5 oz (7 g) baking powder
12 oz (340 g) unsalted butter
0.9 oz (25 g) almond flakes
5.3 oz (150 g) raspberry jam, see recipe on p.19

1. Preheat the oven to 355 °F (180 °C)
2. Sift the flour, cornstarch, vanilla sugar, powdered sugar, and baking powder together on a piece of parchment paper.
3. Blend the softened butter in with the other ingredients; make sure that you do not overwork the dough.
4. Divide the dough down the middle and roll out 2 logs of about 12 inches (30 cm).
5. Cut pieces of about 1.4 oz (40 g) and place them in muffin cups on a baking sheet.
6. Make an indent in the dough by dipping an egg in warm water and pushing it down.
7. Fill about 0.3 oz (10 g) raspberry jam in each indent.
8. Sprinkle almond flakes over.
9. Bake the raspberry grottoes for about 25–30 minutes.
10. Cover them with powdered sugar when they have cooled down.

STORAGE:
Raspberry grottoes are good for about 3 days at room temperature, and they can be frozen.

NAPOLEON HATS

This tasty pastry can only be found in Scandinavia and, surprisingly enough, not in France. In our neighboring country Denmark, every pâtisserie sells Napoleon Hats and I see why. They are delicious and quick to bake.

ABOUT 25 HATS

17.6 oz (500 g) almond paste 50/50
1 lemon, yellow and ripe
1 oz (30 g) egg white (approx. 1)
1 batch classic short-crust dough, see basic recipe p.27
Egg wash, see p.47
1 batch apricot icing, see p.17
0.9 oz (25 g) chopped apricot almonds for decorating
3.5 oz (100 g) fondant, see recipe p.16
0.3 oz (10 g) rum
1 drop of red food coloring, preferably natural
7 oz (200 g) dark chocolate, preferably Valrhona
   Grand Cru Caraque 66% for dipping

1. Preheat the oven to 390 °F (200 °C).
2. Clean and grate the outer zest of the lemon. Blend the zest with the almond paste and egg white until you have a smooth mass.
3. Roll the paste out and cut pieces of about 0.7 oz (20 g). Roll them to small balls with the help of a little wheat flour.
4. Roll out the short-crust dough about 1/8 of an inch (3 mm) thick and cut out bottoms, with a 3 1/3 inch (85 mm) diameter cookie cutter.
5. Place the bottoms on two baking sheets lined with parchment paper, brush them with egg wash, and place the ball in the middle.
6. Fold up the short-crust dough from three sides and press together.
7. Bake the cakes golden brown until the short-crust dough is baked all the way through, about 15 minutes.
8. Brush them with apricot icing right away and sprinkle some chopped pistachio nuts on top.
9. Warm the fondant with the liquor and the red color to 95 °F (35 °C).
10. Scoop it into a paper cone and pipe a small dot on each cake.
11. Melt and temper the chocolate, see p.13.
12. Dip the bottom of the cakes in chocolate and scrape off any excess chocolate against the edge of the bowl.
13. Place them on parchment paper to stiffen.

STORAGE:
Napoleon Hats should be eaten fresh, but will keep for 3 days. Good for freezing.

Napoleon Hats

Vanilla Hearts

Orange Breads

Raspberyy Grottoes

Butter Cups

Milano Sticks

BUTTER CUPS

I received this recipe from the always elegant pastry chef Ove Dackas in Hudiksvall. He had learned the trade at Tage Hakanssons Konditori in Lund. When his daughter was getting married, in the seventies, I remember that he came and made a beautiful croquembouche decorated with sugar butterflies. Sadly, Ove is no longer with us, but his memory still lives on. These simple pastries are a good everyday classic that I very much enjoy.

ABOUT 30 CUPS

30 almond mussel cups
8.8 oz (250 g) butter
8.8 oz (250 g) granulated sugar
1.7 oz (50 g) egg (approx. 1)
8.8 oz (250 g) wheat flour

1. Preheat the oven to 430 °F (220 °C).
2. Stir softened butter and sugar light and airy with the wide blade in the food processor. Add the egg.
3. Sift the flour into the bowl and stir.
4. Scoop the batter in a decorating bag and cut a hole in the bottom.
5. Fill the unbuttered almond mussel cups halfway full with the batter.
6. Bake the cakes for 12–15 minutes.
7. Take them out of the oven and knock them out of the cups.

STORAGE:
Store the butter cups in a dry place so that they don't turn chewy.

MILANO STICKS

You can't find Milano sticks in Milan. The nice buttery dough and the slightly chewy almond filling with a fresh taste of lemon is a Swedish specialty. The roasted almond on top makes them especially delicate and makes me think of Rolf Augustsson, the old owner of Konditori Hollandia in Malmö, who would always treat himself to a Milano stick when they were arranged on a plate for the shop. They should be eaten fresh, which shouldn't be difficult.

ABOUT 25 STICKS

Lemon paste:
1 lemon
0.9 oz (25 g) sugar
8.8 oz (250 g) almond paste 50/50
1.5 oz (45 g) egg whites (approx. 1 ½)

Dough:
8.8 oz (250 g) unsalted butter
0.7 oz (20 g) powdered sugar
1 tsp (5 g) real vanilla sugar
1.7 oz (50 g) egg (approx. 1)
6 oz (175 g) wheat flour
Egg wash, see p.47
2.1 oz (60 g) flaked almonds, for decorating

1. Clean the lemon and grate the outer zest on a grater.
2. Stroke the zest with the sugar with the help of a straight spatula until it starts running.
3. Add the almond paste (room temperature). Work the mass smooth with a little egg white until it is pipeable.
4. Work the softened butter in with the sifted sugar.
5. Add the egg and carefully work in the wheat flour so that you obtain a dough. Do not overwork it.
6. Chill the dough wrapped in plastic wrap, for a couple of hours.
7. Roll the dough out to 1/8 of an inch (3 mm) thickness and cut out 2 inch (5 cm) wide strips with the length of a baking sheet.
8. Squeeze lemon paste on top of the strips. Use a decorating bag with tip no. 12.
9. Brush the one side of the strips with egg wash and sprinkle almond flakes on top.
10. Place the strips in the freezer for about 30 minutes and then cut them in 3 inch (6 cm) long lengths. Place them on a baking sheet lined with parchment paper.
11. Bake the sticks golden brown in 445 °F (230 °C), about 15 minutes.

STORAGE:
If stored in room temperature they will keep for 5 days; they may also be frozen.

ORANGE BREAD

I have never seen this very Swedish pastry in any other country. You can find recipes for this from the early 1900s. They are chewy and tasty, but they have to be fresh; if not, the surface dries easily.

ABOUT 30 PASTRIES

Filling:
1 orange
0.9 oz (25 g) sugar
17.6 oz (500 g) almond paste 50/50
0.5 oz (15 g) lemon juice
5.3 oz (150 g) chopped preserved lemon peels, see p.20
1.7 oz (50 g) egg (approx. 1)

1 batch classic short-crust dough, see p.27
Egg wash, see p.47
1 batch apricot icing, see p.17
1 drop of red food coloring, preferably natural
1 oz (30 g) pistachio nuts

1. Rinse and grate the outer zest of the orange with a grater.
2. Place the zest on a plate with the sugar and stroke it back and forth with a straight spatula until it starts to flow.

3. Squeeze the juice from the orange and blend the almond paste (room temperature) with orange juice, lemon juice, the zest, and the finely chopped preserved orange peels.
4. Divide the almond paste in two pieces of equal size and roll them out to the same length as the baking sheet with the help of a little wheat flour.
5. Work the short-crust dough smooth by hand and roll out to 1/8 of an inch (3 mm) thickness with the help of wheat flour and a rolling pin.
6. Cut 2 strips, the same length as the baking sheet, and 6 inches (15 m) wide. Brush the short-crust dough with egg wash.
7. Place the almond paste strips on top. Roll the almond paste in the short-crust dough into a firm roll. Cut off excess dough.
8. Place the short-crust dough covered rolls on a baking sheet lined with parchment paper with the joint facing down.

9. Preheat the oven to 390 °F (200 °C).
10. Bake the strips to golden brown, for about 15–20 minutes.
11. Brush them with apricot icing (tinted with red food coloring) right away when you take them out of the oven. Sprinkle chopped pistachio nuts on top.
12. Let them cool.
13. When they are cool, cut each length in 15 pieces. Use a sharp knife that you dip in warm water.

STORAGE:
As soon as they're cut in pieces, the cakes should be eaten fresh the same day; they can be kept in the fridge for about 4–5 days.

HALF-MOONS

ABOUT 40 COOKIES

½ batch classic short-crust dough, see p.27

Tea-bread filling:
17.6 oz (500 g) almond paste 50/50
4.2 oz (120 g) egg whites (approx. 4)
½ batch mazarin paste, see p.25
3.4 oz (1 dl) syrup, see recipe on p.17
7 oz (200 g) raspberry jam, see recipe p.19
0.9 oz (25 g) crushed pistachio nuts for decorating
7 oz (200 g) dark chocolate, preferably Valrhona Grand Cru Guanaja 70%, for dipping

1. Preheat the oven to 390 °F (200 °C).
2. Work the cold short-crust dough smooth by hand.
3. Roll out the dough 1/8 of an inch (3 mm) thick and cut out bottoms, about 3 inches (7 cm) in diameter, with a curly cookie cutter.
4. Bake the bottoms half-done for about 5 minutes. Let cool.
5. Work the almond paste (room temperature) smooth by hand and add the egg whites a little at a time until the filling is pipeable.
6. Fill the tea-bread filling in a plastic decorating bag with curly tip no. 12 and pipe a garland around each bottom.
7. Let it dry for about 1 hour so that the mass will dry properly and will get more beautiful contours.
8. Squeeze 0.9 oz (25 g) mazarin paste in the middle of the bottoms.
9 Preheat the oven to 480 °F (250 °C), and bake the cakes golden brown for about 5–7 minutes.

10. Brush the cakes with boiled syrup right away to give them a beautiful shine. Let them cool.
11. Boil the raspberry jam and scoop a spoonful in the indent of each cake.
12. Sprinkle some crushed pistachio on top.
13. Place the cakes in the fridge for 1 hour.
14. Cut the down the middle with a sharp knife.
15. Temper the chocolate, see p.13.
16. Dip the ends in the chocolate and scrape off any excess chocolate on the edge of the bowl.
17. Place the cakes on parchment paper to dry.

STORAGE:
Half-moons will keep in the fridge for 5 days, or you may freeze them and thaw for 15 minutes.

TRUFFLE BOXES

This classic cake, with a strong almond flavor and the contrast of the raw almond paste and the soft ganache, becomes a hit.

ABOUT 40 BOXES

1 batch mazarin paste number 2, see p.25, with the addition of 1.8 oz (50 g) sifted flour
0.4 oz (10 g) sugar to sprinkle on top
3.5 oz (100 g) raspberry jam, see p.19
8.8 oz (250 g) almond paste 50/50
Powdered sugar
½ batch pâtisserie ganache with Valrhona Grand Cru Pur Caribé 66%
14 oz (400 g) dark chocolate, preferably Valrhona Grand Cru Pur Caribé 66%

DAY 1
1. Preheat the oven to 356 °F (180 °C).
2. Place a piece of parchment paper on a baking pan with edges, pour out the almond mass, and spread it evenly with a straight spatula.
3. Bake until golden brown for about 40–45 minutes. Test with a toothpick if it is baked through.
4. Let cool, cover with plastic wrap, and let stand in the refrigerator overnight.
Boil ganache, cover with plastic wrap, and let stand at room temperature.

DAY 2
5. Loosen mazarin paste from the plate by cutting it loose with a small knife.
6. Sprinkle sugar on top and place on parchment paper on a baking tray. Turn it upside down and remove the baking parchment paper.
7. Turn over a baking sheet and invert the tray again so that the cooked side is up.
8. Spread a thin layer of raspberry jam.
9. Work the almond paste (room temperature) smooth with your hand and roll out the same as the mazarin paste with the powdered sugar and a rolling pin.
10. Sprinkle a little powdered sugar and roll up the mass on the rolling pin.
11. Roll it out over the pan and cut off the excess mixture with a sharp knife.
12. Roll over it so that the mass is trapped in the jam.
13. Add the ganache and spread it as evenly as possible with a straight spatula.
14. Comb the surface with a paintscraper—available in paint stores—to make a pattern. Place the layers in the fridge to stiffen.
15. Cut the layers into squares, 40 x 40 mm in diameter, with a knife dipped in hot water.
16. Temper the chocolate, see page 12.
17. Dip pieces in chocolate up to top surface using a fork.
18. Scrape off excess chocolate against the edge of the bowl and put the pieces on a baking sheet to harden.

STORAGE:
Keeps for a week in the refrigerator; they are excellent for freezing.

BRITTLE CONES

Reminiscent of toffee rolls, but rolled on a cone (as shown on pages 88–89). They taste terrific with their nice roasted flavor of almond and hazelnut; combined with the acidic manjari chocolate, they get even tastier! These baked us always to muffins's tiles, which were common in the past.

30 CONES

1 batch brittle mixture, see p.90

Hazelnut cream:
2.8 oz (80 g) roasted hazelnuts
½ batch French buttercream, see p.17
7 oz (200 g) dark chocolate, preferably Valrhona Grand Cru Manjari 64%, for dipping

1. Bake the cones as toffee rolls, but roll on a cone shape instead.
2. Mix the hazelnuts to a paste in a food processor, until there is oiling and the paste has a temperature of 158–162 °F (70–72 °C).
3. Allow the paste to cool completely by pouring it out on parchment paper.
4. Mix the buttercream with the hazelnut paste and fill it in a piping bag.
5. Cut a hole and fill the cones with plenty of cream. Place them on a baking sheet to cool in the fridge.
6. Temper the chocolate, see page 13.
7. Dip the tops in the chocolate and place cones to harden on a baking paper.

STORAGE:
Cones should eaten right away. Otherwise, freeze them and take them out 30 minutes before they will be enjoyed.

TOSCA BITES

40–50 BITES

1 batch classic short-crust dough, see p.27
7 oz (200 g) raspberry jam, see recipe p.19
1 batch mazarin paste number 2, add 1.8 oz (50 g) wheat flour, see p.25
1 batch tosca topping, see tosca cakes, p.40
14 oz (400 g) dark chocolate, preferably Valrhona Grand Cru Pur Caribe 66%

1. Line a baking sheet with edges with parchment paper.
2. Preheat the oven to 374 °F (190 °C).
3. Work pastry smooth with your hand and flour work surface lightly. Roll out the dough about 1/8 inch (3 mm) thick, slightly larger than the baking sheet.
4. Flour lightly on the surface and roll it up on the rolling pin. Unroll it over the baking paper and cut off excess dough to cover bottom of baking sheet.
5. Poke the bottom carefully with a fork so as not to inflate the dough during baking.
6. Half-bake it about 10 minutes; it will be baked again.
7. Remove the plate and lower the temperature to 356 °F (180 °C).
8. Spread a thin layer of raspberry jam on the bottom.
9. Using a straight spatula spread the almond pastry mass evenly.
10. Bake until golden brown for about 45 minutes.
11. Let cool about 1 hour.
12. Preheat the oven to 446 °F (230 °C).
13. Boil the tosca topping and spread it over the layers evenly using a straight spatula.
14. Bake the cake to golden brown for about 7–8 minutes; watch carefully, it is easy to burn tosca pastries.
15. Let the tray stand at room temperature until the next day.
16. Cut off the sides of the layers so that they detach from the tray.
17. Place a sheet of parchment and a baking pan on top and carefully turn everything upside down.
18. Peel the parchment paper and cut up pieces with a ruler, 2 inches x ¾ inch (55 x 20 mm).
19. Temper the chocolate, see p.13.
20. Turn the pieces with tosca side up, place them on a fork, and dip them in chocolate. Scrape off excess chocolate on the edge of the bowl. The chocolate starts to thicken when dippin, so warm it gently without exceeding 32 degrees.
21. Put the pieces todry on the parchment paper.

STORAGE:
Keep tosca bites in the fridge for 1 week.

Brittle Rolls

Brittle Cones

Tosca Bites

Florentines

FLORENTINES

This classic pastry may be found in pâtisseries all over the world. My good friend Calle Widell is a fan, as am I.

ABOUT 25 PASTRIES

2.8 oz (80 g) sugar
1.4 oz (40 g) unsalted butter
5.3 oz (150 g) whipping cream 40%
2.8 oz (80 g) honey
7 oz (200 g) almond flakes
5.3 oz (150 g) preserved, chopped orange peels, see recipe on p.20
7 oz (200 g) dark chocolate, preferably Valrhona Grand Cru Guanaja 70% for brushing

1. Blend sugar, butter, cream, and honey in a saucepan and boil to 235 °F (114 °C), while stirring occasionally, or do a marble-test, see p.40.
2. Brush the inside of the pot with a brush dipped in cold water to avoid crystallization.
3. Stir in the chopped orange peels and the almonds, and pour the batter out on sheet metal to cool.
4. Preheat the oven to 355 °F (180 °C).
5. Weigh pieces of 0.9 oz (25 g) and use your palm to push them out, about 5 per piece of parchment paper. (Remember that they will spread out a little.)
6. Bake the Florentines golden brown, about 10–12 minutes. You may use a cookie cutter that is slightly larger than the baked cakes to cut the Florentines. Let the cakes cool.
7. Temper the chocolate, see p.13.
8. Brush a thin layer of chocolate on the backside of the Florentines and let them dry on parchment paper.
9. Then spread another thin layer of chocolate on the cakes with the help of a straight spatula and comb the surface with a paint or glue scraper (may be found in paint stores).
10. Let them dry on parchment paper.

STORAGE:
Store in the fridge, or freeze the cakes and thaw them for 30 minutes before serving.

BRITTLE ROLLS

I first baked these cakes when I was fifteen years old, and I think they're just as delicious today. You had to be quick to manage both baking and rolling them in a decent amount of time. The filling was always chocolate buttercream, and when we dipped the ends in tempered dàrk chocolate, we used Mazetti chocolate back then.

30 ROLLS

Brittle mixture:
4.5 oz (125 g) butter
5.3 oz (150 g) sugar
2.2 oz (65 g) glucose or honey
2.6 oz (75 g) whipping cream 40%
4.5 oz (125 g) finely grated almond with shell

2.8 oz (80 g) dark chocolate, preferably Valrhona Grand Cru Guanaja 70%, to flavor the buttercream
½ batch Italian buttercream, see p.17
7 oz (200 g) dark chocolate, preferably Valrhona Grand Cru Guanaja 70% for dipping

1. Preheat the oven to 300 °F (150 °C).
2. Boil all of the ingredients for the brittle mixture, except the almonds, to 230 °F (110 °C) while stirring now and then. (Brush the inside of the pot with a brush dipped in cold water to prevent crystals.)
3. Stir the almonds in with the mass and pour it out on a tin sheet to cool.
4. Weigh pieces of 0.7 oz (20 g) on a scale and place 6 pieces on each piece of parchment paper with room in between so that they don't spread together during baking.
5. Bake the brittle mass golden brown for 6–8 minutes.
6. Remove them from the oven and place the next batch in the oven.
7. Roll each piece around a small rolling pin, release them right away, and set aside to cool; continue with the rest of the brittle.
8. Chop 2.8 oz (80 g) chocolate for the buttercream and melt it in the microwave while stirring occasionally.
9. Let the chocolate cool to 85 °F (30 °C) and carefully stir it in the buttercream.
10. Scoop the buttercream in a decorating bag and cut a small hole in the bottom.
11. Fill the roll generously with the buttercream from both sides and place them on parchment paper in the fridge so that they stiffen.
12. Temper the chocolate for dipping, see p.13.
13. Dip both ends in chocolate, about 3/16 inch (5 mm) in, and place them on parchment paper to dry.

STORAGE:
Keep the rolls in the fridge if you are planning to eat them right away. If not, freeze them and thaw them for 30 minutes before serving.

OSLO RINGS

I have no idea how they received the name Oslo Rings, but one thing is certain: I've never seen these in Oslo.

These cakes keep well, and the combination of good chocolate and raw almond paste that's flavored with rum can't really go wrong, can it? Chef Patissier Yngve Malmqvist at the Savoy Hotel in Malmö would always bake these, but he called them Cognac Wreaths instead, as he preferred cognac.

ABOUT 30 RINGS

1 batch classic short-crust dough, see p.27.

Filling:
17.6 oz (500 g) almond paste 50/50
3.5 oz (100 g) dark rum
About 2.6 oz (75 g) syrup, see recipe on p.17
3.5 oz (100 g) roasted almond flakes
14 oz (400 g) dark chocolate, preferably Valrhona
    Grand Cru Pur Caribe 66%, for dipping

1. Preheat the oven to 390 °F (200 °C).
2. Work the cold short-crust dough smooth by hand and roll it out to 1/8 of an inch (3 mm) thickness with a rolling pin and some wheat flour.
3. Cut 30 rings, 2 3/4 inches (70 mm) in diameter, with a curly cookie cutter.
4. Place them on parchment paper. Cut a hole in the middle, 1 inch (30 mm) in diameter, with a cookie cutter.
5 Bake the short-crust dough golden brown, 8–9 minutes.
6. Dissolve the almond paste (room temperature) with the liquor. Then make it pipeable by adding the syrup. Work the filling until very smooth, but not too loose; it should be just pipeable.
7. Squeeze about 0.7 oz (20 g) filling on each bottom, with tip no. 12.
8. Dip the rings in the almond flakes so that they stick to the mass and place them back on the baking sheet. Let them dry for 2 hours.
9. Temper the chocolate, see p.13.
10. Dip the rings with the almond side pointing downwards in the chocolate and carefully shake off excess chocolate.
11. Let them sit on parchment paper to dry.

STORAGE:
Store in the fridge and they will keep for 1 week. You may also freeze these.

WALNUT TOPS

The walnuts from Grenoble in France are viewed as the best in the world, with full aroma and very little bitterness. Similarly, walnuts from Sorrento in Italy are of good quality. Walnuts from California look beautiful, but they lack aroma compared to Mediterranean walnuts. The fat content is 50–55%. This moist cake with its tasty chocolate shell is a given favorite on the coffee table.

35 CAKES

½ batch classic short-crust dough, see p.27

Filling:
17.6 oz (500 g) almond paste 50/50
3.5 oz (100 g) cognac
3.5 oz (100 g) crushed walnuts
1.7 oz (50 g) basic syrup, see recipe on p.17
14 oz (400 g) dark chocolate, preferably Valrhona
    Grand Cru Pur Caribe 66%, for dipping
35 walnuts as décor

1. Preheat the oven to 390 °F (200 °C).
2. Work the cold short-crust dough smooth by hand and roll it out 1/8 of an inch (3 mm) thick.
3. Cut out 35 bottoms, 1.5 inch (40 mm) in diameter, with a cookie cutter, preferably curly.
4. Place the bottoms on parchment paper.
5. Bake the short-crust dough golden brown, 7–8 minutes.
6. Remove the sheet from the oven and let the bottoms cool.
7. Dissolve the almond paste (room temperature) with the liquor and work it smooth; you should have a mass free of lumps.
8. Add the crushed walnuts and adjust the texture with syrup till you have a stiff, but pipeable mass.
9. Scoop the mass in a decorating bag with curly tip no. 15.
10. Pipe a beautiful top of about 0.7 oz (20 g) on each cake bottom.
11. Let the cakes dry at room temperature for about 2 hours.
12. Temper the chocolate, see p.13; dip the tops and shake off excess chocolate.
13. Place them on a piece of parchment paper and decorate with a walnut.

STORAGE:
These will keep for at least one week in the fridge and you may freeze them as well.

Oslo Rings

Brittle Mounds

Walnut Tops

BRITTLE MOUNDS

Good caramel mixed with corn flakes is placed on top of a baked short-crust dough bottom with a spoonful of almond paste dissolved with rum. When they are stiff they are dipped halfway in dark chocolate.

I was fifteen-years-old the first time I baked this cake as well, but it is just as relevant today in any fine selection of cakes at a pâtisserie.

40 CAKES

½ batch classic short-crust dough, see p.27

Rum paste:
5.3 oz (150 g) almond paste 50/50
1.4 oz (4 cl) rum

Caramel:
7 oz (200 g) butter
7 oz (200 g) sugar
4.8 oz (135 g) whipping cream 40 %
4.8 oz (135 g) glucose

Cornflakes
7 oz (200 g) dark chocolate, preferably Valrhona Grand Cru Pur Caribe 66%, for dipping

1. Preheat the oven to 390 °F (200 °C)
2. Roll out the short-crust dough about 1/8 inch (3 mm) thick.
3. Cut out 40 bottoms, about 1 1/3 inch (35 mm) in diameter, with a curly cookie cutter.
4. Place them on parchment paper and bake them golden brown for about 7–8 minutes. Let them cool.
5. Dissolve the almond paste (room temperature) with rum, a little at a time, till you have a smooth mass without lumps. If needed, add more rum to make the mass pipeable.
6. Scoop the mass in a decorating bag and cut a small hole in the bottom.
7. Squeeze out a small marble of rum paste on each short-crust dough bottom.
8. Boil all of the ingredients for the caramel while occasionally stirring to 240 °F (115 °C), or perform a so-called caramel test by dipping your fingers in cold water and forming a marble of the mass. Do not forget to brush the inside of the pot with a brush dipped in cold water to prevent sugar crystals.
9. Stir the cornflakes in the pot with a light hand. Stir until the cornflakes are completely covered and do not float. It is hard to estimate the exact amount; the best way is to see as you go.
10. Place a tablespoon of caramel on each short-crust bottom with the help of a finger dipped in cold water.
11. Let the cakes stiffen at room temperature or in the fridge for about 1 hour.
12. Temper the chocolate, see p.13.
13. Dip the cakes in the chocolate so that it covers the short-crust dough bottom and scrape off excess chocolate against the edge of the bowl. Let them dry on a piece of parchment paper.

STORAGE:
These cakes are really at their best when they are fresh, but you can keep them in the fridge for 3 days or you may freeze them.

RUM PASTRIES

A Swedish classic that's prepared in a variety of ways. Short-crust dough with mazarin paste as a contrast to the rum flavored filling, and everything dipped in dark chocolate, is delicious. I remember the first time I was preparing to bake these; I practiced writing the R on a paper before I was allowed to write on the cakes.

20 PASTRIES

20 mazarin molds
½ batch classic short-crust dough, see p.27
¼ batch mazarin paste 1, see p.25
0.3 oz (10 g) sugar for sprinkling

Rum filling:
5.3 oz (150 g) almond paste 50/50
1.4 oz (40 g) unsalted butter
0.5 oz (15 g) dark rum
About 1 oz (30 g) syrup, see p.17
10.5 oz (300 g) dark chocolate, preferably Valrhona Grand
    Cru Guanaja 70%
2.8 oz (80 g) milk chocolate, preferably Valrhona
    Jivara Lactée 40%
Candied rose petals (you can buy these in certain
    specialty stores and with spice vendors)

1. Preheat the oven to 370 °F (190 °C).
2. Line the mold like described for classic
   mazarins, see p.36.
3. Fill the molds half full with mazarin paste
   with the help of a decorating bag. Cut a
   hole in the bottom or use tip no. 12.
4. Bake the cakes golden-yellow, about
   18 minutes.
5. Sprinkle sugar on top and turn the cakes out
   on a piece of parchment paper. Remove the
   molds.
6. Let them cool and place them in the freezer
   for 30 minutes so that they stiffen.
7. Dissolve the almond paste with butter and
   the liquor. It should be an even mass; add
   the syrup so that the paste is spreadable.
8. Remove the cakes from the freezer and
   spread the paste on top.
9. Leave them in the fridge for 30 minutes.
10. Remove them from the fridge. Let them sit in room
    temperature for 15 minutes.
11. Temper the dark chocolate, see p.13.
12. Dip the cakes in chocolate and scrape off excess
    chocolate against the edge of the bowl.
13. Temper the milk chocolate the same way, pour it in a
    small paper cone and write an R, as pictured.
14. If you wish, decorate with a candied rose petal.

STORAGE:
The cakes will keep for a week in the fridge and are also
ideal for freezing.

Bienstick Bites

Mint Truffle

French Softies

Orange Moons

Rio-Boats

Truffle Boats with Candied Violet

Mont Blanc Tops

94

MONT BLANC TOPS

This classic pastry is usually topped with white chocolate, but I've chosen milk chocolate because I personally think that white chocolate is too sweet.

35 CAKES

1 batch brown linzer dough, see p.55

Butter ganache:
14 oz (400 g) dark chocolate, preferably Valrhona Grand Cru
    Manjari 64%
5.3 oz (150 g) fondant, see p.16
5.3 oz (150 g) unsalted butter
3.5 oz (100 g) Kirschwasser or arrack

14 oz (400 g) dark chocolate, preferably Valrhona Grand Cru
    Guanaja 70%, for dipping
3.5 oz (100 g) milk chocolate, preferably Valrhona Jivara
    Lactée 40%, for the top
Granulated sugar for the top

1. Preheat the oven to 390 °F (200 °C).
2. Work the cold dough smooth by hand and roll it out to 1/8 of an inch (3 mm) thickness.
3. Cut out 35 bottoms with a cookie cutter, about 1 2/3 inch (45 mm) in diameter.
4. Place them on a baking sheet.
5. Bake them until golden brown, 7–8 minutes.
6. Take the sheet out of the oven and let them cool.
7. Chop and melt the dark chocolate in a microwave until it reaches a temperature of about 130 °F (55 °C).
8. Stir fondant and softened butter until light and airy, add the liquor, and whisk well.
9. Temper the chocolate, see p.13.
10. Pour the chocolate in the butter mixture while carefully stirring. Whisk it smooth for 1 minute.
11. Pour into a decorating bag. Cut a hole in the bottom or use tip no. 12.
12. Squeeze out tops on the cookies, about 0.7 oz (22 g) each. Let them stiffen in the fridge for about 1 hour.
13. Take them out and let them sit in room temperature for 15 minutes.
14. Temper the dark chocolate for dipping, see p.13.
15. Dip the top in the dark chocolate and scrape off excess chocolate against the edge of the bowl.
16. Place them on a piece of parchment paper to dry.
17. Temper the milk chocolate the same way and pour it in a small paper cone. Cut a hole in the bottom.
18. Squeeze out a small peak that runs down on each top and sprinkle a little granulated sugar on top before the chocolate is dry.

STORAGE:
Will keep in the fridge for about 14 days and may also be frozen.

TRUFFLE BOATS WITH CANDIED VIOLETS

20 boat molds 4x2 inches (10x5 cm)
½ batch classic short-crust dough, see p.27
¼ batch mazarin paste 1, see p.25
½ batch pâtisserie ganache with Valrhona Grand Cru Pur
    Caribe 66%, see p.14
10.5 oz (300 g) dark chocolate, preferably Valrhona Grand
    Cru Caribe 66%, for dipping
Candied Violets for decorating

1. Bake the boats by following the recipe for Rio-Boats, see p.96.
2. Spread the ganache thinly on a tin sheet and let it stiffen for 2 hours at room temperature.
3. Spread the ganache on top of the boats, somewhat arched, with the help of a small straight spatula.
4. Place them in the fridge and let them stiffen for about 30 minutes.
5. Take them out and let them sit in room temperature for about 15 minutes.
6. Temper the dark chocolate, see p.13.
7. Dip the boats in the chocolate and scrape off excess chocolate against the edge of the bowl.
8. Place them on a piece of parchment paper and decorate with violets before the chocolate has dried.

STORAGE:
Truffle boats will keep for about 1 week in the fridge. You may also freeze these.

RIO-BOATS

20 boat molds, 4x2 inches (10x5 cm)

Caramel ganache:
2.6 oz (75 g) glucose (corn syrup)
7 oz (200 g) sugar
3.5 oz (100 g) heavy whipping cream 40%
2.2 oz (65 g) butter
½ vanilla bean, preferably from Tahiti
1 tsp (5g) salt, preferably fleur de sel
3.5 oz (100 g) milk chocolate, preferably Valrhona Jivara
    Lactée 40 %

½ batch classic short-crust dough, see p.27
¼ batch mazarin paste 1, see p.25
1 batch apricot icing, see p.17
10.5 oz (300 g) dark chocolate, preferably Valrhona Grand
    Cru Guanaja 70%, for dipping
2.8 oz (80 g) milk chocolate, preferably Valrhona Jivara Lac-
    tée 40%, for decorating
Candied lilac as décor

1. First make a ganache by boiling the glucose until golden brown in a small saucepan. Warm the sugar in the microwave oven for a few minutes and add to the glucose.
2. Caramelize by stirring into a light brown caramel.
3. Bring cream and butter to a boil with the vanilla bean (cut and scraped) and salt.
4. Pour it over the caramel and boil everything to 220 °F (105 °C).
5. Remove the ganache from the stove and stir in the finely chopped milk chocolate. Stir until the chocolate has melted.
6. Mix with a hand mixer until homogeneous.
7. Pour the ganache out onto an edged pan to cool down at room temperature.
8. Preheat the oven to 370 °F (190 °C).
9. Line the molds as described for classic mazarins, see p.36.
10. Fill them barely half-full with mazarin paste with the help of a decorating bag. Cut a hole in the bottom or use tip no. 12.
11. Bake the cakes golden brown for about 18 minutes.
12. Sprinkle a little sugar on top, move them onto a piece of parchment paper, and remove the molds right away.
13. Let cool, then place them in the freezer for 30 minutes.
14. Brush apricot icing on the cakes.
15. Use a small straight spatula to spread a layer of stiff ganache on the boat cakes; make the layer quite arched, as pictured on p.94.
16. Place the cakes in the fridge for 30 minutes, then take them out and let them sit in room temperature for 15 minutes.
17. Temper the dark chocolate, see p.13.
18. Dip the boats in the chocolate and scrape off excess chocolate against the edge of the bowl.
19. Place them on a piece of parchment paper to dry.
20. Temper the milk chocolate, see p.13, and pour it in a paper cone. Cut a small hole in the bottom.
21. Squeeze out lines of milk chocolate on top of the cakes and make a small dot in the middle to fasten the candied lilac.

STORAGE:
The Rio-Boats will keep in the fridge for about 1 week, and you may also freeze them.

HORSESHOES

I remember these delicious cakes well from my youth. You needed to keep a fast pace making these, but they always turned out great. When I glazed the cakes, the secret was to be quick enough so that it wouldn't crack. Remember not to add acid to the icing, because it will crack once you start shaping the horseshoes.

ABOUT 40 CAKES OF 0.7 OZ (20 G)

3 oz (90 g) almond paste 50/50
9.7 oz (275 g) unsalted butter
0.7 oz (20 g) powdered sugar
0.7 oz (20 g) real vanilla sugar
11.5 oz (325 g) wheat flour
3 oz (85 g) potato flour
1 batch of icing, see p.180
1.7 oz (50 g) red currant jelly, see recipe in my book, *The Jam and Marmalade Bible,* or use your own

1. Work the almond paste (room temperature) with some of the butter by hand into a smooth mixture without lumps.
2. Blend butter and almond paste with the sugars.
3. Sift the wheat flour onto the baking table and shape it into a ring. Place the butter mass in the middle.
4. Work into dough; be careful not to overwork it. Wrap it in plastic wrap and leave it in the fridge for about 1 hour.
5. Preheat the oven to 355 °F (180 °C).
6. Roll the dough out to a 1/3 inch (10 mm) thickness and spread a thin layer of loose icing with the help of a straight spatula.
7. Cut out 2 inch (5 cm) wide strips with a sharp knife.
8. Squeeze out lines, as pictured, with red currant jelly and add a few dots in between.
9. Divide the lengths in ½ inch-wide strips, which you bend into horseshoes. Place on a baking sheet lined with parchment paper.
10. Bake the horseshoes golden brown for about 10–12 minutes.

STORAGE:
The horseshoes will keep fresh for 5–7 days in room temperature.

RAILROAD TRACK BREAD

These delicious cakes, lightly chewy and sweet with a well-baked short-crust dough as a base, should not weigh more than 0.7 oz (20 g) when you cut them. Remember that you can keep short-crust dough in the freezer, and you can thaw it when you need it. The three tracks made out of almond paste symbolize the railroad.

ABOUT 45 PIECES

½ batch classic short-crust dough, see p.27

Tea-bread filling:
10.5 oz (300 g) almond paste 50/50
(60–70 g) egg white (approx. 2)

3.5 oz (100 g) raspberry jam, see recipe on p.19
3.5 oz (100 g) apple jam, see recipe on p.18
1 oz (30 g) almond flakes
1 batch of apricot icing, see p.17
Preheat the oven to 390 °F (190

1. Roll out the cold, smooth short-crust dough to about 1/8 of an inch (3 mm) thickness and cut three strips, about 2 1/3 inches (60 mm) wide and the length of a baking sheet.
2. Roll them onto the rolling pin and roll them out on a baking sheet lined with parchment paper.
3. Poke them with a fork and bake them half-way done, 7–8 minutes. Take them out and let them cool.

4. Dissolve the almond paste (room temperature) with the egg whites, a little at a time, into a mixture without lumps.
5. Scoop the mixture into a decorating bag with curly tip no. 10–12.
6. Squeeze out a line down the middle of the short-crust lengths and two along the sides.
7. Fill a paper cone with raspberry jam and make a line of raspberry jam in the void between the two lines on the one side, and make a line between the other two with apple jam. Sprinkle almond flakes on top.
8. Preheat the oven to 465 °F (240 °C).
9. Bake the strips until golden brown, about 5–7 minutes (look after them, they burn easily at this point). Let the strips cool.
10. Boil the apricot icing and brush the strips.
11. Cut them with a sharp knife in bites of 0.7 oz (20 g).

STORAGE:
Store them in the fridge. They will keep fresh for 3 days. Freeze the rest for another time. Let them thaw for 30 minutes in room temperature before serving.

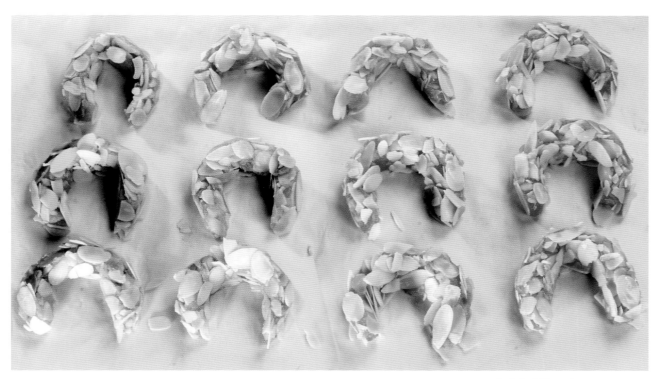

HORSESHOES WITH PISTACHIOS

ABOUT 30 HORSESHOES

Tea-bread dough with pistachios:
17.6 oz (500 g) almond paste 50/50
1.7 oz (50 g) pistachio paste, see p.25
1 oz (30 g) egg white (approx. 1)
1 drop of orange flower water
1 drop of green food coloring, preferably natural

3.5 oz (100 g) almond flakes
1 batch syrup, see p.17
7 oz (200 g) dark chocolate, preferably Valrhona Grand Cru
   Guanaja 70%

DAY 1
1. Dissolve the almond paste with pistachio paste and egg white, a little at a time. Blend into a smooth mixture free of lumps.
2. Add a drop of orange flower water and green food coloring.
3. Spread the almond flakes out on a piece of parchment paper. Pour the mixture in a plastic decorating bag with tip no. 12 and squeeze out 3 inch (9 cm) long bites of about 0.9 oz (25 g) directly onto the almonds.
4. Roll the bites in the almonds and shape them as horseshoes.
5. Place them on parchment paper and let them dry in room temperature overnight.

DAY 2
6. Preheat the oven to 480 °F (250 °C).
7. Bake the horseshoes so that they become golden brown for 5–7 minutes. Do not leave the oven unattended, as they burn easily.
8. Brush them with syrup right away after removing them from the oven. Let cool.
9. Temper the chocolate, see p.13.
10. Dip the horseshoes in the dark chocolate and scrape off excess chocolate against the edge of the bowl.
11. Place them on parchment paper to dry.

STORING
Horseshoes will stay fresh for about 5 days in the fridge. You may also freeze them.

HORSESHOES WITH CANDIED CHERRIES

ABOUT 30 HORSESHOES

17.6 oz (500 g) almond paste 50/50
2.1 oz (60 g) egg whites (approx. 2)
3.5 oz (100 g) almond flakes
3.5 oz (100 g) candied red cherries, chopped
1 batch syrup, see p.17
7 oz (200 g) dark chocolate, preferably Valrhona Grand Cru
   Guanaja 70%
Prepare as described for Horseshoes with Pistachios, but add the cherries to the tea-bread dough.

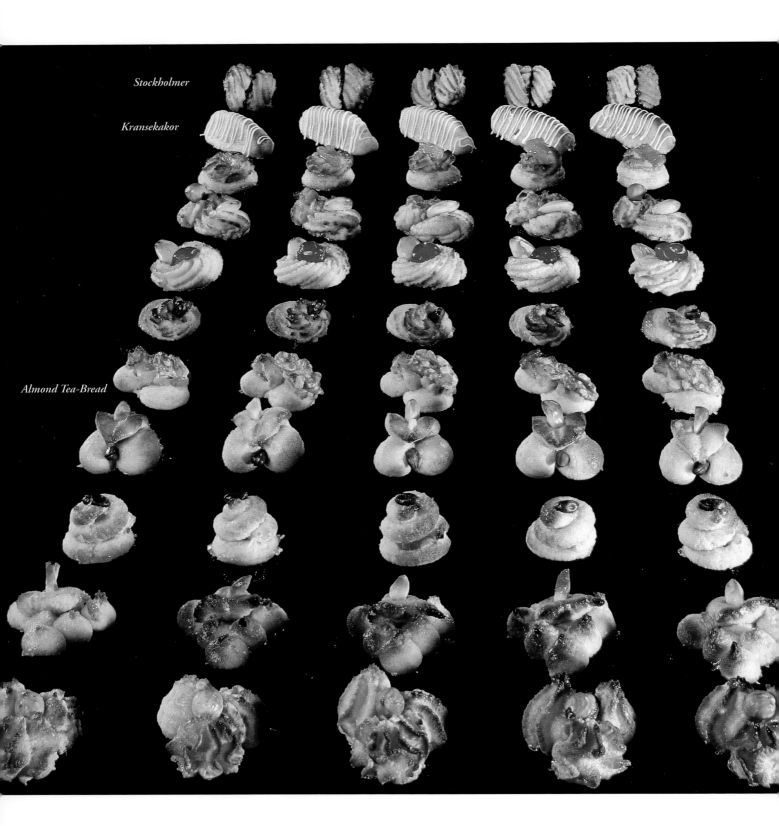

Stockholmer

Kransekakor

Almond Tea-Bread

ALMOND TEA-BREAD

These tasty confectionary-look-alikes may be shaped in a variety of ways. The dough may be colored and garnished with almonds, nuts, and candied fruits. They consist of almond paste 50/50 with a little egg white to make the mass pipeable. It is important that you squeeze them out and let them dry overnight before you bake them so that the contours are sharper.

Tea-bread is an important part of obtaining the journeyman certificate as a pastry chef. They should not weigh more than 0.7 oz (20 g) each.

2.2 lb (1 kg) almond paste 50/50
3-4 oz (90-120 g) egg whites (approx. 3-4 eggs)
Green food coloring, preferably natural
Red food coloring, preferably natural
Candied pineapple, preserved orange peels, almonds, nuts, pistachio nuts, almond flakes, walnuts, and so on, for the décor.
1 batch base syrup, see recipe on p.17

DAY 1

1. Dissolve the almond paste in stages with the egg whites until it is a smooth mixture without lumps.
2. Squeeze out uncolored almond mass as grape clusters, windmills, acorns, and pears.
3. Decorate with dough in different colors with the help of the curly tip, as pictured with the various toppings.

DAY 2

4. Preheat the oven to 445 °F (230 °C).
5. Bake them on double baking sheets lined with parchment paper so that their bottoms don't burn, about 5–7 minutes. (Do not leave the oven unattended, they burn easily.)
6. Brush the tea-breads with syrup right away after taking them out of the oven.
7. Let them cool. Turn the parchment paper upside down with the cakes and brush the underside with water. Loosen the cakes from the paper.

STORAGE:
Tea-bread will stay fresh for 5 days in the fridge. If you want to store them for longer, you can dip the bottoms in dark chocolate. You may also freeze them.

STOCKHOLMER

These tasty almond tea-breads were not only baked in Stockholm; they were a classic in most pâtisseries. They were especially popular as part of tea-bread plates. They would be baked on a water drenched wooden plate, but you can also bake them using my method: place a wet newspaper on a baking sheet.

17.6 oz (500 g) almond paste 50/50
1.7 oz (50 g) sugar
2.1 oz (60 g) egg whites (approx. 2)
1 drop green food coloring, preferably natural
1 drop red food coloring, preferably natural
1 batch syrup, see recipe on p.17
3.5 oz (100 g) raspberry jam, see recipe on p.19.

DAY 1

1. Dissolve the almond paste (room temperature) and the sugar with egg whites, a little at a time, into a mass without lumps. If it is too hard to pipe, then carefully add more egg whites.
2. Color half of the mass with green food coloring and the other half with red food coloring.
3. Place in a decorating bag and squeeze out rosettes of 0.3 oz (10 g) of both colors on a piece of parchment paper. Let them dry in room temperature overnight.

DAY 2

4. Preheat the oven to 480 °F (250 °C).
5. Move the parchment paper onto a double baking sheet with a wet newspaper under the parchment paper. Bake the cakes for 5-7 minutes until they are golden brown.
6. Brush them with syrup right after you take them out of the oven.
7. Turn the parchment paper upside down and brush the backside with water. Let it rest for 5 minutes before you pull the paper off.
8. Squeeze out a spoonful of raspberry jam on the bottom of the cakes and stick one green and one red cake together.

STORAGE:
The Stockholmer will keep for a couple of days in the fridge, but you may also freeze them.

KRANSEKAKOR

These taste great baked with 2.2 lb (1 kg) almond paste and then frozen. When I was a boy, they baked these Danish cookies in every pâtisserie in Skane, but they never tasted as good as they did in Denmark. The Danes use more bitter almonds in the almond paste, and unfortunately they also use apricot cores, which gives a bitter taste. With my friend, Gitte Kikk, at the sandwich shop Slottskallaren in Copenhagen, I eat these good cookies with coconut mounds as a dessert with my coffee.

The pastry chef that bakes for the shop brings fresh cookies everyday from the house of Kransekaker.

About 38 cookies (if you think this is too many you can easily make half the batch)

2 1/5 lb (1 kg) almond paste 50/50
4.2 oz (120 g) egg white (approx. 4)
1 batch icing, see p.180

1. Blend the almond paste (room temperature) with the egg whites, a little at a time in a bowl into a smooth paste.
2. Boil water in a saucepan and set the bowl in the water, as in a double boiler. Let the water simmer.
3. Simmer the mixture while stirring to about 122 °F (50 °C). The dough should feel dry on the surface when you touch it with your hand.
4. Lift the bowl out and cover with plastic wrap. Let it cool for 1 hour.
5. Pipe kransekakor of about 1 oz (30 g), 3 inches (7 cm) in length, on a baking sheet lined with parchment paper using tip no. 14, or cut a hole in the tip of the bag.
6. Fold a small piece of stiff carton, about 3 inches (8 cm) long and 1 ½ inches (4 cm) tall, lengthwise and dip it in cold water. Shape the cakes with it so that they get the classic spine on top.
7. Let them dry for 2 hours in room temperature.
8. Preheat the oven to 480 °F (250 °C).
9. Bake the cakes in the oven, on double baking sheets so that the bottoms don't burn, until they are golden brown underneath.
10. Pipe a light and airy icing on top while they are still warm.

STORAGE:
Kransekakor will keep for 3 days in the fridge, but these are also great to freeze.

CHERRYBALLS WITH PISTACHIO TEA-BREAD DOUGH

ABOUT 35 BALLS

1 batch tea-bread dough, as for the horseshoes with pistachios, see p.99.
3.5 oz (100 g) almond flakes
35 red candied cherries, soaked in 3.5 oz (100 g) dark rum
1 batch syrup, see p.17
10.5 oz (300 g) dark chocolate, preferably Valrhona Grand Cru Pur Caribe 66%

Kransekakor   *Almond Tea-Brea*

Piped Almond Tea-Bread dough.

DAY 1

1. Make the tea-bread dough as described for horseshoes.
2. Pipe balls of 0.7 oz (20 g) in the almond flakes. Add one candied cherry and roll it in the tea-bread dough.
3. Place the balls on parchment paper and let them dry in room temperature overnight.

DAY 2

4. Preheat the oven to 480 °F (250 °C).
5. Bake the balls until golden brown. Do not leave the oven, as they burn easily.
6. Brush them with syrup right away after removing them from the oven and let the balls cool completely.
7. Temper the chocolate, see p.13.
8. Dip the balls in chocolate. Place on parchment paper to stiffen.

CHERRYBALLS WITH RED CANDIED CHERRIES

ABOUT 35 BALLS

1 batch tea-bread dough, see p.99
35 red candied cherries soaked in 3.5 oz (100 g) dark rum
3.5 oz (100 g) almond flakes
1 batch syrup, see p.17
10.5 oz (300 g) dark chocolate, preferably Valrhona Grande Cru Pur Caribe 66%

Prepare as described for cherryballs with pistachio tea-bread dough.

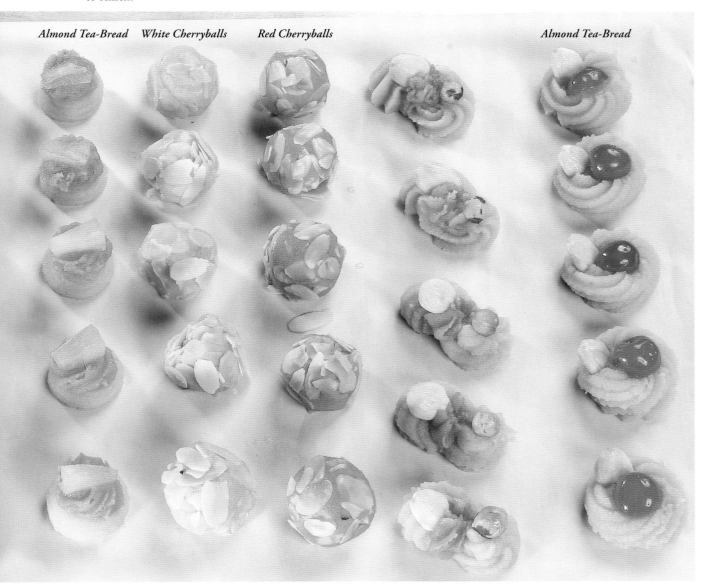

Almond Tea-Bread *White Cherryballs* *Red Cherryballs* *Almond Tea-Bread*

ALMONDS AND DUTCH ALMOND MACAROONS

These old classics are just as good as they are beautiful. They should be moist in the middle and baked on a wet newspaper just like the Stockholmer. The picture also shows Dutch Macaroons. They are made with the same dough, but are piped as rounds and have a cross on top.

ABOUT 50 ALMONDS

17.6 oz (500 g) almond paste
7 oz (200 g) sugar
3 oz (90 g) egg whites (approx. 3)
0.7 oz (20 g) cocoa powder + 0.3 oz (10 g) water
½ batch chocolate ganache with dark chocolate, preferably Valrhona Grand Cru Pur Caribe 66%, see p.14

DAY 1

1. Dissolve the almond paste with the sugar and the egg whites into a dough without lumps.
2. Divide the dough in two equally sized parts, and stir cocoa and water in one of them.
3. Pipe almond shaped bottoms of about 0.2 oz (7–8 g) with the help of a plastic decorating bag with tip no. 12, and let them dry overnight.

DAY 2

4. Preheat the oven to 445 (230 °C).
5. Cut a slit over the middle with a sharp knife dipped in water.
6. Move onto parchment paper on a wet newspaper and bake the almonds for about 5–6 minutes, until they are golden brown.
7. Let them cool. Turn the parchment paper upside down, brush the underside with water. Let it rest for 5 minutes.
8. Pull off the paper and pipe a small spoonful of dark chocolate ganache, about 5 g, on half of the bottoms.
9. Stick one light and one brown bottom together.

STORAGE:
The almond cookies will keep for 3 days in the fridge, but you may also freeze these.

Almonds

Dutch Almond Macaroons

LEMON OR ORANGE RINGS

These pastries are extra moist if they are dipped in citrus syrup with agar-agar that makes it thick. With ends dipped in chocolate they taste even better. You can buy agar-agar in most Chinese stores.

ABOUT 25 RINGS OR 50 COOKIES

25 small ring molds
1.7 oz (50 g) butter for the molds
Wheat flour for the molds

Agar-agar jelly for dipping the rings:
0.3 oz (10 g) agar-agar
3.5 oz (100 g) water
12.3 oz (350 g) sugar
6 oz (175 g) lemon juice

2 lemons or oranges
1 1/3 lb (600 g) almond paste 50/50
7 oz (200 g) butter
5.6 oz (160 g) yolks (approx. 8)
1.7 oz (50 g) cornstarch
7 oz (200 g) dark chocolate for dipping, preferably Valrhona Grand Cru Manjari 64%

DAY 1
  1. Soak the agar-agar for the jelly in the water overnight.
DAY 2
  2. Bring the water and agar-agar to a boil while stirring in sugar and lemon juice, then set aside.
  3. Grease the molds with the softened butter. Powder flour in the molds and shake out the flour that doesn't stick.
  4. Grate the cleaned lemons or oranges (depending on whether you wish to make lemon or orange rings) on a fine grater. Only grate the outer zest.

  5. Blend the almond paste (room temperature) with one third of the butter and the citrus zest into a dough without lumps. Add the remaining butter, a little at a time, till you have a smooth mass.
  6. Stir in the yolks one at a time without stirring the mass too much. Sift in the cornstarch and fold it in with a spatula.
  7. Pour the mass in a decorating bag. Cut a hole in the bottom or use tip no. 12.
  8. Fill the molds three-fourths full.
  9. Preheat the oven to 370 °F (190 °C).
10. Bake the cakes golden brown, about 15 minutes. Take them out of the oven and let them rest for 5 minutes.
11. Sprinkle sugar on a piece of parchment paper. Turn the molds out on the sugar and remove the molds.
12. Let the rings cool. Place them in the fridge for 1 hour before you dip them in the syrup.
13. Make sure that the syrup keeps a temperature of about 185–195 °F (85–90 °C). Dip the rings with the help of a skimmer and let them drain on a grid.
14. Roll the rings in granulated sugar and divide them down the middle with a knife dipped in cold water.
15. Temper the chocolate, see p.13, and dip the ends of the cakes in the chocolate. Let them dry off on a piece of parchment paper.

STORAGE:
They will stay fresh in the fridge for about 7 days. They taste just as good after freezing.

SACHER BITES

20 BITES

This chocolate bite tastes like real chocolate, and the contrast of apricot and chocolate glaze with the preserved orange peels makes it a real treat. It goes well with both coffee and tea, as well as with whipped cream as a dessert. It's just like a real Sacher tart, but this is lighter and tastier.

20 round cups that hold about ¼ cup
0.9 oz (25 g) butter for the cups
Wheat flour for the cups

5.3 oz (150 g) butter
3.5 oz (100 g) almond paste 50/50
3.5 oz (100 g) yolks (approx. 5)
3.5 oz (100 g) sugar
5.3 oz (150 g) dark chocolate, preferably Valrhona Grand Cru Guanaja 70%
6 oz (175 g) egg whites (approx. 6)
1 tsp lemon juice
1.7 oz (50 g) sugar
5.3 oz (150 g) wheat flour

1 batch apricot icing, see p.17
1 batch ganache for glazing, see p.15
20 strips of preserved orange peel, see p.20

1. Grease the cups with softened butter and powder wheat flour on top. Shake off the wheat flour that doesn't stick and place the cups on a baking sheet.
2. Preheat the oven to 390 °F (200 °C).
3. Stir the softened butter, almond paste, yolk, and sugar until foamy in a food processor with a smooth blade.
4. Warm the chopped chocolate while stirring until it reaches a temperature of 130 °F (55 °C).
5. Fold the chocolate into the butter mass with a spatula.
6. Whisk egg whites and lemon juice to foam in a bowl that is completely clean. Add the sugar and increase the speed of the whisking. Whisk into a firm meringue.
7. Fold the meringue in the chocolate mixture with a spatula for a light and airy mass. Sift in the wheat flour and carefully fold that in as well.
8. Pour the mixture in a decorating bag. Cut a hole in the bottom and fill the cups three-fourths full.
9. Bake the cakes for 8–10 minutes; make sure that they are baked all the way through using the tip of a knife.
10. Knock the cakes out of the cups and let them cool on a cooling rack.
11. Brush the cold cakes with boiling apricot icing.
12. The glaze them by dipping them in the ganache.
13. Garnish each cake with a strip of preserved orange peel.

STORAGE:
The bites will keep for 5 days in the fridge.

STRAWBERRIES

These tasty old-fashioned petits-fours deserve a renaissance. Fine mazarin paste with extra yolk baked in small round cups is combined with a good strawberry jam, then dipped in a jelly with strawberry purée and rolled in sugar. The bottom is dipped in chocolate to make it keep longer.

The first step is to make a special strawberry jam that is easy to pipe. It will be more strawberry jam than you need, but the jam tastes great on toast for breakfast as well.

30 STRAWBERRIES

30 small marble cups, should hold about
   0.7 oz (20 g) of filling
1.7 oz (50 g) butter for the cups
Wheat flour for the cups

Filling:
10.6 oz (300 g) almond paste 50/50
3.5 oz (100 g) butter
3.5 oz (100 g) egg yolks (about 5)
0.9 oz (25 g) cornstarch

Agar-agar jelly:
0.3 oz (10 g) agar-agar
3.5 oz (100 g) water
1.7 oz (50 g) lemon juice
7 oz (200 g) strawberry purée mixed with frozen strawberries
12.3 oz (350 g) sugar
1 drop red food coloring, preferably natural

1 batch strawberry jam, see p.20
7 oz (200 g) granulated sugar to roll it in
7 oz (200 g) dark chocolate, preferably, Valrhona
   Grand Cru Manjari 64%.

DAY 1

1. Grease the cups with softened butter and powder them with wheat flour. Shake out the flour that doesn't stick.
2. Preheat the oven to 355 °F (180 °C).
3. Work the almond paste (room temperature) smooth with 1/3 of the butter. Work into a mass without lumps.
4. Work in the remaining butter and add the yolks one at the time.
5. Sift in the cornstarch and fold in with a spatula (do not overwork the filling, as it will seep over the edges of the cups).
6. Pour the filling in a decorating bag. Use tip no. 10 or cut a hole in the bottom.
7. Fill the cups and bake the cakes golden brown, about 10–12 minutes. Turn out on a grid right away to cool.
8. Wrap them in plastic wrap and freeze them overnight.
9. Soak the agar-agar for the jelly in water overnight.

DAY 2

10. Boil agar-agar with the water while stirring, and add lemon juice, strawberry purée, sugar, and color. Set aside.
11. Spread the granulated sugar out on a serving plate.
12. Take the almond cakes out of the fridge and place half of them with the flat side upwards.
13. Scoop strawberry jam in a paper cone and pipe a small mound on half of the cakes. Stick the others on top.
14. Dip them in the jelly with a skimmer and let them drain on a grid.
15. Roll the cakes in granulated sugar and place them on a piece of parchment paper.
16. Temper the chocolate, see p.13.
17. Dip the strawberries in chocolate and scrape of excess chocolate against the edge of the bowl. Place them on parchment paper to dry. Add a strawberry stem if you can find them (it used to be possible to buy artificial strawberry stems that were used for marzipan strawberries).

STORAGE:
The strawberries will keep for 1 week in the fridge. You can freeze them as long as they are packed in an air-tight container, but without the stems as those will soften.

HORSESHOES DIPPED IN CHOCOLATE

This elegant cake should taste of pistachios and be rolled in pistachio nuts. It is dipped in good dark chocolate; my favorite Valrhona Grand Cru Manjari is great for this with its tart tone against the pistachio nuts.

ABOUT 25 HORSESHOES OF 1.4 OZ (40 G)

17.6 oz (500 g) almond paste 50/50
0.9 oz (25 g) Kirschwasser or dark rum
3.5 oz (100 g) pistachio paste, see p.25
1 drop of orange flower water (may be found in specialty stores)
1 drop green food coloring, preferably natural
Optional, 1 batch syrup, see p.17

7 oz (200 g) pistachio nuts
14 oz (400 g) dark chocolate, preferably Valrhona Grand Cru Manjari 64%

DAY 1
1. Blend the almond paste (room temperature) with the liquor and then add the pistachio paste a little at time. Blend into a smooth mass.
2. Flavor with orange flower water, add the color, and control the texture. It should be just pipeable, and not looser; you may add some syrup if it is too firm.
3. Crush the pistachio nuts coarsely with a rolling pin.
4. Scoop the mass in a decorating bag. Use tip no. 12 or cut a hole in the bottom. Pipe small lengths of 0.9 oz (25 g) on top of the almonds and lightly roll them.
5. Let stand and dry until the next day

DAY 2
5. Temper the chocolate, see p.13.
6. Dip the horseshoes in the chocolate with the help of a fork and scrape off excess chocolate against the edge of the bowl. Place the horseshoes on a piece of parchment paper to dry.

STORAGE:
Keep the horseshoes in a cool place and they will last for at least 1 month.

Strawberries

Pistachio Horseshoes Dipped in Chocolate

Princess Rings

Napoleon Hats Dipped in Chocolate

NAPOLEON HATS DIPPED IN CHOCOLATE

I created these treats at the Conditori Lundagard in Lund, and they became very popular. Just like the Charlie Chaplin Hats, they consisted of almond gianduja with cognac truffle dipped in dark chocolate.

ABOUT 28 HATS

Cognac truffle:
7 oz (200 g) dark chocolate, preferably Valrhona
    Grand Cru Pur Caribe 66%
5.3 oz (150 g) whipping cream 40%
0.5 oz (15 g) Swedish honey
1.7 oz (5 cl) cognac
0.5 oz (15 g) unsalted butter
Powdered sugar for rolling the cakes

Orange paste:
2 oranges
0.9 oz (25 g) granulated sugar
17.6 oz (500 g) almond paste 50/50
0.5 oz (15 g) lemon juice
1.3 oz (4 cl) Grand Marnier
1 batch syrup, see p.17
Powdered sugar for rolling out the dough

14 oz (400 g) dark chocolate for dipping, preferably
    Valrhona Grand Cru Pur Caribe 66%
1.7 oz (50 g) chopped pistachio nuts for decorating

DAY 1

1. Finely chop the dark chocolate for the truffle.
2. Boil whipping cream with the honey and empty it right away over the chocolate. Stir with a ladle into a thick ganache.
3. Mix into a smooth batter (it should have the same texture as mayonnaise).
4. Mix in the cognac and the butter.
5. Pour the mass onto a tin sheet to stiffen.
6. Fill a decorating bag with the truffle mixture once it has stiffened; this usually takes 2 hours in room temperature. Use tip no. 12 or cut a hole in the bottom and pipe approximately 28 marbles of about 0.5 oz (15 g) each.

7. Place the marbles in the fridge for 1 hour.
8. Take them out and sift powdered sugar on top. Quickly roll into spheres by hand.
9. Clean the oranges and grate the outer zest finely. Only grate the outer zest, otherwise it will have a bitter taste.
10. Place granulated sugar on the orange zest and stroke it with a straight spatula until it starts floating (this is the best way to release the essential oil from the orange peel).
11. Blend the almond paste (room temperature) with the orange zest, lemon juice, and liqueur into a smooth mass. Adjust with syrup till you have the right texture, it should be easy to roll out.
12. Roll the mass out to 1/8 of an inch (3 mm) thickness with the help of powdered sugar and cut out bottoms. Use a curly cookie cutter with a diameter of 3 inch (80 mm).
13. Place the bottoms on parchment paper and brush them with a thin layer of syrup.
14. Place a truffle marble in the middle of each bottom and fold the marzipan upwards as for a Napoleon Hat, so that the mass sticks to the truffle.
15. Let the hats dry on parchment paper overnight in room temperature.

DAY 2

16. Temper the chocolate, see p.13
17. Dip the Napoleon Hats in the chocolate with the help of a fork and scrape off excess chocolate against the edge of the bowl.
18. Sprinkle some chopped pistachio nuts on top and let them dry on parchment paper.

STORAGE:
Store the Napoleon Hats in a cool place and they will keep for about 1 month. You may also freeze them, but wrap them thoroughly.

PRINCESS RINGS

Sweden is the land of the green tarts. One may wonder why they are not white like they are in Norway. There they call it marzipan cake, and in Bergen they call it white lady. In these tasty small rings are mazarin paste and dark praline filling.

ABOUT 50 RINGS

1 batch mazarin paste no. 2, see p.25
1.7 oz (50 g) wheat flour

Praline filling:
8.8 oz (250 g) whole unpeeled almonds
7 oz (200 g) sugar
3.5 oz (100 g) water
½ vanilla bean, preferably Tahitian
7 oz (200 g) dark chocolate, preferably Valrhona
    Grand Cru Guanaja 70%

1 batch green roll-out marzipan, see p.23
1 batch syrup, see p.17
7 oz (200 g) roasted and peeled hazelnuts for decorating

DAY 1
1. Preheat the oven to 370 °F (190 °C).
2. Sift the wheat flour in the mazarin paste and stir with a spatula.
3. Line an edged baking sheet with parchment paper and spread the dough out evenly with a straight spatula.
4. Bake it golden brown for about 40 minutes, and test that it is cooked all the way through with a toothpick.
5. Once it has cooled, wrap well with plastic wrap and place it in the fridge overnight.
6. Preheat the oven to 390 °F (200 °C).
7. Roast the almonds for the praline filling until golden brown for about 10 minutes.
8. Boil sugar and water with the cut vanilla bean to 240 °F (115 °C) or do a marble-test, see p.40.
9. Add the roasted almonds and boil until they start snapping.
10. Stir with a ladle until the sugar begins to whiten. Continue stirring until the sugar is golden brown and caramelized.
11. Pour onto a piece of parchment paper and let it cool.
12. Crush the mixture and mix it in a food processor into a liquid, oily mass with a temperature of 158 °F (70 °C). Chop the chocolate and mix it until it is melted. Empty everything on an edged baking sheet lined with parchment paper. Cover with plastic wrap and let it sit at room temperature.

DAY 2
13. Loosen the mazarin paste from the sheet with the help of a small knife. Sprinkle some sugar on top and turn it out on parchment paper.
14. Cut out rounds with a 1.5 inch (40 mm) diameter using a smooth cookie cutter and place them on parchment paper.
15. Roll out the marzipan about 1/16 (2 mm) thick with the help of a rolling pin and powdered sugar.
16. Cut out lengths, about 4 2/3 inches (120 mm) long and 1 1/3 inches (35 mm) wide, with the help of a ruler.
17. Brush one side of the marzipan with syrup.
18. Place the marzipan around the mazarin bottoms and fasten it with the syrup brushed on the side. Continue until all of the bottoms are wrapped.
19. Work the praline filling smooth by hand and warm it while stirring until it reaches the exact temperature of 82 °F (28 °C) (once it's warmer, white dots will form on the surface; this is called fat bloom). Scoop the filling into a decorating bag with tip no. 10 or cut a hole in the bottom.
20. Pipe praline filling in the rings until they are almost full and decorate with a roasted hazelnut.

STORAGE:
The Princess Rings keep for at least 14 days in the fridge, but may also be frozen. In that case, thaw them slowly in the fridge to prevent the marzipan from becoming moist.

CHESTNUTS

I always baked this beautiful pastry at the Konditori Hollandia in Malmö, and even today, many years later, this tradition is still alive and they bake chestnuts during autumn when the chestnuts fall. My mother and I would walk and pick chestnuts in fall in Kungsparken that we would later roast and eat with stirred butter. My relationship with chestnuts has been lifelong, and I have therefore worked a lot with chestnuts over the years. At Pâtisserie Dupont in Paris and various pâtisseries in Switzerland, we made chestnuts, but always in different ways, which was interesting for a young professional. (At the Confiserie Hanhold in Zurich, we made the best ones, even if the filling in Basil was very good as well.)

20 CHESTNUTS

White marzipan:
7.9 oz (225 g) almonds
7.9 oz (225 g) sugar
3.5 oz (100 g) water
2.6 oz (75 g) glucose (corn syrup)
1.7 oz (50 g) dark rum

Pistachio marzipan:
2.6 oz (75 g) almonds
5.3 oz (150 g) pistachio nuts
7.9 oz (225 g) sugar
3.5 oz (100 g) water
2.6 oz (75 g) glucose (corn syrup)
1.7 oz (50 g) Kirschwasser or Maraschino, alternatively dark Rum
2 drops orange flower water

1 batch syrup, see p.17

Hazelnut gianduja:
5.3 oz (150 g) roasted hazelnuts
3.5 oz (100 g) powdered sugar
5.3 oz (150 g) dark chocolate, preferably Valrhona Grand Cru Pur Caribe 66% or Caraque 56%

Icing:
3.5 oz (100 g) powdered sugar
1 oz (30 g) egg white (approx. 1)
1 tsp (5g) lemon juice

DAY 1
The same preparation applies to both marzipans:
1. Preheat the oven to 212 °F (100 °C).
2. Scald and peel the almonds. Let dry for 1 hour in the oven.
3. Mix almonds (and pistachio nuts) to fine powder in a food processor with the jagged knifes.
4. Blend sugar and cold water in a small saucepan.
5. Boil and remove foam from the surface with a tea strainer. Dip a brush in cold water and brush the sugar crystals on the inside of the walls down into the syrup.
6. Add the glucose.
7. Boil the syrup to 251 °F (122 °C). Check the temperature with a sugar thermometer or do a marble-test, see p.40.
8. Pour the syrup in the food processor and mix for 1 minute into a marzipan paste. Add liquor (and orange flower water) and blend well. Scrape the mixture out of the machine, wrap it in plastic wrap, and let it mature overnight in room temperature.

DAY 2
9. Mix hazelnuts and powdered sugar for the gianduja in a food processor to a temperature of 158 °F (70 °C).
10. Chop the chocolate, add it, and mix until it's melted.
11. Pour it out on a marble slab or clean kitchen counter. Spread thinly with a straight spatula and let it cool.
12. Work the mass smooth with your hand until it has a marzipan-like texture.
13. Weigh pieces of about 0.7 oz (20 g). Roll them around with some powdered sugar and place them on parchment paper to stiffen for 30 minutes.
14. Temper the dark chocolate, see p.13.
15. Dip the marbles in the chocolate with a fork. Scrape off excess chocolate against the edge of the bowl.
16. Set to dry on parchment paper.
17. Roll out the white marzipan with powdered sugar, about 1/16 inch (2 mm) thick. Cut out round bottoms with a cookie cutter, about 1.9 inch (4.8 cm) diameter.
18. Roll out the green marzipan the same way and cut out the same number of bottoms.
19. Brush the green bottoms with a thin layer of syrup. Place a white bottom on top.
20. Place 2 green-white bottoms next to each other so that the overlap slightly. Brush with a thin layer of syrup.
21. Place a gianduja marble dipped in chocolate at the middle of the joint. Fold the marzipan inwards over the marble so that a small opening is left on top (see picture) and roll them round.
22. Sift powdered sugar in a bowl. Add egg whites and lemon juice. Whisk with a hand beater into a firm and peaked icing.
23. Scoop the icing in a paper cone (cover the remaining icing with a damp cloth so that it doesn't dry up). Cut a small hole in the bottom and squeeze it out as pictured.

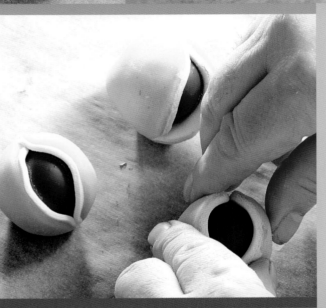

TIP!
If you wish you can spray the chestnuts with brown food color with a paint mister (you may find this in arts and crafts shops).

113

BISKVIER AND MACAROONS

BISKVIER

Biskvier (macaroons) come from the city Nancy, in France, where they are called *macarons de Nancy.* They are supposed to have a beautifully cracked, shiny surface, in contrast to the *macarons de Paris,* which are smooth and may be found in many different colors and flavors in pâtisseries in Paris.

According to the classic recipe, you measure 2 parts granulated sugar for 1 part almonds. Then you add egg whites to obtain a pipeable texture. After baking, you always turn the parchment paper upside down and brush the underside of the paper with water so that the macaroons will let go of the paper easily. You can also freeze them, and they will let go of the paper as well.

4.4 oz (125 g) sugar
2.1 oz (60 g) egg whites (approx. 2)
8.8 oz (250 g) almond paste 50/50

1. Preheat the oven to 355 °F (180 °C).
2. Dissolve the sugar with half of the egg white. Add the almond paste (at room temperature).
3. Blend into a smooth dough without lumps and add the remaining egg white a little at a time for a lump-free mixture.

4. Fill the macaroon mixture in a plastic decorating bag. Cut a hole in the bottom or use tip no. 12.
5. Pipe macaroons the size of a quarter, with even spaces in between, on a baking sheet lined with parchment paper.
6. To obtain the right cracked surface, bake the macaroons golden brown right away, 12–14 minutes.

PISTACHIO BISKVIER

The finest pistachio nuts, with a vibrant green color and a full pistachio aroma, are from Sicily. They have a fat content of 50–55%.

25–30 BISKVIER

1 batch biskvier, see above

Pistachio paste:
1.8 oz (80 g) pistachio nuts, preferably from Sicily
1.3 oz (4 cl) Kirschwasser or dark rum
1 drop orange blossom water

½ batch French buttercream, see p.17
10.5 oz (300 g) dark chocolate, preferably Valrhona
   Grand Cru Pur Caribe 66%, for dipping
0.9 oz (25 g) pistachio nuts for decoration

1. Preheat the oven to 355 °F (180 °C).
2. Pipe the macaroons as arches with smooth tip no. 12, or cut a hole in the bottom of the plastic decorating bag.
3. Bake them right away until they are golden brown, about 12–14 minutes.

4. Let them cool. Turn the parchment paper upside down and brush the paper with water. Let it rest for 5 minutes.
5. Release the macaroons from the paper.
6. Make a pistachio paste by mixing pistachio nuts, liquor, and orange blossom water in a food processor into a smooth paste.
7. Let the paste cool to room temperature and carefully blend it with the airy buttercream.
8. Scoop the cream in a plastic decorating bag. Cut a hole in the bottom or use tip no. 12.
9. Pipe the cream onto the macaroons and place them in the fridge for 30 minutes.
10. Temper the chocolate, see p.13.
11. Dip the macaroons in the chocolate and place them on parchment paper. Decorate with a pistachio.

STORAGE:
Store them in the fridge or freeze them. Take them out of the freezer 30 minutes before serving.

Pistachio Biskvier

Mocha Biskvier

Walnut Biskvier

Chocolate Biskvier

Orange Biskvier

Truffle Biskvier

CHOCOLATE BISKVIER

These tasty and chewy pastries are loved by all. If they're dipped in good chocolate and the buttercream has the right chocolate aroma and the bottom is chewy—well, then they are a delicacy. I love to decorate with gold leaf—I couldn't help it—but you don't have to. Yet it is beautiful, and pâtisseries have for many, many years when they wish to decorate something special.

ABOUT 25–30 BISKVIER

1 batch biskvier, see p.114
2.8 oz (80 g) dark chocolate, preferably Valrhona
    Grand Cru Guanaja 70%
½ batch Italian buttercream, see p.17
10.6 oz (300 g) dark chocolate, preferably Valrhona
    Grand Cru Guanaja 70%, for dipping
1 sheet of gold leaf (may be bought in arts and crafts stores
    and baking supply shops)

1. Make the bottoms as described for the orange biskvier, see the recipe below.
2. Finely chop and melt 2.8 oz (80 g) chocolate in a microwave oven while stirring now and then, or in a water bath.
3. Let the chocolate cool to 85 °F (30 °C) degrees.
4. Fold the melted chocolate in the buttercream with a spatula.
5. Spread the chocolate buttercream slightly tapered on the macaroons with a straight spatula or a butter knife.
6. Cool them in the fridge for 30 minutes.
7. Temper the chocolate, see p.13.
8. Dip the macaroons in the chocolate and place them on a piece of parchment paper. Scrape off excess chocolate against the edge of the bowl.
9. Decorate with a gold leaf on a knife tip right away.

STORAGE:
Store in the fridge or freeze. Let them thaw for 30 minutes before eating.

ORANGE BISKVIER

ABOUT 25 BISKVIER

1 batch biskvier, see p.114
1 batch pâtisserie ganache with Valrhona Grand Cru Manjari 64 %
1.3 oz (4 cl) Cointreau liqueur
1 preserved orange peel, see recipe on p.20
10.6 oz (300 g) dark chocolate, preferably Valrhona
    Grand Cru Manjari 64 %, for dipping

1. Preheat the oven to 355 °F (180 °C) degrees.
2. Pipe 25 macaroon bottoms with a diameter of 1 inch (3 cm) and bake them golden brown right away, 12–14 minutes.
3. Let them cool off. Turn the parchment paper upside down and brush the underside with water.
4. Let them rest for 5 minutes.
5. Release the macaroons from the paper.
6. Stir the liqueur in the chilled ganache.
7. Pipe a mound of ganache on each macaroon.
8. Place them in the fridge for 30 minutes to allow them to stiffen.
9. Let one preserved orange peel drain and cut it in small thin shreds, as pictured.
10. Temper the chocolate, see p.13, and dip the macaroons in the chocolate. Scrap off excess chocolate against the edge of the bowl.
11. Place them on parchment paper and decorate with a strip of preserved orange peel.

STORAGE:
Store them in the fridge or in the freezer until serving. Thaw them for 30 minutes in room temperature.

SMALL TRUFFLE BISKVIER

ABOUT 50 BISKVIER

1 batch biskvier see p. 114
½ batch pâtisserie ganache with Valrhona Grand Cru Pur
    Caribe 66%, see p.14
1.6 oz (300 g) dark chocolate, preferably Valrhona Grand
    Cru Caribe 66%, for dipping

1. Preheat the oven to 355 °F (180 °C).
2. Scoop the macaroon batter into a decorating bag. Cut a hole in the bottom and pipe out 50 bottoms the size of a nickel, on parchment paper.
3. Bake them golden brown right away, 6–7 minutes.
4. Let them cool. Turn the parchment paper upside down and brush the underside with cold water.
5. Let it rest for 5 minutes.
6. Pull the paper off.
7. Pipe 1 tsp (5 g) of ganache on each bottom and let them stiffen in the fridge for 1 hour.
8. Temper the chocolate, see p.13.
9. Let the macaroons sit in room temperature for 30 minutes and then dip them in the chocolate.
10. Let them dry on parchment paper.

STORAGE:
Store them in the fridge or freezer.

WALNUT BISKVIER

These macaroons with a walnut flavor combined with good chocolate and some rum are very good, in my opinion. Remember that everything depends on the quality of the walnuts; try to find French walnuts, as they are so much better.

ABOUT 25–30 BISKVIER

1 batch biskvier, see p.114
½ batch French buttercream. See p.17
2.8 oz (80 g) walnuts
0.7 oz (2 cl) dark rum
10.6 oz (300 g) dark chocolate, preferably
    Valrhona Grand Cru Caribe 66%, for dipping
7 oz (200 g) fine walnuts, preferably from
    Grenoble, for decorating

1. Preheat the oven to 355 °F (180 °C).
2. Pipe 25–30 oval bottoms of the macaroon mixture with a decorating bag. Cut a hole in the bottom or use tip no. 12
3. Bake them until golden brown, 12–14 minutes.
4. Let them cool down, turn the parchment paper upside down, and brush the underside of the paper with water. Let the bottoms rest for 5 minutes.
5. Pull the paper off.
6. Mix the walnuts into a paste in the food processor and stir in the liquor. Fold the mass into the buttercream and whisk it smooth.
7. Scoop the buttercream in a decorating bag. Cut a hole in the bottom or use tip no. 12.
8. Pipe buttercream on the bottoms as beautifully as you can manage.
9. Temper the chocolate, see p.13
10. Dip the macaroons in the chocolate and place them on parchment paper. Scrape off excess chocolate against the edge of the bowl.
11. Decorate with half a walnut.

STORAGE:
Store in the fridge or freezer. Thaw them for 30 minutes before eating.

MOCHA BISKVIER

ABOUT 25 BISKVIER

1 batch biskvier, see p.114
1/5 oz (8 g) Nescafé, dark roasted
1.3 oz (4 cl) dark rum or arrack
½ batch French buttercream, see p.17
10.5 oz (300 g) dark chocolate, preferably Valrhona
    Grand Cru Pur Caribe 66%, for dipping
1.7 oz (50 g) espresso coffee beans

1. Preheat the oven to 355 °F (180 °C)
2. Pipe 25-30 oval macaroon bottoms with the help of a decorating bag. Cut a hole in the bottom or use tip no. 12.
3. Bake them until golden brown, 12–14 minutes.
4. Let them cool down. Turn the parchment paper upside down and brush the underside with water. Let the bottoms rest for 5 minutes.
5. Pull the paper off the bottoms.
6. Dissolve Nescafe in the liquor. Flavor the buttercream with coffee and taste. If needed, dissolve more coffee in liquor till you have a medium-strength flavor; it shouldn't be too weak, but not too strong either.
7. Pipe the buttercream onto the bottoms the same way you did for the walnut macaroons.
8. Chill them for 30 minutes in the fridge.
9. Temper the chocolate, see p.13.
10. Dip the macaroons in the chocolate and place them on parchment paper. Scrape off excess chocolate against the edge of the bowl.
11. Decorate with an espresso bean.

STORAGE:
Store the macaroons in the fridge or freezer. Thaw for 30 minutes before eating.

FRIMURARE — FREEMASONS

This pastry is hard to find at pâtisseries today, although I'm not sure why. They're tasty and moist if you bake them the right way. Migg Sporndly, who was the principal of the pastry chef trade school in Uppsala, would always make sure that we had these for sale there. It can sometimes be hard to find the wafer or edible paper, but you may order them online.

ABOUT 24 FREEMASONS

5.8 oz (165) sugar
3.8 oz (110 g) egg whites (approx. 4)
14 oz (400 g) almond paste
2 wafers or sheets of edible paper, A4 format
2.1 oz (60 g) almond flakes
8.8 oz (250 g) raspberry jam, see p.19
3.5 oz (100 g) fondant, see recipe on p.16
0.3 oz (1 cl) dark rum

1. Blend the sugar with one third of the egg whites and add the almond paste (room temperature). Work the mixture smooth and even.
2. Add the remaining egg whites and work into a spreadable mass without lumps.
3. Stick two wafers together with the help of a little egg white that you brush along the long side.
4. Spread the almond mixture evenly over the wafer with a straight spatula.
5. Cut 12 squares, 3 x 3 inches (80 mm x 80 mm), with a sharp knife. Divide each square diagonally.
6. Sprinkle almond flakes on top and pipe a small mound of raspberry jam in the middle of each cake.
7. Preheat the oven to 390 °F (200 °C).
8. Place the cakes on parchment paper and bake them golden brown right away, about 15 minutes.
9. Let the cakes cool down.
10. Warm the fondant to 95 °F (35 °C) and flavor with a few drops of rum.
11. Scoop the fondant into a decorating bag and pipe a blob on each cake.

STORAGE:
The cakes will keep for 3 days in the fridge, and you may also freeze them.

PISTACHIO MACAROONS

ABOUT 20 MACAROONS

8.5 oz (240 g) granulated sugar
0.3 oz (10 g) real vanilla sugar
3.5 oz (100 g) pistachio nuts
2.6 oz (75 g) egg whites (approx. 2 ½)
1 drop orange flower water
0.7 oz (2 cl) Kirschwasser or dark rum
7 oz (200 g) dark chocolate, preferably Valrhona
    Grand Cru Pur Caribee 66% for dipping
20 pistachio nuts for decorating

The same preparation as described for the Walnut Macaroons, page 120, but exchange the walnuts for pistachio nuts.

Dip the bottom the same way in dark chocolate and garnish with one pistachio nut instead of the walnut.

STORAGE:
All macaroons may be stored in the fridge for 5–7 days or frozen.

Frimurare

Pistachio Macaroons

Hazelnut Macaroons

Walnut Macaroons

Almond Macaroons

HAZELNUT MACAROONS

ABOUT 20 MACAROONS

Prepare the same way described for Walnut Macaroons, p.120, but substitute the walnuts with hazelnuts.

Dip the bottom in dark chocolate the same way and garnish with a lightly roasted, shelled hazelnut instead of a walnut.

ALMOND MACAROON

ABOUT 20 MACAROONS

Prepare the same way described for Walnut Macaroons, see p.120, but exchange the walnuts for almonds with shells.

Dip the bottoms in dark chocolate the same way and garnish with an almond in its skin instead of a walnut.

WALNUT MACAROONS

ABOUT 20 MACAROONS

8 oz (240 g) granulated sugar
0.3 oz (10 g) real vanilla sugar
2.6 oz (75 g) almonds with shell
0.7 oz (2 cl) dark rum
2.6 oz (75 g) egg whites (approx. 2 ½)
7 oz (200 g) dark chocolate, preferably Valrhona
    Grand Cru Pur Caribe 66% for dipping
20 walnuts, preferably French, for decorating

1. Mix granulated sugar, vanilla sugar, walnuts, and almonds to a fine powder in a food processor.
2. Add the rum and egg whites and mix into a smooth mass.
3. Cover with plastic wrap and let it rest for 4 hours.
4. Warm the mass to 77 °F (25 °C) in a saucepan.
5. Stir it together and scoop it into a decorating bag. Cut a hole in the bottom or use tip no. 12.
6. Preheat the oven to 390 °F (200 °C).
7. Pipe 20 oval cookies on a piece of parchment paper and top with a beautiful walnut half. Bake the macaroons right away for about 14–15 minutes, until golden brown and beautifully cracked.
8. Let the cakes cool down.
9. Turn the parchment paper upside down and brush the underside of the paper with water. Let them rest for 5 minutes.
10. Pull the paper off the macaroons.
11. Temper the chocolate, see p.13.
12. Dip the macaroons halfway down in chocolate by using your fingers. Scrape off excess chocolate against the edge of the bowl so that there are no drips.
13. Place them on parchment paper to dry.

STORAGE:
Store in the fridge for 5–7 days or freeze them. Thaw for 30 minutes before eating.

MACARONS DE PARIS

All of the pâtisseries in Paris are packed with macarons in every possible and impossible color. Swedish pâtisseries used to bake macarons as well, but they were called luxemburgerli, since that was their name at the world famous Pâtisserie Sprungli in Zurich. They later disappeared, but are now back in full force at some of the trendy pâtisseries in Sweden. If they are made right, they are really tasty.

Macarons should have a chewy texture with a soft middle. The quality of the almond is essential for the result; they should be smooth with a small edge around the middle. When I interned at Sprungli, we always made macarons with a base of Italian meringue with almond flour from the Bari district of Italy, where the finest almonds grow.

They are best freshly baked, but are almost just as good after freezing.

Macarons naturelles, basic recipe

ABOUT 60 MACARON BOTTOMS, for 30 double macarons

7 oz (200 g) powdered sugar
3.5 oz (100 g) almond flour
3.5 oz (100 g) egg whites (approx. 3)
1 tsp (5g) (1 tsp) lemon juice
1 oz (30 g) granulated sugar

1. Preheat the oven to 340 °F (170 °C), 300 °F (150 °C) if it's a convection oven.
2. Sift powdered sugar and almond flour in a bowl.
3. Whisk the egg whites and lemon juice in a clean metal bowl.
4. Add the granulated sugar and whisk to a stiff foam.
5. Fold the almond sugar in the meringue with a spatula.
6. Line double baking sheets with parchment paper (so that the pastries will not burn underneath).
7. Scoop the mass in a decorating bag with smooth tip no.8. Pipe about 60 bottoms with a diameter of ¾ inch (2 cm).
8. Let them dry on the surface for 15–30 minutes.

Mocha Macaron

Pistachio Macaron

Lemon Macaron

Raspberry Macaron

Chocolate Macaron

9. Bake the bottoms in the oven for 7–8 minutes; the surface should be shiny and the inside should still be soft.
10. Let them rest for 10 minutes so that they cool down somewhat.
11. Turn the parchment paper with the macaroons upside down and brush the underside with cold water. Let the macaroons rest for 5 minutes.
12. Pull the paper off and add a fitting amount of filling.

TIP!
Leftover filling may be frozen and later thawed, whisked, and filled in macarons as needed.

CHOCOLATE MACARONS

1 batch macarons naturelles, see p.120,
    but increase the egg whites in the basic
    recipe to 3.8 oz (110 g); if not, the mixture
    will be too firm
0.7 oz (20 g) Valrhona cocoa powder of the red variety
1 small drop of red food coloring, preferably natural
1 batch pâtisserie ganache with Valrhona
    Grand Cru Guanaja 70%

1. Blend the macaron mass with cocoa powder and red food coloring.
2. Bake as macarons naturelles.
3. Pipe about 0.3 oz (10 g) ganache per macaron on half of the bottoms and place the other half on top.

LEMON MACARONS

1 lemon
1 batch macarons naturelles, see p.120
1 drop lemon-yellow food coloring, preferably natural
½ batch Italian buttercream
1.7 oz (50 g) lemon concentrate, see recipe on p.21

1. Clean and dry the lemon. Finely grate the outer zest and blend the zest with the macaron mixture and the yellow food coloring.
2. Bake as macarons naturelles.
3. Blend the buttercream with the concentrate into a tart, light cream.
3. Fill each macaron with 0.3 oz (10 g) lemon buttercream.

MOCHA MACARONS

1 batch macarons naturelles, see p.120
1 drop brown food coloring, preferably natural
½ batch Italian buttercream, see p.17
1 tsp (5 g) dark roasted Nescafe
0.7 oz (2 cl) dark rum

1. Blend the macaron mass with the brown color.
2. Bake as macarons naturelles.
3. Dissolve the coffee in the liquor and whisk it in the buttercream. Taste it, and add more coffee to taste.
4. Fill each macaron with 0.3 oz (10 g) mocha buttercream.

RASPBERRY MACARONS

1 batch macarons naturelles, see p.120
1 drop red food coloring, preferably natural
½ batch Italian buttercream, see p.17
2.8 oz (80 g) raspberry jam, see p.19

1. Blend the macaron mixture with the red color.
2. Bake as macarons naturelles.
3. Blend the buttercream with the raspberry jam by using a whisk (the raspberry jam should not be right out of the fridge, because the cream will separate).
4. Fill each macaron with 0.3 oz (10 g) raspberry buttercream.

PISTACHIO MACARONS

1 batch macarons naturelles, see p.120,
    but exchange half of the almond flour
    for pistachio nuts that you mix into flour
1 drop green food coloring, preferably natural
½ batch Italian buttercream, see p.17
1.7 oz (50 g) pistachio paste, see recipe on p.25
0.7 oz (2 cl) Kirschwasser or dark rum
1 drop orange flower water

1. Blend the macaron mass with the color.
2. Bake as macarons naturelles.
3. Blend the buttercream with the pistachio paste and flavor with liquor and a drop of orange flower water.
4. Fill each macaron with 0.3 oz (10 g) pistachio buttercream.

TEA-BREAD PLATE

This beautiful plate is initially meant for a birthday. Here I have blown two birds and wrapped them in caramel. Not for beginners!

● SWISS TEA-BREADS

1   Truffle Cake with Gold Leaf
2. Almond and Nougat Shapes
3. Pistachio Paste and Walnut
4. Kirschwasser with Preserved Cherries and Pistachio Nuts
5. Pistachio Gianduja with Chocolate Dipped Top

⬡ WIENER CONFECTIONARY

1. Cherry Heering Paste
2. Walnut Paste and Half a Walnut On Top
3. Tahitian Vanilla Paste and White Fondant with Pistachio
4. Pistachio Filling and Pistachio Fondant
5. Green Chartreuse Liqueur and Preserved Cherries
6. Kirschwasser Paste and Preserved Cherries
7. Truffle and Peppermint

◼ PETITS-FOURS

1. Lemon Petits-Fours
2. Mocha and Walnut Petits-Fours
3. Pistachio Petits-Fours
4. Passionfruit Petits-Fours

SWISS TEA-BREADS

VARIETY 1:

Truffle Cake with Gold Leaf

20 CAKES

20 small cups, 1.5 inches (40 mm) in diameter and with
    1/3 inch (10 mm) high walls
½ batch short-crust dough for wiener
    confectionary, see p.28
¼ batch pâtisserie ganache with Valrhona
    Grand Cru Guanaja 70%
1 sheet gold leaf

1. Preheat the oven to 390 °F (200 °C).
2. Work the cold short crust dough smooth and roll it
   out to about 1/10 inch (2.5 mm) thickness.
3. Place the cups out on the table. Lightly sprinkle flour
   over the dough and roll it onto the rolling pin.
4. Roll the dough out over the cups, powder flour on
   top, and bring the cups close together. Press the dough
   into the cups with another piece of dough.
5. Roll over the cups and place them on a baking sheet
   lined with parchment paper.
6. Bake them until golden brown, 8–10 minutes.
7. Let them cool and knock them out of the cups.
8. Scoop the freshly made ganache into a plastic cone
   and cut a hole in the bottom. Fill the cakes with the
   ganache, almost to the edge.
9. Place a piece of gold leaf on top with the help of the
   tip of a knife.

VARIETY 2:

Almond and Nougat Shapes

Glazed with dark chocolate and decorated with a roasted
almond.

20 CAKES

20 small cups, 1.5 inches (40 mm) in diameter and 1/3 inch
    (10 mm) high edges
½ batch short-crust dough for wiener confectionary, see p.28

Soft almond nougat:
3.5 oz (100 g) roasted, shelled almonds
3.5 oz (100 g) milk chocolate, preferably
    Valrhona Jivara Lactée 40 %
7 oz (200 g) dark chocolate, preferably Valrhona
    Grand Cru Caraque 66% for dipping
20 roasted almonds with skin

1. Line and bake the cups as for truffle cake with gold
   leaf, see above.
2. Pour the roasted almonds in a food processor and mix
   into an oily paste with a temperature of 338 °F (170 °C).
3. Add the chopped milk chocolate, and mix to a smooth paste.
4. Temper the nougat by stroking it back and forth,
   preferably on a marble slab or another cold surface,
   until it has a temperature of 82 °F (28 °C).
5. Scoop the nougat in a decorating bag and cut a hole in
   the bottom tip.
6. Fill the cups almost completely full with the nougat.
   Stroke them even with a straight spatula.
7. Place them in the fridge to stiffen for 30 minutes. Take them
   out and let them sit in room temperature for 15 minutes.
8. Temper the chocolate, see tempering on p.13. Dip the
   top part of the cake in the chocolate and scrape off
   excess chocolate against the edge of the bowl.
9. Place them on parchment paper and decorate with a
   roasted almond.

VARIETY 3:

Pistachio Paste and Walnut

210 PASTRIES

20 small cups, 1.5 inches (40 mm) in diameter and
    with a 1/3 inch (10 mm) tall edge
½ batch short-crust dough for wiener confectionary, see p.28

Alexander mixture:
3.5 oz (100 g) almond paste 50/50
1.7 oz (50 g) egg (approx. 1)

Pistachio mixture:
2.8 oz (80 g) almond paste 50/50
0.7 oz (20 g) pistachio paste, see p.25
0.3 oz (10 g) Kirschwasser or dark rum
1 drop orange flower water
1 drop green food coloring, preferably natural
Syrup, see p.17
0.7 oz (20 g) walnut halves, preferably French
    from Grenoble

1 batch apricot icing, see p.17

1. Line and bake the cups as described for truffle cake
   with gold leaf, see p.126.
2. Dissolve the almond paste (room temperature) with
   the eggs, a little at a time.
3. Scoop the mass into a plastic cone and cut a small hole
   in the bottom. Divide the mixture evenly in the cups.

4. Bake them until golden brown for about 7–9 minutes.
5. Take them out of the oven and let them cool down. Knock them out of the cups and place them on a piece of parchment paper.
6. Dissolve the almond paste with pistachio paste, liquor, and orange flower water. Add a drop of green food coloring.
7. Adjust the texture with the syrup; the mixture should be barely pipeable and absolutely not too loose.
8. Scoop the mixture into a paper cone and cut a small hole in the bottom.
9. Pipe a small green dome on each cake and press half a walnut in each.
10. Place them in the fridge for 30 minutes to stiffen.
11. Brush the boiling apricot icing over the cakes.

VARIETY 4:
Kirschwasser with Preserved Cherries and Pistachio Nuts

20 CAKES

20 small cups, 1.5 inches (40 mm) in diameter and
     with a 1/3 inch (10 mm) high edge
½ batch short-crust dough for wiener confectionary, see p.28

Alexander mass:
3.5 oz (100 g) almond paste 50/50
1.7 oz (50 g) egg (approx. 1)

0.7 oz (20 g) preserved cherries
2.8 oz (80 g) almond paste 50/50
0.7 oz (2 cl) Kirschwasser or dark rum
Syrup if needed, see p.17
20 pistachio nuts
1 batch apricot icing, see p.17

1. Follow the recipe above up until step 5.
2. Finely chop the preserved cherries and blend them with the almond paste (room temperature), liquor, and food coloring. Blend a mixture without lumps.
3. Adjust the texture with syrup. The mixture should not be too loose, it should be barely pipeable.
4. Scoop the mass into a paper cone and cut a hole in the bottom.
5. Pipe a dome of the pink mass on each cake.
6. Decorate with a pistachio.
7. Set the cakes in the fridge for 30 minutes to stiffen.
8. Brush boiling apricot icing over the cakes.

VARIETY 5:
Pistachio Gianduja with Chocolate Dipped Top

20 CAKES

20 small cups, 1.5 inches (40 mm) in diameter and 1/3 inch
     (10 mm) tall edge.
½ batch short-crust dough for wiener confectionary, see p.28

Alexander mixture:
3.5 oz (100 g) almond paste 50/50
1.7 oz (50 g) egg (approx. 1)

Pistchio gianduja:
1 oz (30 g) roasted, shelled sweet almonds
1 oz (30 g) pistachio nuts
1 oz (30 g) powdered sugar
1.7 oz (50 g) milk chocolate, preferably
     Valrhona Jivara Lactée 40%

7 oz (200 g) dark chocolate, preferably Valrhona Grand Cru
     Caraque 66% for dipping
20 pistachio nuts

1. Follow the recipe for pistachio paste and walnut up until step 5, see p.126.
2. Mix the almonds and powdered sugar in a food processor to a liquid mixture with a temperature of 160 °F (70 °C).
3. Add the chopped milk chocolate and mix the mass smooth.
4. Temper it just like chocolate by stroking it back and forth until it starts thickening; at that point it is at about 82 °F (28 °C).
5. Scoop the mass into a decorating bag. Use smooth tip no. 10 or cut a small hole in the bottom.
6. Pipe a dome on each cake.
7. Place them in the fridge for 30 minutes to stiffen. Take them out and let them sit in room temperature for 15 minutes.
8. Temper the dark chocolate, see p.13.
9. Dip the domes in the chocolate and scrape off excess chocolate against the edge of the bowl.
10. Place them on parchment paper and decorate with a pistachio.

WIENER CONFECTIONARY

VARIETY 1:

To the far right of the tea-bread plate

½ batch short-crust dough for wiener confectionary, see p.28

1. Preheat the oven to 390 °F (200 °C).
2. Roll out the wiener confectionary dough about 1/8 of an inch (3 mm) in thick with the help of a rolling pin and a little wheat flour.
3. Cut out 40 round bottoms with a smooth cookie cutter, 1 inch (30 mm) in diameter.
4. Place them on a baking sheet lined with parchment paper.
5. Bake them golden brown for about 8 minutes (do not leave the oven, this happens quickly). Let them cool.

Filling 1:

20 PASTRIES

Cherry Heering paste:
6.3 oz (180 g) almond paste 50/50
2 ½ cl Cherry Heering-liqueur
Syrup, see p.17

1. Dissolve the almond paste (room temperature) with the liqueur, a little at a time, until you have a smooth paste. If needed, adjust with syrup. The paste should be just pipeable and absolutely not too loose.
2. Scoop the mass into a decorating bag with smooth tip no. 12 and pipe about 0.3 oz (10 g) filling on half of the bottoms.
3. Place the remaining bottoms on top with the flat side facing upwards.

Filling 2:

40 PASTRIES

3.5 oz (100 g) almond paste 50/50
0.3 oz (1 cl) Cointreau
Syrup, see p.17

1 batch apricot icing, see p.17

1. Dissolve the almond paste (room temperature) with the liqueur and syrup, a little at a time, till you have a mixture without lumps. The mass should be just pipeable and absolutely not too loose.
2. Scoop it into a paper cone, cut a hole in the bottom and pipe a dome of 1 tsp (5 g) on top of each cake. Add a shelled almond.
Brush them with the boiling apricot icing.

VARIETY 2:

WALNUT PASTE AND HALF A WALNUT ON TOP

20 PASTRIES

½ batch short-crust dough for wiener confectionary, see p.28

Walnut paste with Maraschino liqueur:
7 oz (200 g) almond paste 50/50
0.5 oz (1.5 cl) Maraschino liqueur
1.7 oz (50 g) walnuts
Syrup, see p.17

20 walnut halves for decorating, preferably French from Grenoble
1 batch apricot icing, see p.17

1. Bake 40 bottoms with 1 inch (30 mm) diameter as described in variety 1.
2. Dissolve the almond paste (room temperature) with the liqueur.
3. Crush the walnuts to a powder with a rolling pin and add it to the paste.
4. Adjust the texture with the syrup so that you get a smooth and just pipeable mass.
5. Scoop the mixture into a decorating bag. Use smooth tip no. 12 or cut a hole in the bottom.
6. Pipe a marble of 1/3 oz (10 g) on half of the bottoms. Save walnut mixture for the décor later on.
7. Place the remaining bottoms on top with the flat side facing upwards.
8. Pipe a blob of filling on top and decorate with half a walnut.
9. Boil the apricot icing and brush over the cakes.

VARIETY 3:
TAHITIAN VANILLA PASTE AND WHITE FONDANT WITH
PISTACHIO NUTS

20 PASTRIES

½ batch short-crust dough for wiener-confectionary, see p.28

Tahitian vanilla paste:
1 Tahitian vanilla bean
7 oz (200 g) almond paste 50/50
0.5 oz (1.5 cl) dark rum
Syrup, see p.17

1 batch apricot icing, see p.17
1 batch fondant, see p.16
20 pistachio nuts for decorating

1. Bake 40 bottoms with 1 inch (30 mm) diameter as for variety 1, see p.128.
2. Cut the vanilla bean lengthwise and scrape the seeds out with a knife. Spread them onto the almond paste.
3. Dissolve the paste with liquor and syrup so that you get a pipeable mass.
4. Scoop the mixture into a decorating bag. Use smooth tip no. 12 or cut a hole in the bottom. Pipe domes of 0.3 oz (10 g) on 20 of the bottoms.
5. Place the remaining 20 bottoms on top with the flat side facing upwards.
6. Boil the apricot icing and brush over the cakes.
7. Warm the fondant to 95 °F (35 °C), scoop it into a paper cone, and cut a small hole in the bottom.
9. Pipe a small dot on each cake and add a pistachio.

VARIETY 4:
Pistachio Filling and Pistachio Fondant

20 PASTRIES

½ batch short-crust dough for wiener confectionary, see p.28

Pistachio filling:
(170 g) almond paste 50/50
0.3 oz (1 cl) Kirschwasser or dark rum
1 oz (30 g) pistachio paste, see p.25
Syrup, see p.17

1 batch apricot icing, see p.17
1 batch fondant, see .16
1 drop green food coloring, preferably organic
20 pistachio nuts for decorating

1. Bake 40 bottoms with 1 inch (30 mm) diameter just like described in variety 1, see p.128.
2. Dissolve the almond paste (room temperature) with liquor and pistachio paste, a little at a time, till you have a mass without lumps. Adjust with syrup if needed. The mass should be just pipeable and absolutely not too loose.
3. Scoop the mixture into a decorating bag. Use smooth tip no. 12 or cut a hole in the bottom.
4. Pipe a dome of 0.3 oz (10 g) on half of the bottoms.
5. Place the remaining bottoms on top with the flat side facing upwards.
6. Brush boiling apricot icing on top.
7. Warm the fondant to 95 °F (35 °C) and color it wit some green food coloring.
8. Scoop the fondant into a paper cone and cut a hole in the bottom.
9. Pipe a dot of fondant on each cake and decorate with a pistachio.

VARIETY 5:
Green Chartreuse Liqueur and Preserved Cherries

20 PASTRIES

½ batch short-crust dough for wiener confectionary, see p.28
9.7 oz (275 g) almond paste 50/50
0.9 oz (25 g) green chartreuse
Syrup, see p.17
10 red preserved cherries, cut in half
1 batch apricot icing, see p.17

1. Bake 40 bottoms with 1 inch (30 mm) diameter as described for variety 1, see p.128.
2. Dissolve the almond paste (room temperature) with the liqueur, and blend into a smooth mass. Adjust the texture with syrup; it should not be too loose.
3. Scoop the mixture into a decorating bag. Use smooth tip no. 12 or cut a hole in the bottom.
4. Pipe a dome of 0.3 oz (10 g) on 20 bottoms and place the remaining bottoms on top with the flat side facing upwards.
5. Pipe the remaining pass on top and decorate with half a preserved cherry.
6. Brush boiling apricot icing over the cakes.

VARIETY 6:
Kirschwasser Paste and Candied Cherries

20 PASTRIES

½ batch short-crust dough for wiener confectionary, see p.28
9.7 oz (275 g) almond paste 50/50
0.8 oz (2.5 cl) Kirschwasser
1 drop red food coloring, preferably natural
Syrup, see p.17
19 candied green cherries, cut in half
1 batch apricot icing, see p.17

1. Bake 40 bottoms with 1 inch (30 mm) diameter as described for variety 1, see p.128.
2. Dissolve the almond paste (room temperature) with the liquor and a drop of color. Work it into a smooth mass without lumps. Adjust the texture with syrup so that the mass is just pipeable.
3. Scoop the paste into a decorating bag. Use tip no. 12 or cut a hole in the bottom. Pipe a dome of 0.3 oz (10 g) on half of the bottoms and place the remaining bottoms on top with the flat side facing upwards.
4. Pipe the remaining mixture on top and decorate with half a candied green cherry.
5. Brush the cakes with boiling apricot icing.

VARIETY 7:
Truffle and Peppermint

20 PASTRIES

½ batch short-crust dough for wiener confectionary, see p.28

Butter truffle:
5.3 oz (150 g) dark chocolate, preferably Valrhona Grand Cru Pur Caribee 66%
5.3 oz (150 g) unsalted butter
5.3 oz (150 g) fondant, see recipe on p.16
1 drop peppermint oil

1. Bake 40 bottoms with 1 inch (30 mm) diameter as described for variety 1, see p.128.
2. Chop and melt the chocolate to 130 °F (55 °C).
3. Add the cold butter and whisk it in lightly with an electric beater until it's melted.
4. Scoop the mass into a decorating bag. Use curly tip no.8 and pipe a rosette of 0.3 oz (10 g) on half of the bottoms.
5. Place the remaining bottoms on top with the flat side facing upwards.
6. Pipe a ring of the remaining butter truffle around the cake.
7. Warm the fondant to 95 °F (35 °C) and flavor it with a few drops of peppermint oil.
8. Let the fondant cool to about 82 °F (28 °C) (if not, the truffle will melt).
9. Fill the hole with peppermint fondant. Use a small paper cone with a small hole in the bottom.

PETITS-FOURS

Petit-fours can come in an infinite number of varieties. In the past, they were always glazed with fondant like these four examples. At the Savoy Hotel in Malmö, we baked large batches of fresh petits-fours every morning, since we served them with every dessert.

VARIETY 1:
Lemon Petits-Fours

Glazed with white fondant and with a cross of brown cake-decorating gel.

ABOUT 40 PETITS-FOURS

1 batch petit-four wrap, see p.30
½ batch lemon curd, see p.26
½ batch Italian butter cream, see p.17
1 batch marzipan, see p.112
1 batch fondant, see p.16
1 batch syrup, see p.17
Brown decorating gel
40 strips preserved lemon zest, see p.20

1. Blend the cold lemon curd and the buttercream with a whisk.
2. Spread out 90% of the cream on one petit-four bottom with the help of a straight spatula.
3. Cover with the other bottom and press it even with a baking sheet.
4. Spread the remaining cream on top with the straight spatula.
5. Roll out the marzipan to the same size as the petit-four layers, about 1/16 (2 mm) thick, with the help of powdered sugar.
6. Roll it on top of the layers and cut off excess marzipan.
7. Place it in the fridge to stiffen for about 2 hours.
8. Dip a knife in warm water and cut the mold with the marzipan facing downwards. Use a ruler and cut it in squares of about 1.5 x 1.5 inch (40 x 40 mm).
9. Warm the fondant to 95 °F (35 °C), dilute it with about ½ cup (1 dl) syrup, and control the temperature carefully.
10. Dip the bites in the fondant with the help of a fork with the marzipan side facing downwards; afterwards turn the marzipan side upwards.
11. Place the cakes on a cooling rack to drain.
12. Fill brown decorating gel in a small paper cone and make two crossing stripes with gel on the cake. Decorate with a strip of preserved lemon.

VARIETY 2:
Mocha and Walnut Petits-Fours

ABOUT 40 PETITS-FOURS

1 batch petit-four wrap, see p.30
2.8 oz (80 g) milk chocolate, preferably Valrhona Jivara Lactée 40%
0.3 oz (10 g) dark roasted Nescafe
1.4 oz (40 g) arrack or dark rum
1.7 oz (50 g) chopped walnuts, preferably French from Grenoble
½ batch Italian buttercream, see p.17
1 batch white marzipan, see recipe for chestnuts on p.112
1 batch fondant, see p.16
1 batch syrup, see p. 17
0.3 oz (10 g) Nescafe
0.7 oz (20 g) arrack or rum

1. Finely chop and warm the chocolate in the microwave to a temperature of 84-86 °F (29–30 °C).
2. Dissolve 0.3 oz (10 g) Nescafe in 1.4 oz (40 g) liquor, finely crush the walnuts with a rolling pin and blend everything with the buttercream so that you get a beautiful filling.
3. Spread it out as you did for the lemon petits-fours, variety 1, see previous recipe.
4. Place the marzipan on top as in the previous recipe.
5. Cut the cold layers with the marzipan on the bottom in squares of 1.5 x 1.5 inch (40 x 40 mm) with a sharp knife dipped in warm water.
6. Warm the fondant to 95 °F (35 °C) and dilute it with about ½ cup (1 dl) syrup. Add 0.3 oz (10 g) Nescafe dissolved in 0.7 oz (20 g) liquor and stir well. Make sure that the temperature is still 95 °F (35 °C)
7. Dip the bites in the fondant with the marzipan side facing downwards and then later turn it around. Use a fork for the dipping.
8. Place the cakes on a cooling rack to drain off.

VARIETY 3:
Pistachio Petits-Fours

ABOUT 40 PETITS-FOURS

1 batch petits-fours wrap, see p.30

2.8 oz (80 g) pistachio paste, see p.25
½ batch Italian buttercream, see p.17
0.7 oz (2 cl) Kirschwasser or dark rum
1 drop orange flower water
1.7 oz (50 g) chopped pistachio nuts
1 batch pistachio marzipan, see chestnuts on p.112
1 batch fondant, see p.16
1 batch syrup, see p.17
0.7 oz (2 cl) Kirschwasser or dark rum
1 drop green food coloring, preferably natural
Brown decorating gel
40 pistachio nuts for decorating

1. Blend the pistachio paste with the buttercream and flavor with liquor, orange flower water, and finely chopped pistachio nuts.
2. Spread the mass out as described for lemon petits-fours, variety 1, see p.131.
3. Place the pistachio marzipan on top as well.
4. Cut the cold layers with the marzipan on the bottom in squares of 1.5 x 1.5 inch (40 x 40 mm) with a sharp knife dipped in warm water.
5. Warm the fondant to 95 °F (35 °C) and dilute it with about ½ cup (1 dl) syrup and liquor. Add a drop of green food coloring.
6. Use a fork to dip the squares in the fondant with the marzipan side facing downward first, and then turned around.
7. Place the cakes on a cooling rack to drain off.
8. Garnish with a line of brown decorating gel and a pistachio.

VARIETY 4:
Passionfruit Petits-Fours

ABOUT 40 PETITS-FOURS

1 batch petits-fours wrap, see p.30

½ batch passionfruit curd, see p.26
½ batch Italian buttercream, see p.17
1 batch white marzipan, see chestnuts on p.112
1 batch fondant, see p.16
0.3 oz (1 cl) dark rum for the fondant
1 batch syrup, see p.17
1 drop yellow food coloring, preferably natural
Brown decorating gel
Pistachio nuts for decorating

1. Whisk the cold passionfruit curd and the buttercream together.
2. Spread the mixture out as described for the lemon petits-fours, variety 1, see p.131.
3. Cover with the marzipan the same way.
4. Turn the layers so that the marzipan faces downwards and cut out round bottoms with a smooth cookie cutter, 1.5 inch (40 mm) in diameter, dipped in warm water.
5. Place them on a piece of parchment paper with the marzipan facing upwards.
6. Warm the fondant to 95 °F (35 °C). Dilute it with about ½ cup (1 dl) syrup and add a drop of color. Control the temperature carefully.
7. Use a fork to dip the cakes in the fondant, first with the marzipan side facing downwards and then with the marzipan side facing upwards.
8. Place the cakes on a cooling rack to drain off.
9. Decorate with a piped spiral of decorating gel and a pistachio.

FLARN (CRISPY BISCUITS)

These crunchy treats are called tuiles in France, and they should be as thin as tulle curtains, crispy, and light. If you want to make these last longer, you may brush them with tempered dark chocolate.

OAT FLARN

We always baked these tasty oat flarn at Blekingborg's Pâtisserie in Malmö. Sometimes we brushed them with chocolate so that they kept better, and we would stick them together (in which case they would be flat and not arched) with arrack buttercream and decorate them with chocolate lines. That was delicious as well.

ABOUT 35 FLARN

4.5 oz (125 g) eggs (approx. 2 ½)
9.7 oz (275 g) granulated sugar
2.6 oz (75 g) butter
0.5 oz (15 g) baking powder
1.4 oz (40 g) wheat flour
6 oz (175 g) oats

1. Whisk eggs and sugar until light and airy for 5 minutes. Melt the butter and set it aside.
2. Sift the baking powder and the wheat flour into the egg batter and work it in with a spatula.
3. Add the oats and the melted butter and let it rest for 30 minutes.
4. Preheat the oven to 390 °F (200 °C)
5. Scoop the mixture into a decorating bag with smooth tip no. 15 and pipe balls of about 0.7 oz (20 g) per sheet of parchment paper.
6. Bake them golden brown for about 10-12 minutes, 1 sheet at a time.
7. Take them out of the oven and let them rest for 1 minute. Place them over a rolling pin to stiffen.

STORAGE:
Store them in an airtight container so they don't go soft.

COCONUT FLARN

ABOUT 20 FLARN

4.5 oz (125 g) sugar
4.5 oz (125 g) butter
0.9 oz (25 g) honey
4.5 oz (125 g) grated coconut
2.6 oz (75 g) wheat flour

1. Preheat the oven to 390 °F (200 °C)
2. Work all of the ingredients together into a smooth mixture.
3. Divide the dough in 4 parts and roll them out with the help of a little wheat flour.
4. Cut pieces of 0.7 oz (20 g) and place 4 on each baking sheet lined with parchment paper.
5. Bake them until golden brown for about 12–15 minutes. Bend them on a rolling pin right away.
6. Set them aside as soon as they have cooled.
7. Continue baking until the entire dough is used.

STORAGE:
Store the flarn in an airtight container so that they don't go soft.

Oat Flarn

Tosca Flarn

Coconut Flarn

TOSCA FLARN

These tasty, crispy flarn are perfect for desserts and with coffee or tea. Remember to keep them dry in a container with a lid; if not, they will go soft and lose their flavor and shape. They should be crunchy and have the nice flavor of fine chocolate. The intense guanaja chocolate from Valrhona is perfect for this pastry.

25–30 FLARN

3.5 oz (100 g) butter
3.5 oz (100 g) sugar
3.5 oz (100 g) whipping cream 40%
3.5 oz (100 g) honey
3.5 oz (100 g) almond flakes
0.9 oz (25 g) wheat flour
7 oz (200 g) dark chocolate, preferably Valrhona
    Grand Cru Guanaja 70%, for brushing

1. Preheat the oven to 340 °F (170 °C).
2. Boil butter, sugar, cream, and honey to 240 °F (115 °C), or do a marble-test, see p.40. Remember to brush the inside of the saucepan with a brush dipped in cold water to prevent the caramel from forming crystals.
3. Stir in the almonds and wheat flour, pour the mixture out, and let it cool.
4. Weigh pieces of 0.7–0.9 oz (20–25 g) and place 6, evenly spaced, on each parchment paper (remember that the caramel will make them spread out a little, so do not place them too close to one another).
5. Bake the flarn until golden brown, 10–12 minutes.
6. Let them stiffen a little as you take them out of the oven. Then place them on a rolling pin to harden completely so that they bend. Continue until they are all baked.
7. Temper the chocolate, see p.13.
8. Dip a brush in the chocolate and brush the backside of the cookies. Place them on parchment paper to dry.

STORAGE:
Store the flarn in the fridge until serving. You may freeze them the same way as brittle rolls.

WAFER PASTRIES

WOOD SHAVINGS

These tasty, crisp pastries used to be served on tea-bread plates and with ice cream desserts. The last time I received these with my coffee was at the famous restaurant Troigros in Roanne. They colored half of the dough with cocoa so they looked like marble, which was very pretty. The fantastic pâtisserie Bernachon always keeps them as part of their selection in Lyon, as does Paul Bocuse, where they are served as petits-fours with the coffee.

4.5 oz (125 g) almond paste 50/50
1 oz (30 g) egg white (approx. 1)
2.2 oz (65 g) wheat flour
1.7 oz (50 g) powdered sugar
0.5 oz (15 g) real vanilla sugar
1 oz (30 g) milk 3%

1. Blend the almond paste (room temperature) with the egg white, a little at a time, to form a dough without lumps.
2. Sift in the wheat flour and sugars, and blend into a smooth dough. Dilute with the milk.
3. Pipe 10 inch (26 cm) long, narrow strips on a baking sheet lined with parchment paper. Use a decorating bag and cut a small hole in the bottom with scissors.
4. Spread the strips out somewhat with the straight spatula to flatten them a little.
5. Bake them until golden brown at 430 °F (220 °C).
6. Remove the sheet from the oven and immediately roll the strips around rolling pins (you may also use pens and similar items). Leave them to stiffen. This is quick and then it should be easy to pull them off. Continue until you've used all of the batter.

STORAGE:
Store these crispy pastries in a dry place with a lid so that they don't go soft.

CAPRI ROLLS

I used to bake this good cake often as an apprentice, and I learned to spread the batter out quickly and get it onto the rolling pin even quicker. The good filling with a generous amount of pistachios makes these rolls especially festive. If you dip them in chocolate, they will keep longer and be even tastier to eat. Maybe Alex Munthe ate these in Capri . . .

ABOUT 20 ROLLS

4.2 oz (120 g) egg whites (approx. 4)
1 tsp (5 g) lemon juice
0.7 oz (20 g) granulated sugar
2.6 oz (75 g) almond flour
0.3 oz (10 g) wheat flour
2.6 oz (75 g) powdered sugar
1 drop green food coloring, preferably natural
1.7 oz (50 g) chopped pistachio nuts for decorating
1 batch pistachio buttercream, see p.150
7 oz (200 g) dark chocolate, preferably Valrhona
   Grand Cru Pur Caribe 66%

1. Preheat the oven to 355 °F (180 °C)
2. Whisk the egg whites and the lemon juice into meringue with the granulated sugar.
3. Sift almond flour, wheat flour, and powdered sugar into the bowl and fold in with the meringue. Add a drop of color.
4. Carve out a large round stencil, about 4 inches (10 cm) in diameter, from a thick carton with a small sharp knife or an exacto knife (you may find these in arts and crafts stores, and they are the best to work with). Spread the mass out with the stencil on a piece of parchment paper, only 4 at a time; if not, you'll have trouble with the timing when you try to roll them before they crack.
5. Sprinkle chopped pistachio nuts on top.
6. Bake them until golden brown, about 5 minutes.
7. Take them out of the oven, quickly roll them onto sticks and let them cool.
8. Fill the rolls with pistachio buttercream from both ends with the help of a plastic decorating bag. Chill them for 30 minutes.
9. Temper the chocolate, see p.13.
10. Dip the ends in dark tempered chocolate and place them on parchment paper to dry.

STORAGE:
Capri Rolls will keep in the fridge for a week. You may also freeze them as long as they're packed tightly.

Capri Rolls

Almond Rolls

Lemon Rolls

LEMON ROLLS WITH COCONUT

Beautiful crispy rolls of "cigarette dough" topped with coconut that's roasted during baking. The rum-flavored filling goes well with coconut and a good chocolate; this makes a nice petit-four. My good friend Matti Touminem, who keeps the monastery pâtisserie in Lund, was very speedy when he made the lemon rolls during our time working together at Conditori Lundagard in Lund.

25–30 ROLLS

Cigarette dough:
1 lemon, yellow and ripe
3.5 oz (100 g) butter
3.5 oz (100 g) powdered sugar
3.5 oz (100 g) wheat flour
3.5 oz (100 g) egg whites (approx. 3)
1.7 oz (50 g) grated coconut
½ batch French buttercream, see p.17
0.9 oz (25 g) dark rum
7 oz (200 g) dark chocolate, preferably Valrhona
    Grand Cru Pur Caribe 66%

1. Preheat the oven to 355 °F (180 °C).
2. Clean and grate the lemon zest; only use the outer zest, as the inner zest will make it bitter.
3. Blend the zest with the softened butter, sift in the powdered sugar and wheat flour, and stir with a spatula into a smooth dough.
4. Add egg whites at room temperature, a little at a time, for a mixture without lumps.
5. Spread the dough out thinly with a stencil, like with the Capri Rolls.
6. Sprinkle grated coconut on top.
7. Blend the butter cream with the liquor and fill the rolls from both ends with the buttercream by using a decorating bag. Use smooth tip no. 10 or cut a hole in the bottom. Place them in the fridge to harden for 30 minutes.
8. Temper the chocolate, see p.13.
9. Dip both ends of the rolls in the chocolate and let them dry on parchment paper.

STORAGE:
The rolls will keep for 1 week in the fridge. You can freeze these with tight packaging.

ALMOND ROLLS

Wafer pastry rolls filled with lean vanilla flavored cream with crispy nougat—an extra treat is the crispy shell covered in roasted almond and fine chocolate on the ends.

25–30 ROLLS

Nougat:
1.7 oz (50 g) sugar
1 tsp (5 g) lemon juice
1.7 oz (50 g) roasted almond flakes
1 knife tip of baking soda
0.5 oz (15 g) butter

½ batch French buttercream, see p.17

Wafer pastry dough:
5.3 oz (150 g) powdered sugar
3.5 oz (100 g) almond flour
2.1 oz (60 g) egg whites (approx. 2)
1 oz (30 g) wheat flour
4.5 oz (125 g) milk 3%

1.7 oz (50 g) almond flakes

1. Melt the sugar for the nougat with 1 tsp (5 g) lemon juice so that it attains a brownish color.
2. Stir in almonds, baking soda, and butter.
3. Let the nougat cool completely and then crush it with a rolling pin. Fold the nougat into the buttercream with a spatula.
4. Blend all of the ingredients for the wafer pastry dough in a food processor with jagged knifes so that you get a smooth batter; add the milk towards the end, a little at a time.
5. Let the batter rest for at least 1 hour.
6. Preheat the oven to 355 °F (180 °C).
7. Spread them out with a stencil as described for the Capri Rolls.
8. Sprinkle almond flakes and bake and then roll them onto a rolling pin like the Capri Rolls.
9. Fill the rolls with the nougat buttercream from both ends with a decorating bag. Use smooth tip no. 10 or cut a small hole in the bottom.
10. Place in the fridge to cool for 30 minutes.
11. Temper the chocolate, see p.13.
12. Dip both ends in the chocolate and let them dry on parchment paper.

STORAGE:
The rolls will keep for 1 week in the fridge. You can also freeze them.

HAZELCONES

These delicious cones are made with so-called waffle pastry dough. They can be tricky to make the first time, but later on rolling these will become second nature. The result is fantastic, and it's hard to find cakes that taste better than these. When I was young and worked at the Confiserie Brandli in Basil, I was assigned to bake these cones on the confectionary post for 14 days before they allowed me to bake their beautiful nougat pralines. If you ever go to Basil, don't miss this place; it is located on Barfusserplatz in the old town. Try their fantastic pralines and fine Swiss confectionary.

ABOUT 30 PASTRIES OF 0.3 OZ (10 G)

8.8 oz (250 g) almond paste 50/50
1.7 oz (50 g) egg whites (approx. 2)
0.2 oz (7 g) wheat flour
1.7 oz (50 g) milk 3%
0.2 oz (7 g) butter

Gianduja:
3.5 oz (100 g) roasted, shelled hazelnuts
3.5 oz (100 g) powdered sugar
3.5 oz (100 g) milk chocolate, preferably
  Valrhona Jivara Lactée 40%

7 oz (200 g) dark chocolate, preferably
  Valrhona Grand Cru Guanaja 70%, for dipping

DAY 1

1. Dissolve the almond paste (room temperature) with egg whites, a little at a time, to a form nice mixture without lumps; add the flour, and dilute the mixture with the milk till you have a thin batter.
2. Pass it through a sieve.
3. Melt the butter and blend into the batter with a spatula.
4. Cover with plastic wrap and let the batter rest overnight.
5. Mix nuts and powdered sugar in a food processor with jagged knife blade until the mass reaches a temperature of about 160 °F (70 °C).

6. Add the chopped milk chocolate and mix until it has melted completely.
7. Pour the gianduja in a bowl, cover with plastic wrap, and leave at room temperature overnight.

DAY 2

8. Make a stencil out of stiff paper, like cake carton. Cut a round with a sharp knife.
9. Cut so that you make a handle, see the drawing.
10. Spread the mass out evenly in the stencil on parchment paper, approximately 8 circles per paper.
11. Preheat the oven to 390 °F (200 °C).
12. Bake the waffle pastry dough until it starts getting some color, 3–5 minutes. Take the baking sheet out of the oven and repeat with the next one. Place the first sheet back in the oven and bake it light brown.
13. Remove the sheet from the oven and quickly roll the waffle rounds into cones on the tip of a wooden cone, see picture of brittle cones on p.88–89. (If you don't have one, you may roll them and place them in a shot glass instead; it is just as effective.) Continue until you've used up the batter.
14. Stir the gianduja with a ladle and mix it smooth with a mixer. Let it stiffen for a couple of minutes.
15. Scoop the gianduja in a decorating bag with smooth tip no. 10.
16. Fill the cones to the edge with gianduja mass and leave them to dry on parchment paper.
17. Temper the dark chocolate, see p.13, and dip the top of the cones. Let them dry on parchment paper.

STORAGE:
Store them in a tight container so they don't go soft. They keep for at least 14 days.

TIP!
The reason why we bake it in two rounds is to obtain an even color and not make their surface rugged. This goes for all kinds of so-called wafer pastries.

MERINGUE

In the book *The Practical Pastry Chef* from 1915 the following is written:

Egg white whisking
As a bowl for egg white whisking you should preferably use a dry, well-cleaned, untinned copper kettle. Aluminum or tinned bowls will not do, as the egg whites will neither become stiff nor good in them.

The steel whisk is best made by hand: You hammer two nails in an old table quite close to one another and then a third nail right in front of the space between these as afar away as you assume will make a nice whisk.

50 penny wire, bought at a hardware store, is wrapped around the nails, until you have a medium sized whisk. Then you release the wire from the nails, hammer the whisk even with a hammer, and warp it tightly with a finer wire that you fasten to a doorknob in order to be able to pull it really hard. It should be wrapped lightly, and in one layer only, so that the handle is steady and easy to maneuver.

You stick the end of the wire in the whisk, so it doesn't poke the hand that is holding the whisk.

Just like the bowl where you whisk, the whisk itself needs to be properly cleaned. You should use one whisk for egg whites and another for yolk, just like you need a separate whisk for whipping cream.

In order for the egg whites to whisk well, it has to be completely clean of the yolk. If you can use the same bowl for egg white whisking every time, that would be ideal.

Yes, everything is so much easier nowadays; today we can simply buy a whisk or an electric beater when we are going to make meringue.

Nostalgic beehive with meringue the way they were made during the 1800s with apple flowers, bees, and butterflies in caramel—everything placed on rock sugar.

MERINGUE CHICKS

These cozy Easter decoration are nice to serve as dessert with coffee. If they seem complicated, then draw the body and head on the parchment paper before you start piping. To pastry chefs, the decorating bag is like a second hand, and I remember how I would practice piping when I was too young to control the bag. Give it a try, and if it doesn't turn out as beautiful, it will still be just as tasty. Don't give up—I never do.

Traditional (French) Meringue, so-called cold-whipped:

The traditional French meringue can vary much in both appearance and texture. If the temperature never exceeds 212 °F (100 °C), the meringue will maintain its shape when you bake it. If you increase the temperature to 265 °F (130 °C) the meringue will increase in volume and easily caramelize. It will get a chewy texture on the inside and a crisp surface. This is not ideal when you, for instance, are making figures that have to maintain their shape, as they will crack.

The meringue baked in lower temperatures keeps for a long time and may be packed in bags, which you cannot do with meringue baked in higher temperatures that you have to eat fresh.

TIP!
One recipe rule is to use twice as much sugar as egg white.

7 oz (200 g) refrigerated egg whites (approx. 7)
2 tsp lemon juice (approx. 10 g)
3.5 + 3.5 oz (100 + 100 g) sugar
7 oz (200 g) powdered sugar
1 drop yellow food coloring, preferably natural

3.5 oz (100 g) shelled almonds
0.9 oz (25 g) currants for eyes
0.9 oz (25 g) pistachio nuts for beaks
10.5 oz (300 g) dark chocolate, preferably Valrhona Grand Cru Guanaja 70% for dipping

1. Preheat the oven to 212 °F (100 °C).
2. Whisk the egg whites and the lemon juice until they start to foam.
3. Sprinkle on 3.5 oz (100 g) granulated sugar and whisk with large movements with a hand whisk or on medium speed with a hand beater.
4. Add the remaining sugar during whisking and increase to full speed. Whisk until stiff peaks form.
5. Sift the powdered sugar in the bowl and fold into the foam with a spatula, along with the yellow food color.
6. Pipe small chicks on a baking sheet lined with parchment paper.
7. Add a shelled almond as a wing, a currant as the eye, and one pistachio to make the beak.
8. Bake them for 90 minutes. Leave them in the oven until they are dry. Let cool.
9. Temper the dark chocolate, see p.13.
10. Dip the underside of the chickens in the chocolate and scrape off excess chocolate against the edge of the bowl.
11. Let it stiffen on parchment paper.

TIP!
If you have a vent on your oven, open it when you bake meringue!

MERINGUE RABBITS

1. Follow the recipe above up until step 5, but do not color the meringue.
2. Pipe the rabbit's body on a baking sheet lined with parchment paper.
3. Then pipe the head and add currants as eyes and the mouth.
4. Bake them as in the above step 8.
5. Temper the chocolate and dip three-fourths of the hares. Let them dry on parchment paper.

EASTER NEST

These classic macaroons are a nice snack with coffee during Easter.

1. Make chocolate biskvier, see recipe on p.116, but pipe the chocolate cream around the top of the cookies instead of spreading it.
2. Dip them in dark chocolate and place a small yellow marzipan chicken next to it. Place a few colored eggs in the middle.

MERINGUE MUSHROOMS

These decorative meringues used to be very common and were used for decorating desserts, even ginger bread houses.

1 batch classic meringue, see p.140
0.7 oz (20 g) cocoa, preferably Valrhona
3.5 oz (100 g) dark chocolate, preferably Valrhona Grand Cru Guanaja 70%

1. Preheat the oven to 212 °F (100 °C).
2. Follow the recipe for classic meringue, but pipe one third as small domes for tops with a 1.5 inch (40 mm) diameter on a baking sheet lined with parchment paper.
3. Powder cocoa on top with a sieve.
4. Pipe the remaining meringue as mounds, about 2 1/3 inches (7 cm) tall, finish with a tip.
5. Bake and dry them for about 90 minutes until they feel completely dry.
6. Temper the chocolate, see p.13.
7. Dip the tips of the stems in the chocolate, add a mushroom hat and let it dry.

MERINGUES AUX AMANDES

These delicious meringues are always flavored with vanilla sugar and topped with almond flakes. They tower in the windows of most French pâtisseries, freshly baked every day. The difference between these and regular meringues is that you bake them at a higher temperature so that they get a crispy surface and a chewy cream inside, which makes them such a delicacy.

You can dip the bottom in dark chocolate—that tastes even better.

ABOUT 30 MERINGUES

8.8 oz (250 g) egg whites (approx. 8)
1 tsp (5 g) lemon juice (approx. 1 tsp)
8.8 oz (250 g) granulated sugar
7.9 oz (225 g) powdered sugar
0.9 oz (25 g) real vanilla sugar
2.1 oz (60 g) almond flakes for decorating

1. Preheat the oven to 265 °F (130 °C).
2. Whisk the meringue the same as for the chicks, see p.140.
3. Dip a large tablespoon in lukewarm water and shape beautiful meringues by placing them on the baking sheet and pulling a line towards you with the spoon so that a spine forms on top. Sprinkle almond flakes on top.
4. Bake them for about 60 minutes until they feel dry and light.

MERINGUE WREATHS

It used to be common to bake lots of meringues, and many were colored pink, yellow, and green and attached to one another with chocolate.

1 batch French meringue, see p.140
2.1 oz (60 g) almond flakes for decorating

1. Preheat the oven to 212 °F (100 °C)
2. Pipe the meringue as garlands with the help of a decorating bag with curly tip no. 12. Sprinkle almond flakes on top.
3. Bake them for about 90 minutes.
4. Let cool.

Meringues aux Amandes   *Meringue Wreaths*

Marbled Chocolate Meringues   *Pistachio Meringues*   *Almond Mounds*   *Grenoble Meringues*

GRENOBLE MERINGUES

We named these Grenoble Meringues because the best walnuts are from Grenoble. These chewy, warm-whipped meringues may be varied indefinitely. With pistachio nuts we might call them Palermo Meringues since the finest pistachio nuts grows in Sicily.

With hazelnuts they're called Piedmont Meringues, and Almond Mounds have flaked almonds. Dip the bottom in dark chocolate and they won't be as sweet; furthermore the chocolate protects the meringue from drying out.

8.8 oz (250 g) egg whites (approx. 8)
16.8 oz (475 g) powdered sugar
0.9 oz (25 g) vanilla sugar
1 tsp (5 g) lemon juice (approx. 1 tsp)
7 oz (200 g) walnuts
10.5 oz (300 g) dark chocolate, preferably Valrhona
    Grand Cru Guanaja 70%

1. Preheat the oven to 300 °F (150 °C).
2. Pour egg whites, powdered sugar, vanilla sugar, and lemon juice in a metal bowl. Whisk to blend everything well.
3. Place over a saucepan with simmering water. Whisk properly until the batter reaches a temperature of 122–140 °F (50–60 °C).
4. Then whisk the meringue cold with the lowest speed on the hand beater or slowly by hand.

5. Crush the walnuts roughly and fold them in the meringue.
6. Arrange the meringue as pictured with a spoon on a baking sheet lined with parchment paper. Let it dry for 30 minutes.
7. Bake them for about 45 minutes or until they easily let go of the paper. Let them cool.
8. Temper the chocolate, see p.13.
9. Dip the meringue in the chocolate and scrape off excess chocolate against the edge of the bowl. Let them dry on parchment paper.

MARBLED CHOCOLATE MERINGUES

1 batch warm-whipped meringue, see previous recipe, but substitute the walnuts with 7 oz (200 g) roasted almond flakes.

2.8 oz (80 g) dark chocolate, preferably Valrhona
    Grand Cru Guanaja 70%
10.5 oz (300 g) dark chocolate Grand Cru Valrhona
    Guanaja 70%, for dipping

1. Follow the instructions for Grenoble meringue up until step 5.
2. Finely chop 2.8 oz (80 g) chocolate and heat it in the microwave oven or a water bath to about 113–122 °F (45–50 °C). Stir occasionally.
3. Fold the chocolate haphazardly in the almond meringue and arrange with a spoon, like small uneven mounds. The meringue should be marbled so do not stir too much.
4. Let it dry for 30 minutes.
5. Bake as described for Grenoble meringue.
6. Dip the bottom as described for Grenoble meringue.

JAPONAIS *(The Japanese)*

These cakes were a specialty of the Conditori Lundagard in Lund when I worked there. The ovens were full of Japanese bottoms all day long because the demand for this hazelnut flavored cake was so great. We made it as a tart as well. The recipe is originally from Switzerland, and Max Hammerli, who was a janitor, brought it from his home country. Max later opened a pâtisserie in Malmö, where he also made The Japanese.

This cake is fantastic, if made the proper way. Pastry chefs spread the meringue with a plastic stencil, but you can also pipe the bottoms, which is the original method. Originally, they would pipe chocolate fondant on top, but I am using dark chocolate instead, which is not as sweet.

TIP!
If you can't get a hold of cocoa butter at the store, then stop by a pâtisserie and ask if you can buy cocoa butter there.

ABOUT 30-35 PASTRIES

14 oz (400 g) hazelnuts for sprinkling
3 oz (90 g) almonds with shell
3 oz (90 g) sugar
0.9 oz (25 g) milk 3%

Meringue:
9.5 oz (270 g) egg whites (approx. 9)
4.2 oz (120 g) sugar
1 tsp (5 g) lemon juice

Japonaise-Cream:
14 oz (400 g) sugar
7 oz (200 g) water
7 oz (200 g) almonds with peel
7 oz (200 g) hazelnuts
5.3 oz (150 g) cocoa butter
10.5 oz (300 g) unsalted butter

2.8 oz (80 g) dark chocolate, preferably Valrhona
    Grand Cru Guanaja 70%

1. Preheat the oven to 390 °F (200 °C).
2. Empty the nuts for sprinkling on an edged baking sheet. Roast them until golden brown while stirring occasionally until the shells start falling off.
3. Shell the hazelnuts by rubbing them in a dish towel until the shells fall off.
4. Finely grind them in a grinder.
5. Preheat the oven to 230 °F (110 °C).
6. Make a TPT by mixing the almonds with shells and sugar in a food processor with jagged knifes to form a fine powder.
7. Blend TPT with the milk to a smooth mass in a bowl.
8. Whisk the egg whites on medium speed with the lemon juice and one-fourth of the sugar for meringue. Add the remaining sugar a little at a time and whisk into stiff meringue. Increase the speed of the whisking towards the end so that the meringue is really stiff.
9. Blend a handful of meringue into the TPT-blend. Stir smooth and carefully fold it in the meringue with a spatula.
10. Draw 60–70 circles on parchment paper, about 2 inches (50 mm) in diameter. Scoop the almond meringue in a decorating bag with smooth tip no. 12 and squeeze out rounds, about 3/16 inch (5 mm) thick, on the parchment paper.
11. Bake them until golden brown, about 2 hours.
12. Pull the paper off the bottoms as soon as they've cooled and place them in a large tin with a lid so that they do not go soft.
13. Boil sugar and water for the Japonaise-cream to 230 °F (110 °C).
14. Add almonds and nuts and boil until they start snapping. Stir now and then. Increase the stirring when the sugar starts to whiten and crystalize.
15. Stir forcefully until the sugar has turned to golden caramel. Empty onto parchment paper and let it cool.
16. Mix the mass in a food processor until it starts oiling and turns creamy. The temperature should be about 160 °F (70 °C). Let the mass cool.
17. Chop the cocoa butter finely and melt it in a small saucepan; do not let it exceed 122 °F (50 °C).
18. Add the cocoa butter and the softened butter and stir the cream until light and airy with an electric beater on medium speed. If the cream is not turning light and airy or lifting, then chill it for 30 minutes and start whisking again.
19. Place half of the bottoms on a baking sheet and pipe a ball of cream on each one with a decorating bag. Cut a hole in the bottom or use tip no. 12.
20. Place the remaining bottoms on top with the flat side facing upwards. The cake should weigh about 1 oz (30 g).
21. Press down with a baking sheet to make the cakes even and set them in the fridge for 10 minutes.
22. Take them out two at a time. It is easiest to glaze them if they are leaning on each other. Spread cream on the sides with a straight spatula.
23. Spread a thin layer of cream on each cake. Place them with the cream side facing down in the hazelnuts. Stick them back together with the sprinkle sides against each other and roll them so that the sides are covered with hazelnuts. Repeat on the rest of the cakes.

24. Temper the chocolate, see p.13.
25. Scoop the chocolate into a paper cone, cut a hole in the bottom, and pipe a dot the size of a nickel on top of each cake.

STORAGE:

Store in the fridge until eating. They will keep for about 3 days.

SWISS KISSES

These tasty chocolate meringues are some of the finest pastries a pastry chef can make, in my opinion. They, too, were a specialty at Conditori Lundagard in Lund. The tart specialist Sven Malmborg always baked these once or twice a week. We baked them on soaked wooden plates so that they wouldn't get any heat from below. If you can't find wooden plates, you can use double baking sheets with a wet newspaper under the parchment paper.

ABOUT 30 KISSES

Boiled chocolate meringue:
4.5 oz (125 g) water
8.8 oz (250 g) sugar
3.5 oz (100 g) egg whites (approx. 3)
1 tsp lemon juice
0.9 oz (25 g) sugar
5.3 oz (150 g) dark chocolate, preferably Valrhona
    Grand Cru Guanaja 70%
1.4 oz (40 g) lukewarm water

1. Pour 4.5 oz (125 g) water in a saucepan that can hold 5 cups (1 liter).
2. Add sugar and stir with a whisk to dissolve.
3. Boil and skim.
4. Brush the inside of the saucepan with a brush dipped in cold water.
5. When the syrup reaches 230 °F (110 °C) start whisking egg whites, lemon juice, and 0.9 oz (25 g) sugar into meringue.
6. Boil the syrup on high temperature to 250 °F (122 °C), use a sugar thermometer or do a marble test, see p.40.
7. Pour the boiling syrup in the meringue while constantly stirring.
8. Whisk on low speed until the meringue is cool, about 10 minutes.
9. Finely chop the chocolate. Melt it in the microwave oven or in a water bath to 130 °F (55 °C).
10. Stir the chocolate with a spatula. Add the lukewarm water and stir into cream.
11. Stir the chocolate cream in with the meringue using a spatula. You should obtain an airy meringue.
12. Preheat the oven to 300 °F (150 °C).
13. Pipe about 60 very small oval meringues on a parchment paper, with a decorating bag. Cut a small hole in the bottom or use tip no. 12.
14. Place one sheet in the oven at a time and bake them for 6–9 minutes, until a crust forms.
15. Stick the cakes together in doubles with the bottoms facing each other. Use a small straight spatula to glue together, with a ganache if you choose, and be careful when you stick them together. Repeat the same process with the second sheet of meringues.

STORAGE:
Eat them the same day or freeze them and let them thaw for 15 minutes before eating.

Double Chocolate Meringues with Hazelnuts and Manjari Ganache   *Swiss Kisses*

DOUBLE CHOCOLATE MERINGUES WITH HAZELNUTS AND MANJARI GANACHE

A variety of the same chocolate meringue that will not leave any sweet tooth wanting. The chewy chocolate meringue with a soft ganache center is a true delicacy.

1 batch boiled chocolate meringue, see p.146
3.5 oz (100 g) roasted chopped hazelnuts
½ batch pâtisserie ganache with Valrhona Grand Cru Manjari 64%, see p.14

1. Follow the directions for Swiss Kisses up until step 11.
2. Preheat the oven to 345 °F (175 °C).
3. Pipe the meringue as 2 inch 95 cm) long tongues with a decorating bag. Cut a hole in the bottom or use smooth tip no. 12.
4. Crush the roasted walnuts roughly and sprinkle them on half of the meringues.

5. Bake the meringues for about 30 minutes until they feel somewhat resilient, but not dry.
6. Let them cool and pipe ¼ tsp (5-6k pa g) ganache on the meringue without nuts. Place the meringues with the nuts on top like a lid.

STORAGE:
Stored in the fridge, they should be slightly chewy. May also be frozen.

147

SOFT FRAGILITÉ

Rolf Augustsson at Konditori Hollandia in Malmö always baked this cake. This cake is fantastically tasty and chewy and is great with coffee after a good dinner. Store rolls in the freezer. You can cut pieces as needed and always serve freshly baked cakes.

ABOUT 45 CAKES

10.5 oz (300 g) almond paste 50/50
3.5 oz (100 g) milk 3%
10.5 oz (300 g) egg whites (approx. 10)
1 tsp (5 g) lemon juice (approx. 1 tsp)
3.5 oz (100 g) sugar
2.1 oz (60 g) almond flakes
Sugar for sprinkling on top
1 batch chocolate ganache with Valrhona Grand
    Cru Manjari 64%, see p.14.

Pistachio filling:
½ batch Horseshoes dipped in chocolate, see p.108
Follow recipe up until step 2

Powdered sugar
1.7 oz (50 g) dark chocolate, preferably Valrhona Grand Cru Manjari 64%

1. Preheat the oven to 390 °F (200 °C).
2. Dissolve the almond paste (room temperature) with the milk and work to a smooth mixture by hand.
3. Whisk the egg whites with the lemon juice on medium speed and add one third of the sugar, Continue whisking, add an additional third of the sugar, and whisk for 3 minutes. Add the remaining sugar, increase the speed of the whisking, and whisk until stiff peaks form.
4. Blend some of the meringue into the dissolved almond paste. Fold the meringue in with the paste to form a light and airy mass.
5. Spread the mixture out on two baking sheets lined with parchment paper. Sprinkle with almond flakes and bake them until golden brown for about 20 minutes.
6. Move them onto a cold surface right away so that they do not cool on the baking sheet; if they do, they can dry up and be hard to roll.
7. Sprinkle sugar on top of the bottoms, cover with a piece of parchment paper, and turn upside down. Brush the paper with water underneath and pull off.
8. Spread ganache on each bottom.
9. Divide each bottom lengthwise and pipe a line of pistachio filling on the lengths with a decorating bag. Cut a hole in the bottom or use smooth tip no. 12.
10. Roll the lengths together like a Swiss Roll with the help of the paper, and clamp them with the help of a ruler.
11. Freeze the rolls for at least 1 hour wrapped in plastic wrap.
12. Take the lengths out of the freezer and cut medium sized cakes with a sharp knife, about 1 oz (30 g).
13. Once they've thawed, dust some powdered sugar on top.
14. Temper the chocolate, see p.13. Scoop the chocolate in a paper cone and cut a hole in the bottom. Line the lengths with chocolate.

Soft Fragilité

Jitterbug

Biarritz

Progresser

Palermo

Almond Mounds Dipped in Chocolate

Ristori

PALERMO

These tasty, chewy pastries with pistachio nuts are filled with real pistachio cream and taste as they should without artificial aromas.

4.5 oz (125 g) shelled sweet almonds
4.5 oz (125 g) pistachio nuts
2.6 oz (75 g) powdered sugar
2.6 oz (75 g) wheat flour

Meringue:
8.8 oz (250 g) egg whites (approx. 8)
1 tsp (5 g) lemon juice (approx. 1 tsp)
2.6 oz (75 g) granulated sugar

1.7 oz (50 g) chopped pistachio nuts

Pistachio buttercream:
2.8 oz (80 g) pistachio paste, see p.25
0.7 oz (20 g) Kirschwasser or dark rum
Optional 1 drop orange flower water (you can find this in specialty grocery stores)
½ batch French buttercream, see p.17

7 oz (200 g) dark chocolate, Valrhona Grand Cru Guanaja 70%

1. Preheat the oven to 285 °F (140 °C).
2. Make a so-called TPT of sweet almonds, pistachio nuts, powdered sugar, and wheat flour. Mix it all in a food processor with a jagged blade to form a powder.
3. Whisk the egg whites and lemon juice with half of the granulated sugar to a meringue on medium speed. Add the remaining sugar while whisking. Increase the speed and whisk until stiff peaks form.
4. Fold in the TPT with a spatula to an airy blend.
5. Empty the blend into a decorating bag. Cut a hole in the bottom or use smooth tip no. 12.
6. Pipe 4 inch (10 cm) long tongues on a baking sheet lined with parchment paper and sprinkle some chopped pistachio nuts over half of them.
7. Bake them for about 35–45 minutes until the let go of the paper.
8. Once they're out of the oven, remove them from the paper right away and let them cool down.
9. Blend pistachio paste, liquor, and optional 1 drop orange flower water with the buttercream.
10. Place half of the bottoms with the flat side up and cover with 0.7 oz (20 g) pistachio buttercream.
11. Put the remaining bottoms on top. Place the meringues in the fridge and let them stiffen for 30 minutes.
12. Temper the chocolate, see p.13.
13. Dip the one end in chocolate and let them dry on parchment paper.

BIARRITZ

These lovely hazelnut meringues with hazelnut cream are a pâtisserie specialty that not only exists in Sweden, but on the entire continent. At Pâtisserie Dupont in Paris, these are baked every single day. The contrast of the chocolate makes them unforgettable. Try to get a hold of Italian or Spanish hazelnuts. Pâtisseries that bake larger batches usually spread the meringue in rubber stencils, but you can also pipe them.

ABOUT 20 MERINGUES

5.6 oz (160 g) egg whites (approx. 5-6)
1 tsp (5 g) lemon juice (1 tsp)
7 oz (200 g) sugar
7 oz (200 g) roasted, finely chopped hazelnuts
2.8 oz (80 g) roasted, roughly crushed hazelnuts
¼ batch French buttercream, see p17.
2.8 oz (80 g) hazelnut paste, see recipe p.25
2.8 oz (80 g) dark chocolate, preferably Valrhona Grand Cru Guanaja 70%

1. Preheat the oven to 300 °F (150 °C).
2. Draw about 40 circles, 3 inches (75 mm) in diameter, on parchment paper.
3. Whisk egg whites with lemon juice and one third of the sugar on medium speed to medium peaks.
4. Add the remaining sugar in two rounds. Increase the speed and whisk to stiff peaks.
5. Fold in the grated nuts with a spatula.
6. Scoop the meringue in a decorating bag. Cut a hole in the bottom or use smooth tip no. 10.
7. Pipe about 1/8 of an inch (3 mm) thick meringue in the drawn rings (not too thick)
8. Sprinkle crushed hazelnuts on half the bottoms.
9. Bake them until golden brown, for about 45 minutes, when they should feel dry and light. Take them out of the oven and let them cool.
10. Blend the buttercream and the hazelnut paste with a spatula and pipe about 0.7 oz (20 g) of filling on half of the bottoms. Place the bottom with the hazelnuts on top and press down a little.
11. Set in the fridge to stiffen
12. Temper the chocolate, see p.13.
13. Scoop the chocolate into a paper cone. Cut a small hole in the bottom and make lines on the cakes with the chocolate.

STORAGE:
Store the cakes in the fridge; they will keep for about 4–5 days and may also be frozen.

JITTERBUG

My mother would occasionally bake these tasty pastries, and my good friend, the chef garde manger Kerstin Forsberg, wanted all the ones I baked for the book. They're her favorite. A chewy and sweet cake.

Special short-crust dough:
1.4 oz (40 g) powdered sugar
0.3 oz (10 g) real vanilla sugar
8.8 oz (250 g) wheat flour
1 tsp (5 g) baking powder
8.8 oz (250 g) butter
1.7 oz (50 g) egg (approx. 1)

Warm-whipped meringue:
4.5 oz (125 g) egg white (approx. 1)
1 tsp (5 g) lemon juice
10 oz (290 g) powdered sugar
0.3 oz (10 g) real vanilla sugar

Egg wash, see p.47

1. Sift powdered sugar, vanilla sugar, wheat flour, and baking powder through a sieve onto parchment paper.
2. Blend the softened butter with the egg; that should stay room temperature.
3. Carefully add the sifted blend and stir into a dough, but do not overwork it.
4. Cool the dough for at least 2 hours wrapped in plastic wrap.
5. Pour egg white, lemon juice, powdered sugar, and vanilla sugar in a metal bowl. Wisk till everything is blended properly.
6. Place the bowl over a saucepan with simmering water.
7. Whisk until the batter has reached a temperature of 122–140 °F (50–60 °C).
8. Then whisk the meringue cold on the lowest speed with the electric beater or slowly by hand.
9. Work the cold short-crust dough smooth by hand.
10. Roll it out 1/16 (2 mm) thick and about 8 inches (20 cm) wide.
11. Spread the cold meringue on top with a straight spatula. Brush egg wash along the bottom edge so that the roll will stick together with the help of parchment paper; roll it just like a Swiss Roll.
12. Place the roll on parchment paper and let it stiffen for 1 hour in the freezer.
13. Preheat the oven to 300 °F (150 °C).
14. Cut slices of 2.1 oz (60 g) with a knife dipped in warm water.
15. Bake them golden brown for about 25 minutes.

STORAGE:
Store them in a dry place so that they do not go soft.

RISTORI

This chewy almond cake becomes a delicacy with vanilla buttercream with real Tahitian vanilla as a filling.

ABOUT 15 CAKES

7 oz (200 g) almond paste 50/50
2.1 oz (60 g) egg whites (approx. 2)

Meringue:
8.8 oz (250 g) egg whites (approx. 2)
1 tsp (5g) lemon juice (approx. 1 tsp)
3.5 oz (100 g) sugar

1.7 oz (50 g) wheat flour
1.7 oz (50 g) almond flakes
½ batch French buttercream, see p.17
7 oz (200 g) dark chocolate for dipping, preferably Valrhona Grand Cru Guanaja 70%

1. Preheat the oven to 285 °F (140 °C).
2. Draw about 30 circles on two baking sheets, approx. 2 1/3 inches (60 mm) in diameter.
3. Dissolve the almond paste with the two egg whites, a little at a time, until you have a mass without lumps.
4. Whisk the egg white with the lemon juice and a third of the sugar to medium peaks on shifting speeds. Add the remaining sugar in turns while constantly whisking. Increase the whisking speed and whisk until stiff peaks form.
5. Fold one-fourth of the meringue into the dissolved almond paste and blend so that there are no lumps. Sift in the wheat flour.
6. Fold the mass into the meringue with a spatula.
7. Scoop the mixture into a decorating bag. Cut a small hole in the bottom or use smooth tip no. 12.
8. Pipe bottoms starting in the middle of the circles and working your way out, about 1/8 of an inch (3 mm) thick, no more.
9. Sprinkle almond flakes on top.
10. Bake the meringues for approx. 35–40 minutes, until they feel dry and light and you can pull them off the paper; if not, then bake them a while longer.
11. Let them cool and remove the paper. Place half of them with the flat side facing upwards.
12. Scoop the buttercream into a decorating bag. Cut a hole in the bottom or use smooth tip no. 12.
13. Pipe about 0.9 oz (25 g) buttercream on half of the meringues and place the others on top. Place them in the fridge to stiffen.
14. Temper the chocolate, see p.13.
15. Dip the meringues halfway in chocolate and let them dry on parchment paper.

STORAGE:
Meringues will keep for about 3 days, but you may also freeze them.

CLASSIC FRAGILITÉS WITH VANILLA OR MOCHA FILLING

This good and chewy cake used to exist in most pâtisseries in Sweden and can also be prepared as a tart. I remember how many fragilité strips we baked at Conditori Lungard in Lund, with the word "fragilité" sifted on top with the help of cocoa and a stencil. The filling was either vanilla or mocha buttercream.

20 bites
The cakes will serve about 12 people

Vanilla buttercream:
1 sheet gelatin (approx. 2 g)
8.8 oz (250 g) milk 3 %

½ vanilla bean
2.1 oz (60 g) egg yolks (approx. 2)
2.6 oz (75 g) sugar
0.7 oz (20 g) cornstarch
15 oz (425 g) unsalted butter

For the mocha filling add:
0.3 oz (10 g) dark roasted Nescafe
0.8 oz (2.5 cl) rum

8.8 oz (250 g) almond paste 50/50
2.6 oz (75 g) milk 3%
8.8 oz (250 g) egg whites (approx. 8)
1 tsp (5g) lemon juice (approx. 1 tsp)
10.5 oz (300 g) sugar
1 oz (30 g) almond flakes

Décor:
Powdered sugar
0.7 oz (20 g) cocoa
Espresso coffee beans

DAY 1

1. Soak the gelatin leaf in a generous amount of cold water for at least 10 minutes.
2. Cut the vanilla bean down the middle and scrape the seeds out in a small saucepan with the milk.
3. Bring the milk to a boil with the vanilla seeds and bean. Set aside to absorb the vanilla flavor for 10–15 minutes.
4. Whisk the yolks with the sugar and cornstarch and pour the milk over it. Blend well.
5. Bring the cream to a boil while constantly stirring.
6. Pull the gelatin sheet out of the water and let it drain off. Whisk it into the cream until it's melted.
7. Whisk half of the butter in with the cream.
8. Cool the cream to a temperature of 68 °F (20 °C) in a water bath.
9. Add the remaining butter and whisk everything until light and airy on medium speed; if you whisk too fast, the cream may become too dense and runny.
10. For mocha cream: dissolve the coffee in the liquor and fold in the buttercream.
11. Preheat the oven to 265 °F (130 °C).
12. Dissolve the almond paste (room temperature) with the milk by hand.
13. Whisk the egg whites with the lemon juice on medium speed and add one third of the sugar. Continue whisking, add another third of the sugar, and whisk for 3 minutes. Add the remaining sugar and increase the speed of the whisking, forming stiff peaks.
14. Blend some of the meringue into the dissolved almond paste. Fold the smooth mass into the meringue to form a light and airy mass.
15. Divide the mass on 3 baking sheets lined with parchment paper and spread it out evenly and carefully so that it covers the entire sheet.
16. Sprinkle almond flakes over one of the plates.
17. Bake all three at once for approx. 45 minutes. Feel free to move the sheets around a bit during baking for a more even color. Let them cool on the sheets.
18. Lightly dust powdered sugar over the bottoms. Turn them upside down and pull the paper off the underside of the bottoms by brushing some cold water on it.
19. Place one bottom with the shiny side downwards, and spread a layer of vanilla or mocha buttercream on top. Layer another bottom on top and spread the remaining cream on top (save a little mocha cream for decorating).
20. Place the plate with the almond flakes on top and press down with the help of a baking sheet so that the cake will stick together.
21. Set the cake in the fridge overnight so it's easier to slice. If not, it will crack and fall apart.

DAY 2

22. Cut squared pieces, 1.5 x 1.5 inches (40 x 40 mm), and dust powdered sugar on top.
23. With mocha filling: Set a grid on top and sift cocoa powder on top, preferably Valrhona. Use a sieve. Decorate with small peaks of mocha buttercream using a paper cone, and place a coffee bean on each cake.

Long pastries:
1 batch classic fragilities
2.1 oz (60 g) roasted almond flakes

1. Follow the recipe above up until step 21, but save some of the vanilla buttercream or mocha buttercream.
2. Cut the layers lengthwise with a sharp jagged knife.
3. Spread a thin layer of vanilla buttercream or mocha buttercream on the sides and sprinkle them with roasted almond flakes.
4. Sift powdered sugar on top. For the mocha variety: Make a grid with sifted cocoa. Decorate with mocha buttercream and espresso beans.

STORAGE:
Will keep for approx. 5 days in the fridge, but you may also freeze it.

PROGRESSER

This pastry is a clear favorite with mocha buttercream as a filling, topped with roasted hazelnuts, and decorated with fine chocolate—almost sinfully good. Pastry chef Yngve Malmqvist taught me how to bake these at the Savoy Hotel in Malmö.

ABOUT 20 CAKES

6 oz (170 g) almond paste 50/50
2.1 oz (60 g) egg whites (approx. 2)

Meringue:
7 oz (200 g) egg whites (approx. 7)
1 tsp (5g) lemon juice (approx. 1 tsp)
14 oz (400 g) sugar

3.5 oz (100 g) roasted, chopped hazelnuts for decorating

0.3 oz (10 g) Nescafe
0.9 oz (25 g) arrack or punch
½ batch French buttercream, see p.17
2.9 oz (80 g) dark chocolate, preferably Valrhona
   Grand Cru Guanaja 70%
Powdered sugar

1. Preheat the oven to 300 °F (150 °C)
2. Dissolve the almond paste (room temperature) with the two egg whites, a little at a time, so that the mass is free of lumps.
3. Whisk the cold egg whites and lemon juice for the meringue until the foam starts lifting.
4. Sprinkle 1.7 oz (50 g) sugar in the bowl and whisk with large movements by hand or with an electric beater on medium speed.

5. Add the remaining sugar in small batches during constant whisking and increase the whisking to full speed.
6. Stir one-fourth of the meringue in with the dissolved almond paste to an even batter.
7. Carefully fold the batter in the meringue with a large spatula to form a light and airy meringue mass.
8. Scoop the mass into a decorating bag. Cut a hole in the bottom or use smooth tip no. 14.
9. Pipe domes, 2 inches (5 cm) in diameter, of the mixture on two baking sheets lined with parchment paper.
10. Sprinkle chopped hazelnuts on top and bake until golden brown for about 25 minutes.
11. Take them out of the oven and let them cool.
12. Dissolve the Nescafe in the liquor and fold in the buttercream with a spatula.
13. Scoop the buttercream into a decorating bag with curly tip no. 12 and pipe one large rosette on the flat side of half of the meringues.
14. Set the other bottom on top as a lid.
15. Temper the chocolate, see p.13. Pour it into a paper cone and cut a small hole in the bottom.
16. Decorate the meringues with lines, as pictured.
17. Dust powdered sugar on top.

STORAGE:
Store the meringues in the fridge. They will keep for 5 days or you may also freeze them.

YOLK MERINGUES OR "THE CHINESE"

These sandy sweet delicacies are reminiscent of meringues, but melt in your mouth. It is important to le the surface of the cakes dry properly before you bake them. Pastry chef Gosta Wenneberg at the Hotel d'Angleterre in Copenhagen served these with the first rhubarb compote of spring, which was very luxurious.

3.5 oz (100 g) yolks (approx. 5)
0.7 oz (2 cl) dark rum
1 lb (475 g) powdered sugar
0.9 oz (25 g) real vanilla sugar
0.2 oz (7 g) ammonium carbonate (also called baker's ammonia)

1. Lightly whisk the yolk with the liquor.
2. Sift powdered sugar and vanilla sugar with the ammonium carbonate into the bowl.
3. Boil 5 cups (1 liter) of water in a saucepan. Place the bowl in the water bath and whisk constantly until the mass reaches a temperature of 104 °F (40 °C)

4. Then whisk the mixture cold on alternating speeds.
5. Scoop the mixture into a decorating bag. Cut a hole in the bottom or use smooth tip no. 12.
6. Pipe round balls, 1 inch (25 mm) in diameter and 1/8 of an inch (3 mm) thick, on parchment paper.
7. Let them dry for 1 hour before they bake. Preheat the oven to 300 °F (150 °C).
8. Bake "The Chinese" for 15 minutes. If they're properly done they should be golden brown and rise straight upward during baking to multiple times the piped size.
9. Let them cool and store in a dry place.

COCONUT AND HAZELNUTS

ROASTED NUTCAKES

These tasty nutcakes obtain their moist texture through the roasting of the dough, and they stay fresh for a long time. When I was a boy it was common to add a little apple jam in the dough to make it even moister. You can adjust the texture as you wish. If you want it to spread out like the picture, then follow the recipe; but if you wish to make them taller, decrease the amount of egg white. My mother loved these nutcakes, and so do I.

ABOUT 40 NUTCAKES

8.8 oz (250 g) finely grated hazelnuts
8.8 oz (250 g) almonds with the shell
17.6 oz (500 g) sugar
3 oz (90 g) egg whites (approx. 3)
3.5 oz (100 g) roasted hazelnuts for decorating
1 batch basic syrup, see p.17
10.5 oz (300 g) dark chocolate, preferably Valrhona
    Grand Cru Manjari 64%

1. Blend nuts, almonds, sugar, and egg whites in a saucepan and roast while constantly stirring to 114–122°F (45–50°C).
2. Pipe balls of 0.9 oz (25 g) with the help of a decorating bag. Cut a hole in the bottom or use smooth tip no. 12.
3. Stick a roasted hazelnut in the cake. Let them dry for 30 minutes.
4. Preheat the oven to 445 °F (230 °C). Bake the cakes golden brown.
5. Brush them with syrup right away.
6. Let the cakes cool down. Place them in the fridge for 30 minutes to stiffen.
7. Temper the chocolate, see p.17.
8. Dip the bottom of the cake in the chocolate and scrape off excess chocolate against the edge of the bowl. Let them dry on parchment paper.

Storage:
These will keep in the fridge for about 1 week or you can freeze them.

CHOCOLATE AND COCONUT MACAROONS WITH RASPBERRY JAM

These chewy coconut macaroons with chocolate flavor are delicious and were some of my favorites as an apprentice.

ABOUT 25 MACAROONS

8.8 oz (250 g) finely grated coconut
17.6 oz (500 g) sugar
4.2 oz (120 g) egg whites (approx. 4)
0.9 oz (25 g) cocoa, preferably Valrhona
7 oz (200 g) raspberry jam, see recipe on p.19
3.5 oz (100 g) syrup for glazing, see p.17
7 oz (200 g) dark chocolate, preferably Valrhona
    Grand Cru Guanaja 70%, for dipping

1. Blend coconut, sugar, egg whites, and cocoa in a bowl and set it in a saucepan with simmering water. Roast the mass while stirring until it reaches a temperature of 140 °F (60 °C).
2. Cover with lid and let the batter simmer for 1 hour.
3. Scoop the mixture into a decorating bag. Cut a large hole in the bottom or use smooth tip no. 14.
4. Pipe buns of about 1.5 oz (45 g) of the mass on a baking sheet lined with parchment paper.
5. Dip an egg in warm water and use it to make an indent in the cake.
6. Scoop the raspberry jam in a paper cone and cut a hole in the bottom. Squeeze out 1 tsp (5 g) raspberry jam in each cake.
7. Let them dry for 1 hour.
8. Preheat the oven to 390 °F (200 °C).
9. Bake the coconut macaroons until golden brown for 12–14 minutes.
10. Brush them with syrup as soon as you take them out of the oven to give them a beautiful shine. Let them cool on the sheet.
11. Temper the chocolate, see p.13, and dip the bottoms in the chocolate. Scrape off excess chocolate against the edge of the bowl and let the macaroons dry on parchment paper.

STORAGE:
These will keep fresh in the fridge for 3–4 days. You can freeze these.

Roasted Nutcakes

Safari Nutcakes

Nut Tops

Sebastopol Nutcanapés

SEBASTOPOL NUTCANAPÉS

This chewy nutcake with the flavor of delicious apple jam is a fine pastry that deserves a place in a pâtisserie or on the coffee table. If you flavor them with preserved orange peels, they taste even better. Preserve the peels from scratch, see recipe on page 20. Do not buy the dried orange peels you find at the store, as they have nothing to do with good preserved orange peels.

½ batch classic short-crust dough, see p.27

Nut Sebastopol filling:
1 lemon, yellow and ripe
4.5 oz (125 g) ground hazelnuts
1.7 oz (50 g) chopped, preserved orange peels, see recipe on p.20
8.8 oz (250 g) sugar
3.5 oz (100 g) egg white
0.3 oz (10 g) wheat flour

7 oz (200 g) raspberry jam, see recipe on p.18
Egg wash, see p.47
2.8 oz (80 g) dark chocolate, preferably Valrhona
   Grand Cru Guanaja 70%

1. Preheat the oven to 390 °F (200 °C)
2. Work the cold dough smooth by hand and roll it out to 1/8 of an inch (3 mm) thickness and the same length as a baking sheet with a rolling pin and some wheat flour.
3. Cut strips as long as a baking sheet and 3 inches (7 cm) wide, with a large knife or spur.
4. Place three strips on a baking sheet lined with parchment paper.
5. Brush the edges with egg wash, cut 6 pieces, 1/4 inch (6.5 mm) wide, and place them on each side of the lengths.
6. Poke the strips with a fork.
7. Half-bake the short-crust dough for about 7–8 minutes. Take it out and let it cool down.
8. Clean and grate the outer zest of the lemon with the fine side of a grater.
9. Blend all of the ingredients for the nut filling in a bowl and roast it in a simmering water bath while constantly stirring until it reaches a temperature of 113–122 °F (45–50 °C).
10. Scoop the nut filling in a plastic decorating bag. Cut a hole in the bottom or use smooth tip no. 12.
11. First pipe a layer of jam at the bottom of the short-crust dough through a paper cone.
12. Then add the nut filling on the three lengths.
13. Preheat the oven to 390 °F (180 °C)
14. Bake them golden brown for about 12–15 minutes. Let them cool.
15. Temper chocolate, see p.13.
16. Brush the edges of the strips with chocolate. Let dry.
17. Cut pieces of 1 oz (30 g) with a sharp, sturdy knife.

STORAGE:
Will keep for 2 days in the fridge; if you don't cut the strips, they will keep for a few days longer. Fine to freeze.

SAFARI NUTCAKES

Good and moist nutcake with a lovely chocolate flavor.

ABOUT 25 NUTCAKES

8.8 oz (250 g) almond paste 50/50
3.5 oz (100 g) egg whites (approx. 3)
6.5 oz (185 g) sugar
6.5 oz (185 g) finely grated roasted nuts
0.9 oz (25 g) cocoa
3.5 oz (100 g) roasted shelled hazelnuts for decorating
7 oz (200 g) dark chocolate for dipping, preferably Valrhona
   Grand Cru Pur Caribe 66%

1. Blend the almond paste (room temperature) with egg whites, a little at a time, to form a mixture without lumps.
2. Stir in the sugar, nuts, and cocoa and place the bowl in a small saucepan with boiling water.
3. Let the water simmer and roast the mixture while stirring to a temperature of 113–122 °F (45–50 °C).
4. Remove the bowl. Stir the mass cool and scoop it into a decorating bag with curly tip no. 14.
5. Pipe rosettes of about 1 oz (30 g) and stick a hazelnut in the middle of each.
6. Let the cakes dry for 1 hour.
7. Preheat the oven to 480 °F (250 °C)
8. Bake the cakes in the oven to a golden brown color, approx. 4–5 minutes. Cool down.
9. Temper the chocolate, see p.13. Dip the bottom of the cakes in the chocolate and scrape off excess chocolate against the edge of the bowl.
10. Let them dry on parchment paper.

STORAGE:
The cakes keep for 5 days in the fridge, and you may also freeze them.

NUT TOPS

Another of my favorite pastries with an intense hazelnut flavor. crispy outside, moist cream in the center, and fantastic chocolate—can it get any better? The recipe has followed me since I was 15 years old; in other words, I baked them for the first time 45 years ago and I remember it like it was yesterday.

ABOUT 28 NUT TOPS

12.7 oz (360 g) finely ground hazelnuts
11.6 oz (330 g) sugar
6 oz (170 g) egg whites (approx. 5)
7 oz (200 g) dark chocolate, preferably Valrhona
    Grand Cru Guanaja 70%, for dipping

1. Blend hazelnuts, sugar, and egg whites in a bowl.
2. Place the bowl in simmering water and heat the mass with constant stirring to a temperature of 112–122 °F (45–50 °C).
3. Scoop the mixture in a plastic decorating bag. Use smooth tip no. 12 or cut a hole in the bottom.
4. Pipe tops of about 1 oz (30 g).
5. Dip your fingers in water and squeeze the tops up.
6. Let them dry for an hour.
7. Preheat the oven to 445 °F (230 °C)
8. Bake the tops in the oven until they are beautifully brown, about 7 minutes. Let them cool down.
9. Temper the chocolate, see p.13.
10. Dip the bottoms in the chocolate and scrape off excess chocolate against the edge of the bowl.
11. Let them dry on parchment paper.

STORAGE:
Nut Tops will keep for 5 days in the fridge and also freeze very well. They thaw in 15 minutes.

COCONUT MOUNDS

These soft coconut mounds are, as most cakes, best when they're fresh. The vanilla cream and the butter in the dough provide creaminess and a delicious texture, and then they are dipped in chocolate for additional enjoyment.

When I was fifteen years old, the pastry chef Filip Liljekvist and I baked them this way at the Pâtisserie Heidi in Limhams. Unfortunately, the pâtisserie is no longer there.

ABOUT 20 MOUNDS

3 oz (90 g) vanilla cream, see p.15
16 oz (450 g) grated coconut
5.3 oz (150 g) eggs (approx. 3)
2.6 oz (75 g) butter
(225 g) sugar

10.5 oz (300 g) dark chocolate, preferably Valrhona Grand
    Cru Guanaja 70% for dipping

1. Blend the cold vanilla cream with the other ingredients (the butter needs to be at room temperature) with a wooden spoon until it forms a homogeneous dough.
2. Scoop the mixture into a decorating bag. Cut a large hole in the bottom or use smooth tip no. 14.
3. Pipe coconut mounds of 1.7 oz (50 g) on the sheets, dip your fingers in cold water, and shape them beautifully.
4. Let the mounds dry for 1 hour at room temperature.
5. Preheat the oven to 445 °F (230 °C).
6. Bake the coconut mounds in the oven for 7–8 minutes, until they are golden brown. Let them cool down.
7. Temper the chocolate, see p.13.
8. Dip the bottoms of the mounds in the chocolate and scrape excess chocolate off against the edge of the bowl.
9. Let them dry on parchment paper.

STORAGE:
Coconut Mounds will keep for 4 days in the fridge, but you may also freeze them.

Roasted Coconut Mounds

Coconut Canapés

Coconut Mounds

Chocolate and Coconut Macaroons with Raspberry Jam

ROASTED COCONUT MOUNDS

I remember how I used to love these as a child, with their crispy surfaces and soft centers. In Dragor, in our brotherland Denmark, there was a pâtisserie by the square that made the most perfect coconut mounds I had ever tasted. Thankfully the bakery is still there after all this time, which is good news for the future.

18–20 MOUNDS

8.8 oz (250 g) grated coconut
17.6 oz (500 g) sugar
4.5 oz (125 g) egg whites (approx. 4)
0.9 oz (25 g) potato flour

10.5 oz (300 g) dark chocolate, preferably Valrhona Grand Cru Guanaja 70% for dipping.

1. Blend all of the ingredients in a bowl.
2. Place the bowl in a simmering water bath and stir quickly until the mass starts toasting. Make sure that the temperature is 140 °F (60 °C).
3. Remove the bowl from the saucepan and cover it with a lid. Let it rest for 1 hour.
4. Stir the dough with a ladle and scoop into a decorating bag. Cut a large hole in the bottom or use smooth tip no. 14.
5. Pipe tops of about 1.7 oz (50 g) each on a baking sheet lined with parchment paper. Dip your fingers in cold water and shape the tops beautifully.
6. Let them dry for 1 hour.
7. Preheat the oven to 300 °F (150 °C)
8. Bake the coconut mounds for about 20–25 minutes. Let them cool down on the sheet.
9. Temper the chocolate, see p.13, and dip the bottoms of the coconut mounds. Scrape off excess chocolate against the edge of the bowl and let them dry on parchment paper.

STORAGE:
Store the coconut mounds in the fridge; they keep for approximately 4 days or you can freeze them.

COCONUT CANAPÉS

These chewy treats with crunchy outsides and creamy centers on bottoms of classic short-crust dough, with delicious raspberry jam and chocolate on the sides, are classics that should be eaten fresh while the short-crust dough is still crisp. If you freeze them, thaw them on a cooling rack so that the short-crust dough doesn't get too moist.

APPROX. 30 PASTRIES

½ batch classic short-crust dough, see p.27
Egg wash, see p.47
8.8 oz (250 g) raspberry jam, see p.19
1 lemon, yellow and ripe
4.2 oz (120 g) egg whites (approx. 4)
0.7 oz (20 g) dark rum
0.3 oz (10 g) cornstarch
7 oz (200 g) grated coconut
9.7 oz (275 g) sugar
0.9 oz (25 g) real vanilla sugar
3.5 oz (100 g) syrup, see recipe on p.17
2.8 oz (80 g) dark chocolate, preferably Valrhona
    Grand Cru Guanaja 70%

1. Work the cold short-crust dough smooth by hand and roll it out 1/8 of an inch (3 mm) thick and the same length as the baking sheet.
2. Cut three strips, 22 x 3 inches (55 x 7 cm), with the help of a ruler. Place them on a baking sheet.
3. Brush the edges of the lengths with egg wash.
4. Cut 6 dough strips, 3/16 inch (5 mm) thick, and place them along the sides of the lengths.
5. Brush them with egg wash.
6. Preheat the oven to 390 °F (200 °C).
7. Half-bake the lengths for 8 minutes; they should still be very light. Let them cool.
8. Scoop the raspberry jam in a paper cone, cut a hole in the bottom, and pipe a thin layer on the dough bottoms.
9. Clean the lemon and grate the outer zest.
10. Blend lemon zest, egg whites, rum, cornstarch, coconut, sugar, and vanilla sugar in a bowl.
11. Place the bowl in a simmering water bath and cook the mass while constantly stirring to a temperature of 140 °F (60 °C).
12. Cover with a lid and let the mass rest for 1 hour.
13. Scoop it into a decorating bag. Cut a hole in the bottom or use smooth tip no. 12.
14. Pipe the coconut mass on top of the jam on the strips.
15. Preheat the oven to 410 °F (210 °C).
16. Bake the strips until golden brown for 8–10 minutes.
17. Brush the strips with syrup right after they come out of the oven so that they get a beautiful shine. Let them cool completely.
18. Temper the chocolate, see p.13
19. Brush the chocolate on the edges of the short-crust dough lengths, see picture.
20. Let them stiffen and cut them in slanted pieces.

TOSCADA DELICACIES

These are quite a treat, with their wonderfully crispy roasted tosca on top and creamy filling of dark chocolate ganache. Everything is baked in a good almond paste and sealed at the bottom with milk chocolate. You can't help but give in to the temptation, no matter the consequences.

APPROX. 30 DELICACIES

30 small mazarin cups for petits-fours
1.7 oz (50 g) butter for the cups

17.6 oz (500 g) almond paste 50/50
2.1 oz (60 g) egg whites (approx. 2)

1 batch pâtisserie ganache on Valrhona Grand
    Cru Pur Caribee 66%, see p.14
1 batch tosca topping, see p.40, but without almond flakes
5.3 oz (150 g) roasted, shelled hazelnuts and
    1.7 oz (50 g) pistachio nuts
or 6 oz (175 g) shredded, roasted, shelled almond and
    0.9 oz (25 g) pistachio nuts
or 2.6 oz (75 g) shredded, roasted, shelled almonds and
    2.6 oz (75 g) pistachio nuts and 0.9 oz (25 g) chopped,
    preserved orange peels, see p.20.
10.5 oz (300 g) milk chocolate, preferably Valrhona Jivara
    Lactée 40%, for dipping

1. Grease the small mazarin cups with softened butter.
2. Work the almond paste soft and smooth with the egg whites so that you can roll it out.
3. Roll the mixture out 1/8 of an inch (3 mm) thick with a rolling pin and a little wheat flour.

4. Cut rounds in the mass with a curly cookie cutter, somewhat larger than the cups. Push them in the cups to line them with your thumb (dip your thumb in wheat four so that it doesn't stick). Poke the bottom with a fork.
5. Preheat the oven to 480 °F (250 °C).
6. Place the baking sheet with the cups in the oven. If you can, stay by the oven and watch them, as it usually takes about 5 minutes to bake them golden brown, or "flame" them as pastry chefs say.
7. Let the cups cool down. Fill them three-fourths full with freshly boiled ganache; use a decorating bag with smooth tip no.8, or cut a small hole in the bottom.
8. Place them in the fridge to stiffen for 2 hours.
9. Boil the tosca topping to 244 °F (118 °C) with constant stirring to prevent burning.
10. Stir in some of the nut varieties you chose and keep stirring until they are shiny and covered by the batter.
11. Remove the cups from the fridge. Add a teaspoon of tosca topping on top of each cake, see picture, and stir the paste while you do this. Place the cake in the fridge for 1 hour.
12. Remove the cakes from the cups.
13. Temper the milk chocolate, see p.13.
14. Dip the bottoms of the cakes in the chocolate with the help of a fork and scrape of excess chocolate against the edge of the bowl.
15. Let the delicacies dry on parchment paper.

STORAGE:
Store in the fridge, they will keep for at least a week.

NOISETTE RINGS

Very good cakes with their moist nutbottom, wonderfully melting hazelnut cream with roasted hazelnuts, wrapped in melting milk chocolate. If you can get a hold of hazelnuts from Piedmont they will taste fantastic.

ABOUT 40 RINGS

8.8 oz (250 g) finely grated hazelnuts
8.8 oz (250 g) sugar
4.2 oz (120 g) egg whites (approx. 4)
½ batch French buttercream, see p.17
2.1 oz (60 g) hazelnut paste, see p.25
14 oz (400 g) milk chocolate for dipping, preferably Valrhona Jivara Lactée 40%
7 oz (200 g) roasted hazelnuts for decorating

1. Place a water bath with simmering water on the stove.
2. Blend nuts, sugar, and egg whites in a steel bowl and place in the water bath.
3. Toast the mixture while constantly stirring to 113–122 °F (45–50 °C).
4. Draw 40 rings, 2 inches (55 mm) in diameter, on parchment paper.
5. Scoop the mass in a decorating bag with smooth tip no. 12 and pipe rings of 0.5 oz (15 g) inside the drawn circles until you've used up all the mass.

6. Preheat the oven to 355 °F (180 °C)
7. Bake the rings until golden brown for 8 minutes. Let them cool.
8. Turn the paper upside down and brush the underside with water. Let it rest for 5 minutes. Pull the paper off and place the rings on parchment paper with the flat side facing upwards.
9. Blend buttercream and hazelnut paste to a light and airy cream.
10. Scoop the cream into a decorating bag with smooth tip no. 12 and pipe a rather thick garland of cream on top of the rings.
11. Stick 3 hazelnuts on each ring.
12. Place the cakes in the fridge for 30 minutes to stiffen.
13. Temper the chocolate, see p.13.
14. Sip the top of the cakes in chocolate and shake off excess chocolate. Let them dry on parchment paper.

STORAGE:
Store the cakes in the fridge; they keep for 5 days. You can also freeze them.

PRALINE RINGS

APPROX. 30 RINGS

1 batch brown linzerdough, see p.55

Almond gianduja:
8.8 oz (250 g) roasted, shelled hazelnuts
7 oz (200 g) powdered sugar
7 oz (200 g) milk chocolate, preferably Valrhona Jivara
    Lactée 40%

7 oz (200 g) roasted, shelled hazelnuts for decorating
14 oz (400 g) milk chocolate, preferably Valrhona Jivara
    Lactée 40%, for dipping

1. Preheat the oven to 390 °F (200 °C)
2. Work the cold dough smooth by hand and roll it out
   to 1/8 of an inch (3 mm) thickness.
3. Cut rounds, 2 ¾ inches (70 mm) in diameter, with a
   curly cookie cutter. Place them on a baking sheet lined
   with parchment paper.
4. Cut a hole, 1 inch (30 mm) in diameter, in each round
   with a cookie cutter.
5. Bake the rounds beautifully light brown for
   8–9 minutes (watch them carefully, they burn easily).
6. Mix hazelnuts and powdered sugar in a food processor with
   jagged knife blades to a temperature of 160 °F (70 °C).
7. Mix in the chopped chocolate and continue mixing
   until its melted. Empty the mass out on a cold surface
   (marble slab is ideal but the kitchen counter is also fine).
8. Stroke the mass back and forth with a straight spatula
   until it starts to thicken and has a creamy texture.
9. Scoop the mass in a decorating bag. Cut a hole in the
   bottom or use smooth tip no. 12.
10. Pipe a ring of 0.7 oz (20 g) on each bottom.
11. Stick 6 hazelnuts with the tips pointing up in the
    gianduja before it stiffens.
12. Let them stiffen for 1 hour.
13. Temper the chocolate, see p.13.
14. Dip the rings in the chocolate. Scrape off excess
    chocolate against the edge of the bowl.
15. Let the cakes dry on parchment paper.

STORAGE:
Store in the fridge. The cakes will keep for at least 14 days.

TARRAGON CIRCLES

Try to find Spanish or Italian nuts for this good
cake; for added complexity to the crunchy filling
and crisp short-crust dough, combine with delicious
chocolate. Eat this cake with a glass of sweet sherry
and you can imagine that you're sitting at Pâtisserie
Baxia in Barcelona. It doesn't get any better.

30 PASTRIES

1 batch white linzerdough, see p.80
½ batch tosca topping, see p.40
7 oz (200 g) roasted, shelled hazelnuts
10.5 oz (300 g) dark chocolate, preferably Valrhona Grand
    Cru Manjari 64%, for dipping

1. Work the cold linzerdough smooth by hand and roll it
   out 1/8 of an inch (4 mm) thick.
2. Cut out 30 round circles, about 3 inches (80 mm) in
   diameter, with a curly cookie cutter. Place them on a
   baking sheet lined with parchment paper.
3. Cut a hole in the middle with a smooth cookie cutter
   with a diameter of 1 ¾ inches (45 mm).
4. Boil tosca topping to 244 °F (118 °C).
5. Stir in the hazelnuts.
6. Distribute the filling in all of the holes of the rings
   with a teaspoon.
7. Preheat the oven to 390 °F (200 °C)
8. Bake the cakes until golden brown for about
   12–14 minutes (watch them carefully, they burn easily). Let
   them cool.
9. Temper the chocolate, see p.13.
10. Dip the cakes in the chocolate and scrape off excess
    chocolate against the edge of the bowl.
11. Let them dry on parchment paper.

STORAGE:
The cakes will keep for approximately 5 days in room
temperature.

NOUGAT SQUARES

This awfully good cake, as they say in Skane, is a real explosion of enjoyment and comfort in your mouth.

Hazelnut mazarin paste:
8.8 oz (250 g) finely grated hazelnuts
5.3 oz (150 g) sugar
5.3 oz (150 g) butter
3.5 oz (100 g) eggs (approx. 2)
1.7 oz (50 g) wheat flour
0.3 oz (10 g) sugar for sprinkling

Gianduja:
3.5 oz (100 g) apricot jam, see my book *The Jam and Marmalade Bible*
7 oz (200 g) roasted, shelled hazelnuts
5.3 oz (150 g) powdered sugar
7 oz (200 g) milk chocolate, preferably Valrhona Jivara Lactée 40%
14 oz (400 g) dark chocolate, preferably Valrhona Grand Cru Manjari 64%

DAY 1

1. Preheat the oven to 370 °F (190 °C).
2. Blend the finely grated nuts with the sugar into fine powder, so called TPT, in a food processor with jagged knifes.
3. Blend TPT and softened butter to a smooth mass.
4. Add the eggs (room temperature) one at a time.
5. Sift in the wheat flour and stir around with a spatula.
6. Line an edged baking sheet with parchment paper and spread the mass out evenly with a straight spatula.
7. Bake the capsule for approx. 35 minutes until it is golden brown and feels finished when you poke it with a toothpick.
8. Let the capsule cool down. Cover it with plastic wrap and set in the fridge overnight.

DAY 2

9. Loosen the capsule from the paper with a small knife and sprinkle sugar on top.
10. Cover with a piece of parchment paper and turn the capsule upside down.
11. Turn the baked side up. Spread a thin layer of apricot icing over with a straight spatula.
12. Make the gianduja. Mix the hazelnuts and powdered sugar in a food processor into a smooth mass with a temperature of 160 °F (70 °C). Add the chopped milk chocolate.
13. Mix the gianduja until the chocolate is completely melted, and then cool it on a marble slab or stainless sheet to a temperature of 79 °F (26 °C).

14. Spread the gianduja over the layers evenly with a straight spatula.
15. Comb the surface with a glue scraper (you can find this in paint stores) and place the layers in the fridge for about 1 hour.
16. Cut the layers in squares, 1 ½ x 1 ½ inches (40 x 40 mm), with the help of a ruler and a knife that you dip in warm water.
17. Temper the chocolate, see p.13.
18. Dip the bites in the chocolate with the help of a fork, and scrape off the excess chocolate against the edge of the bowl.
19. Let the cakes dry on parchment paper.

STORAGE:
The cakes will keep for 14 days in the fridge and you can also freeze these.

BUTTERDOUGH PASTRIES

DANCE FLOORS

Matti Touminen at the monastery patisserie in Lund always makes these crispy pastries, not to mention delicious macaroons and good Finnish rye bread.

10 PASTRIES

21.2 oz (600 g) butterdough, see p.28
Egg wash, see p.47
Granulated sugar for rolling out
Powdered sugar for glazing
1 batch fondant, see p.16
0.3 oz (1 cl) dark rum
0.9 oz (25 g) chopped pistachio nuts

1. Roll out the butterdough with the help of wheat flour and a small rolling pin.
2. Brush the dough with a thin layer of egg wash. Roll it to a tight roll.
3. Cut the roll in 10 pieces and fold the joint inwards for each one.
4. Roll out each slice in a little sugar, turn and then roll out the other side in a little wheat flour. Roll it into a round cake, about 4 ¾ inch (120 mm) in diameter.
5. Place them on a baking sheet lined with parchment paper and let them sit in the fridge for 1 hour.
6. Bake them at 410 °F (210 °C) degrees for 20 minutes until they are golden brown.
7. Take them out of the oven and sift powdered sugar over them. Set them back in and increase the temperature to 480 °F (250 °C).
8. Bake them so that they get a real shine (watch the oven closely).
9. Take them out and let cool. Warm the fondant to 95 °F (35 °C) with the rum. Scoop it into a paper cone and cut a hole in the bottom. Pipe a dot on top of each cake and sprinkle some chopped pistachio nuts on top.

STORAGE:
The cakes will keep for 1–2 days in a dry place.

CANAPÉS AND BUTTERFLIES

These crispy treats have not only been a favorite of mine to eat, but also to bake. There are many different ways of making canapés and butterflies—I will describe how to fold the easiest ones. They should have the golden color of sugar on the surface.

At Blekingborgs pâtisserie in Malmö we would stick two canapés together with apple jam and dip the bottom in chocolate. Sometimes restaurants would order cheese canapés and we would prepare these the same way, except we used Parmesan cheese mixed with a little chili powder instead.

ABOUT 20 CANAPÉS OF 0.9 OZ (25 g) EACH OR 10 BUTTERFLIES OF 1.7 OZ (50 g) EACH

17.6 oz (500 g) butterdough, see recipe on p. 28
7 oz (200 g) granulated sugar

1. Preheat the oven to 430 °F (220 °C).
2. Roll out the butterdough in granulated sugar, so that it's coated on top and underneath, to 1/8 of an inch (3 mm) thickness. The dough should be about 24 inches (60 cm) long, and 4 ½ inches (12 cm) wide on one end and 4 ¼ inches (11 cm) wide on the other end.
3. Fold the thinner end over the other and roll the dough back out to 3 1/8 of inches (3 mm) in thickness. The width should be 4 ½ inches.
4. Fold both of the long sides toward the middle, and then roll the dough out to 1/8 of an inch (4 mm) thickness, 4 ½ inches (12 cm) width on one end and 4 inches (10 cm) on the other.
5. Fold the thinner end on top of the other and finally fold it lengthwise. Then it's ready for cutting into single and butterfly canapés.
6. For single canapés, you cut 1/8 – 1/4 inch (5–6 mm) thick pieces. Space them out on a baking sheet lined with parchment paper and bake them right away. After half the baking time, when the underside has gained some color, flip them with a straight spatula and bake them until the other side has a nice color as well.
7. For butterfly canapés the dough is cut twice as thick and then you cut a slit in the middle, almost all the way through. Both halves are folded out and they are baked as single canapés.
8. If you want the canapés to have additional shine, preheat the oven to 480 °F (250 °C) and sift some powdered sugar over them. Bake them in the oven, but don't leave the oven door unattended, as they burn easily.

STORAGE:
Canapés should be eaten fresh.

For how to fold butterdough for canapés, see p.239.

APPLE JEALOUSIES

In France, they call these *dartois aux pommes,* and my mother loved to eat Magnhild's apple jealousies when we visited my grandmother in Tomelilla. The pâtisserie was situated right across from Folkets Park and I ate many good cakes there as a child; among others, I often ate Parisian waffles.

10 PASTRIES

1 1/3 lb (600 g) butterdough, see recipe on p.28
Egg wash, see p.47

Cream mass:
7 oz (200 g) almond paste 50/50
3.5 oz (100 g) vanilla cream, see recipe p.15
17.6 oz (500 g) apple compote, see recipe on p.19
Cinnamon sugar, see p.62
1 batch apricot icing, see p.17
3.5 oz (100 g) fondant, see recipe on p.16
0.3 oz (1 cl) dark rum
0.7 oz (20 g) chopped pistachio nuts

1. Roll out half the butterdough with a little flour, about 2.5 mm thick, 5 ½ inches (14 cm) wide, and the length of a baking sheet.
2. Roll it onto the rolling pin and roll it out on a baking sheet lined with parchment paper.
3. Cut away 2 pieces ½ inch (1 cm) wide in length on each side.
4. Brush the length with egg wash and place the ½ inch (1 cm) wide pieces along the edges, like a frame.
5. Brush with the egg wash once more and poke the bottom with a fork.
6. Dissolve the almond paste (room temperature) with the vanilla cream to a mass without lumps.
7. Spread the cream on top of the butterdough sheet.
8. Spread the apple compote over the cream and sprinkle cinnamon sugar on top.
9. Roll out the rest of the butterdough, a little longer than the first piece and 6 ¼ inches (16 cm) wide.
10. Fold lengthwise and make slits with the knife over the fold, almost all the way to the edge, with 3/16 inch (5 mm) spaces between them.
11. Fold it back and carefully roll it onto the rolling pin. Roll the dough over the filling.
12. Brush it with the egg wash and squeeze the edges together with a fork. Make small slits all around with a knife.
13. Let it rest in a cool place for 1 hour.
14. Preheat the oven to 390 °F (200 °C) and bake until golden brown for about 35 minutes. Lower the temperature to 355 °F (180 °C) after 10 minutes.
15. Brush with boiling apricot icing right after taking out of the oven.
16. Warm the fondant with the rum to 95 °F (35 °C) and brush it thinly on top. Sprinkle chopped pistachio nuts on top.
17. Move onto a cooling rack to cool.
18. Cut the edges off and cut into 10 pieces using a ruler and a sharp knife.

STORAGE:
Apple jealousies should be eaten the same day.

APPLES IN BUTTERDOUGH

When I was an apprentice, fall meant a lot of peeling apples for all kinds of good butterdough pastries with apple. These are sometimes called "Drottningapplen" or Queen Apples. Apples baked in butterdough are among the best things out there, especially when served freshly baked with vanilla sauce. Have a glass of nice wine from Alsace with it, or a cup of coffee.

8 APPLES

3.5 oz (100 g) almond paste 50/50
0.9 oz (25 g) unsalted butter
1 tsp (5 g) ground cinnamon
8 apples, preferably Belle de Boskoop or Gravensteiner
17.6 oz (500 g) butterdough, see recipe on p.28
Egg wash, see p.47
1 oz (30 g) almond flakes
0.9 oz (25 g) granulated sugar
0.9 oz (25 g) powdered sugar

1. Dissolve the almond paste with the softened butter and add the cinnamon. Peel the apples and remove the cores.
2. Roll out the butterdough to a roughly 1/16 inch (2 mm) thick square with a rolling pin and a little wheat flour.
3. Cut squares, 4 ½ x 4 ½ inches (12 x 12 cm), with a sharp knife.
4. Whisk the egg wash together, brush the butterdough with it, and place an apple on each square.
5. Divide the cinnamon mixture into 8 parts and stuff them into the hole left from the apple cores.
6. Wrap the butterdough around the apples and squeeze them so that it sticks in place.
7. Place the apples with the joint facing downwards, and brush the entire surface with egg wash.
8. Crumble almonds, blend with the granulated sugar, and roll the apples in the mixture.
9. Place them on a baking sheet lined with parchment paper and let them sit in a cool place for at least 1 hour.
10. Preheat the oven to 445 °F (230 °C).
11. Bake the apples for 5 minutes, lower the temperature to 355 °F (180 °C), and bake them until golden brown, for about 25 minutes.

Apples in Butterdough

Apple Jealousies

12. Take them out of the oven and increase the temperature to 480 °F (250 °C).

13. Sift powdered sugar over the apples and set them back in the oven to allow the sugar to caramelize and become golden brown (be careful, they burn easily).

STORAGE:
These apples should be eaten fresh the same day.

SWISS KRINGLES

You see these tasty, classic kringles all over the world. Sometimes they're baked with regular short-crust dough and butterdough, sometimes there's pure almond paste inside instead of short-crust dough, but that makes them hard. The best kind is this delicious almond short-crust dough and butterdough combination. Bake them until really golden so that they are done all the way through.

ABOUT 10 KRINGLES OF 2.1 OZ (60 G) EACH

Almond short-crust dough:
3.5 oz (100 g) almond paste 50/50
3.5 oz (100 g) unsalted butter
3.5 oz (100 g) wheat flour

10.5 oz (300 g) butterdough, see recipe on p.28
Egg wash, see p.47
0.9 oz (25 g) almond flakes
1 batch apricot icing, see p.17
5.3 oz (150 g) fondant, see recipe on p.16
0.5 oz (15 g) lemon juice

1. Mix the almond paste (room temperature) with the softened butter until well blended (no lumps) and carefully work in the wheat flour. Roll the dough in plastic wrap and leave it in the fridge for 1 hour.

2. Roll out the butterdough so that it is 1/16 on an inch (2 mm) thick and 12 inches (30 cm) wide.

3. Brush egg wash on top and cover with a sheet of the same size of rolled out almond short-crust dough.

4. Cut out about a ½ inch (1 cm) wide piece of 2.1 oz (60 g) of the dough. Twist the pieces and shape them into kringles.

5. Brush the kringles with egg wash and sprinkle almond flakes on top.

6. Place the kringles on a baking sheet lined with parchment paper and let them rest for at least 1 hour.

7. Preheat the oven to 445 °F (230 °C) and bake the kringles until golden brown. Move them onto a cooling rack right away and brush them with boiling apricot icing.

8. Heat the fondant to 95 °F (35 °C) and flavor it with lemon juice. Brush the kringles very thinly with the fondant.

STORAGE:
Store in a dry place and they will keep for 1–2 days.

Swiss Kringles

Twisted Students

TWISTED STUDENTS

You don't encounter these tasty pastries often, but they are delicious! At Tage Hankanssons pâtisserie in Lund they are always part of the selection, as well as at Conditori Lundagard in Lund.

12 PASTRIES

14 oz (400 g) classic short-crust dough, see p.27
14 oz (400 g) butterdough, see p.28
Egg wash, see p.47
Cinnamon sugar, see p.62
1 batch apricot icing, see p.16
0.3 oz (1 cl) dark rum
0.7 oz (20 g) roasted almond flakes

1. Roll out the short-crust dough to ⅛ of an inch (3 mm) thick and 6 inches (15 cm) wide, and brush it with egg wash.
2. Roll the butterdough out the same way and layer it on top of the short-crust dough.
3. Brush with egg wash again and sprinkle cinnamon sugar on top.

4. Cut 12 equally sized strips. Twist them and place them on the baking sheet (see picture).
5. Let the cakes rest for 1 hour in the fridge.
6. Preheat the oven to 445 °F (230 °C).
7. Bake until golden brown, for about 18 minutes.
8. Take them out of the oven and brush them with the boiling apricot icing right away, while they are still warm.
9. Warm the fondant to 95 °F (35 °C) and dilute with the rum. Brush a thin layer of fondant over the pastries.
10. Sprinkle the almonds on top.
11. Let them cool on a cooling rack.

STORAGE:
Dry, they keep for 1–2 days.

PLUM BOXES

In Sweden, apples were the most common fruit, so these pastries were called Apple Boxes, but when I worked abroad we used a lot of apricots and plums instead. Crispy butterdough with tart plums or apricots —you can't go wrong. Serve with lightly whipped cream or vanilla ice cream and suddenly you have dessert.

10 BOXES

17.6 oz (500 g) butterdough, see recipe on p.28

Filling:
3.5 oz (100 g) almond paste 50/50
1.4 oz (40 g) yolk (approx. 2)

10 red plums, or another fruit like apricots or apples
½ batch cinnamon sugar, see p.62
0.7 oz (20 g) almond flakes
1 batch apricot icing, see p.17
3.5 oz (100 g) fondant, see p.16
0.3 oz (1 cl) dark rum

1. Roll the butterdough out into an even square of ⅛ of an inch (3 mm) thickness.
2. Cut into smaller pieces, 3.5 x 3 inches (90 x 80 mm), with a knife.
3. Place them on a baking sheet lined with parchment paper.
4. Dissolve the almond paste (room temperature) with the yolks and pipe 0.4 oz (12 g) mass into a 2 ¾ inches (7 cm) long stripe on each piece of dough.
5. Remove the pits from the plums and place them with the skin facing downward on top of the almond mass. Sprinkle cinnamon sugar and almond flakes on top.
6. Let the pastry rest for 60 minutes.
7. Preheat the oven to 430 °F (220 °C).
8. Bake the plum boxes until golden brown, for approximately 20 minutes, lowering the heat toward the end if needed.
9. Brush with apricot icing right away.
10. Heat the fondant to 95 °F (35 °C).
11. Brush the plum boxes with a thin layer of fondant and place them on a cooling rack to cool.

STORAGE:
Plum boxes should be eaten the same day.

VANILLA MUFFS

These crunchy pastries with a vanilla cream center are delicious. The pastry chef Ingvar Larsson at the pâtisserie Hollandia in Malmö was an expert at making these. In addition to the Napoleon pastries with apple jam, vanilla cream, and whipped cream, we had at least 15 different fresh butterdough pastries everyday.

ABOUT 10 MUFFS

1 1/3 lb (600 g) butterdough, see recipe on p.28
¼ batch vanilla cream, see p.47
1 oz (30 g) powdered sugar
1 batch apricot icing, see p.17
5.3 oz (150 g) fondant, see recipe on p.16
0.3 oz (1 cl) dark rum

1. Roll out the butterdough into an even square 1/8 of an inch (3 mm) thick, and cut out squares of 3.5 x 3.5 inches (90 x 90 mm).
2. Brush the ends of one of the long sides with egg wash.
3. Pipe a line of vanilla cream, about 0.7 oz (20 g), onto each square.
4. Fold the sides in toward the middle so that they overlap a little and turn them around so that the joint faces down. Squeeze the ends with your fingers so that they stay in place.
5. Brush the pastries with egg wash and place them on parchment paper. Let them rest for 1 hour in the fridge.
6. Preheat the oven to 430 °F (220 °C). Bake the vanilla muffs in the oven for 10 minutes. Lower the temperature to 390 °F (200 °C) and bake them for another 10 minutes.
7. Take the muffs out of the oven and increase the temperature to 480 °F (250 °C).
8. Sift powdered sugar over the cakes, return them to the oven and bake them until they acquire a beautiful shine.
9. Brush them with apricot icing right away after you take them out of the oven.
10. Heat the fondant with the rum to 95 °F (35 °C) and brush the pastries with a thin layer of fondant.
11. Let them cool on a cooling rack.

STORAGE:
Vanilla Muffs should be eaten the same day.

Plum Boxes   Vanilla Muffs   Raspberry Bows   Apple Bows

APPLE BOWS

This tasty, simple pastry was one of my favorites as an apprentice. We boiled the delicious apple compote with Gravensteiner apples every day. You can bake hundreds of different kinds of apple pastries with butterdough, and they always taste good.

Many fold these differently, but the taste is the same.

10 BOWS

17.6 oz (500 g) butterdough, see recipe p.28
7 oz (200 g) apple compote, see p.19
Cinnamon sugar, see p.62
Egg wash, see p.47
1 oz (30 g) almond flakes
1 oz (30 g) powdered sugar
1 batch apricot icing, see p.17
5.3 oz (150 g) fondant, see p.16
0.5 oz (15 g) lemon juice

1. Roll out the butterdough 2 1/6 of an inch (4 mm) thick and cut out squares, 3 ½ x 3 ½ inches (90 x 90 mm).
2. Pipe 0.7 oz (20 g) of apple compote in the middle of each square and sprinkle cinnamon sugar on top.
3. Fold one side toward the middle and squeeze the edges together so that the filling is squeezed upward. Brush with egg wash along the folded edge of the dough.
4. Fold the other side so that it looks like an envelope with a hole in the middle.
5. Brush the pastry with the egg wash and sprinkle almond flakes on top.

6. Let the bows rest in a cool place for at least 2 hours to prevent shrinking of the dough.
7. Preheat the oven to 445 °F (230 °C).
8. Place the apple bows on a baking sheet lined with parchment paper, leaving space in between. Bake them for 10 minutes. Lower the heat to 390 °F (200 °C) so that they do not brown too much and bake them for another 10 minutes.
9. Take them out of the oven and increase the temperature to 480 °F (250 °C).
10. Sift powdered sugar over the apple bows and place them back in the oven to be beautifully caramelized (be careful, they burn easily).
11. Transfer them directly onto a cooling rack to cool.
12. Brush the pastries with boiling apricot icing.
13. Heat the fondant and lemon juice to 95 °F (35 °C) and brush over the pastries.

STORAGE:
Eat the apple bows the same day.

RASPBERRY BOWS

In my opinion, this pastry is just as delicious with old-fashioned raspberry flavors.

10 BOWS

Follow the above recipe for the apple bows, but exchange the apple compote with raspberry jam. See recipe on p.19.

172

PISTACHIO SLICES

The talented pastry chef Arne Sandberg introduced these tasty pistachio slices at Vetekattens Konditori in Stockholm. Today, Arne has many prestigious workplaces on his resume, but the first time we met, Arne was fifteen years old and was just starting out as an apprentice at Conditori Lundagard in Lund. Then he moved on to Baur au Lac Hotel in Zurich and Confiserie Honold, and he eventually became managing pastry chef on large cruise ships.

12 PISTACHIO SLICES

17.6 oz (500 g) butterdough, see recipe p.28
Egg wash, see p.47

Pistachio filling:
10.5 oz (300 g) almond paste 50/50
3.5 oz (100 g) butter
1.7 oz (50 g) egg (approx. 1)
1.4 oz (40 g) yolks (approx. 2)
0.9 oz (25 g) wheat flour
0.9 oz (25 g) pistachio paste, see recipe on p.25
1 drop of green food coloring, preferably natural
1 drop orange flower water

0.7 oz (20 g) almond flakes
1 batch apricot icing, see p.17
3.5 oz (100 g) fondant, see recipe on p.16
0.3 oz (1 cl) dark rum
1 oz (30 g) chopped pistachio nuts for topping

1. Roll the dough out to 1/8 of an inch (3 mm) thick and the length of a baking sheet. Roll it out to 12 ½ inches in width (32 cm) so that you can cut one strip that is 5 ½ inches (14 cm) wide and one that is 7 inches (18 cm) wide.
2. Place the 5 ½ inch (14 cm) wide strip on a baking sheet lined with parchment paper and brush the sides with egg wash.
3. Make the pistachio mass:
Dissolve 10.5 oz (300 g) almond paste (room temperature) with one third of the softened butter so that you get a mass without lumps. Work in the remaining butter and add the eggs and yolks one at a time. Sift in the wheat flour and blend it into the batter with the pistachio paste, food coloring, and orange flower water.
4. Scoop the mass into a decorating bag and cut a large hole in the bottom.
5. Pipe the mass into the middle of the strip, stopping about 3/16 inch (5 mm) from the ends.
6. Brush the other strip of butterdough with egg wash and place it on top. Squeeze the dough along the edges with a fork so that the filling can't seep out.

7. Brush the entire surface on top and sprinkle almond flakes on top.
8. Let it rest in a cool place for 60 minutes.
9. Preheat the oven to 430 °F (220 °C).
10. Place in the oven. Lower the temperature to 355 °F (180 °C) after 10 minutes.
11. Bake until golden brown, for 40–45 minutes.
12. Remove from the oven and brush with boiling apricot icing right away.
13. Heat the fondant with the liquor to 95 °F (35 °C) and brush a thin layer of fondant all over the pastry. Sprinkle the chopped pistachio nuts on top.
14. Let cool on a cooling rack for 1 hour.
15. Cut off the ends with a sharp knife and then cut into 12 equally sized pieces lengthwise, using a ruler to measure.

STORAGE:
You should eat the pistachio slices the same day.

Parisian Waffles

Strawberry Waffles

Apple Truffles

APPLE WAFFLES

10 APPLE WAFFLES

3.5 oz (100 g) almond paste 50/50
1.4 oz (40 g) yolk (approx. 2)
3 green apples
12.3 oz (350 g) butterdough, see recipe on p.28
Wheat flour and granulated sugar
½ batch cinnamon sugar, see p.62
Powdered sugar for glazing
Apricot icing, see recipe on p.17

1. Dissolve the almond paste (room temperature) with the yolks so that it becomes pipeable.
2. Peel and core the apples. Cut 6 slices for each waffle.
3. Roll the dough out to ¼ inch (6 mm) thick and cut bottoms with a curly cookie cutter with a diameter of 2 1/3 inch (60 mm).
4. Dip one side of the bottoms in flour and lay the other side in a layer of granulated sugar. Roll them out to 6 x 2 ½ inch (15 x 6 cm) long pieces.

5. Place the pieces of dough on a baking sheet lined with parchment paper that is first moistened with water so that the pastries don't shrink.
6. Make a paper cone and fill with the dissolved almond paste. Pipe a 1/4 inch (8 mm) thick line in the middle of the waffle, but not all the way to the ends.
7. Add 6 apple slices to the top of each waffle, as beautifully as possible.
8. Sprinkle cinnamon sugar over the apples and let them rest in a cool place for 60 minutes.
9. Bake until golden brown, at 355 °F (180 °C) for about 15 minutes.
10. Take them out of the oven and increase the temperature to 480 °F (250 °C).
11. Sift powdered sugar over the waffles and return them to the oven for a short while until they are beautifully caramelized (this happens quickly, so don't burn them).
12. Take them out of the oven and brush them with boiling apricot icing right away. Let the waffles cool on a cooling rack.

STORAGE:
Eat the apple waffles fresh.

PARISIAN WAFFLES

Properly baked crisp and shiny Parisian waffles, filled with French buttercream flavored with arrack or rum, can be the best thing in the world. Many pâtisseries roll them out with special waffle irons, but this isn't necessary, as long as you poke them well.

The pastry has been misrepresented with margarine in the dough and buttercream, as well as through improper baking, so that they are chewy instead of crisp and crunchy.

24.7 oz (700 g) butterdough, see recipe on p.28
Wheat flour and granulated sugar for rolling out
Powdered sugar for glazing
¼ batch French buttercream, see recipe on p.17

1. Roll the dough out to ³⁄₁₆ inch (5 mm) thick with the help of a rolling pin and some wheat flour.
2. Cut out 20 bottoms with a curly cookie cutter about 3/16 inch (5.2 mm) in diameter. Dip one side in the wheat flour and place the other side in a layer of granulated sugar.
3. Roll them out to pieces measuring 6 x 2 ½ inches (15 x 6 cm).
4. Line a baking sheet with parchment paper. Brush the paper with water before you place the waffles on the paper so that they won't shrink in the oven.
5. Roll the bottoms out the same way and place them on the parchment paper.
6. Poke the waffles with a fork to make sure that they don't get too doughy.
7. Let the waffles rest in a cool place for 1 hour to prevent shrinkage during baking.
8. Preheat the oven to 430 °F (220 °C), and bake the waffles until golden brown, for approximately 12 minutes.
9. Remove the waffles from the oven and increase the temperature to 480 °F (250 °C). Sift powdered sugar over the waffles and set them back in the oven to caramelize and become golden brown (watch them closely; these burn easily).
10. Move them directly onto a cooling rack to cool.
11. Scoop the buttercream into a decorating bag with smooth tip no. 12 or cut a hole in the bottom. Pipe a line of buttercream on half of the waffles.
12. Place the other half on top and eat them right away, or at least the same day, if you can wait.

STORAGE:
Parisian waffles are eaten fresh.

STRAWBERRY WAFFLES

We always baked these tasty strawberry desserts at Conditori Lundagard in summertime, and they were very popular with the customers.

10 WAFFLES

12.3 oz (350 g) butterdough, see recipe on p.28
Wheat flour and granulated sugar for rolling out
17.6 oz (500 g) ripe strawberries
3.5 oz (100 g) vanilla cream, see recipe on p.15
5.3 oz (150 g) red currant jelly

1. Follow the recipe for Parisian Waffles up until step 10.
2. Rinse and remove the calyxes of the strawberries. Dry them well and cut them in half.
3. When the waffles have cooled on the cooling rack, scoop the vanilla cream into a small paper cone and pipe a line of cream on each waffle.
4. Garnish with strawberry halves and press them down in the vanilla cream.
5. Boil the red currant jelly and brush on the strawberries.

STORAGE:
Eat the strawberry waffles fresh.

MACAROON SLICES

When I was concentrating on butterdough pastries, I learned to bake many good pastries that are both crispy and moist at the same time. Hand Tidemand, German pastry Chef at Konditori St. Jorgen in Malmö, was a talented pastry chef who had worked in many places. He always baked these. Later on, we worked together at the Savoy Hotel in Malmö. Hans was also great at making ice sculptures and chocolate sculptures, and he taught me a lot over the years.

12 SLICES

8.8 oz (250 g) butterdough, see recipe p.28
Egg wash, see p.47
7 oz (200 g) apple jam, see recipe p.18

Biskvi mass:
8.8 oz (250 g) almond paste 50/50
4.5 oz (125 g) sugar
2.1 oz (60 g) egg white (approx. 2)

0.7 oz (20 g) almond flakes

1. Roll out the butterdough to 1/8 of an inch (3 mm) thick and the same length as a baking sheet. Cut a piece that is 6 inches (15 cm) wide.
2. Brush the edges with egg wash.
3. Cut two dough strips, about 3/16 inch (5 mm) wide, and place them on top of the larger piece, lengthwise along the sides.
4. Brush the surface of the dough with egg wash and stick the strips to the lengths by pressing down with a fork.
5. Set the dough strip on a cold plate to rest for 60 minutes.
6. Preheat the oven to 390 °F (200 °C).
7. Poke the strip several times with a fork and spread on the apple jam with a straight spatula.
8. Blend the almond paste (room temperature) with sugar and one-third of the egg whites. Blend to a smooth mass.
9. Work in the remaining egg white and scoop it into a decorating bag. Use smooth tip no. 10 or cut a hole in the bottom.
10. Pipe the almond mass in a zigzag pattern over the apple jam and sprinkle almond flakes on top.
11. Place in the oven and lower the temperature to 355 °F (180 °C) after 10 minutes. Bake to a golden brown, for 30–35 minutes in total.
12. Let it cool on a cooling rack.
13. First cut the ends off and then cut the pastry into 12 slanted squares with the help of a sharp knife and a ruler.

STORAGE:
Eat the macaroon slices fresh.

KATALANS

This Swedish classic has been around for at least a hundred years, and it is still just as good today. The pastry chef Sigge Lundin in Stockholm baked the absolute best Katalans. Sigge was a visionary within the pastry industry as he started everything with butter, and he was known all over Stockholm for his fine wheat dough.

30 KATALANS

30 round mazarin cups
17.6 oz (500 g) butterdough, see recipe p.28
10.5 oz (300 g) raspberry jam, see recipe on p.19

Filling:
12.7 oz (360 g) almond paste 50/50
12 oz (340 g) unsalted butter
7 oz (200 g) eggs (approx. 4)

0.3 oz (10 g) sugar to sprinkle on top
7 oz (200 g) fondant, see recipe on p.16
0.5 oz (15 g) dark rum

1. Line the cups with butterdough as described for the Gothenburger, see p.180.
2. Preheat the oven to 370 °F (190 °C).
3. Pipe raspberry jam in each cup, about 0.3 oz (10 g) each.
4. Stir the almond paste (room temperature) until smooth with one-third of the butter. Carefully work in the remaining butter a little at a time without stirring the mass too much; if it is overworked it will rise over the cups during baking.
5. Stir in the eggs, one at a time without overworking the mixture.
6. Fill the cups three-fourths full with the mass and bake them for about 25 minutes, or until they are golden brown.
7. Sprinkle sugar on top, cover with parchment paper, and place on a rimmed baking sheet (without the rims, the pastry will easily slide off when you turn it). Turn everything upside down so that the pastries have an even surface.
8. Lift the cups off right away.
9. When the pastries have cooled, boil the remaining raspberry jam and brush a thin layer of jam on top.
10. Warm the fondant to 95 °F (35 °C) and dilute it with rum.
11. Brush the cakes with the icing right away.
12. Set the cakes in the oven with the door ajar for 1–2 minutes so that the glaze stiffens and obtains a shine.

STORAGE:
Eat the katalans fresh.

RUM CAKES

These butterdough cakes are delicious, with their crispy butterdough and lean filling. The contrast of the intense rum-flavored glaze is especially nice. Sometimes one would make the same cake but fill it with equal parts pâte à choux and vanilla cream instead. That is delicious as well; they are called Pont Neuf and in France they are a classic. They should be eaten freshly baked. Pastry Chef Curt Andersson at Residens Schweizeri always baked these, and the glaze would sparkle in the window. Kurt really knew how to glaze and maintain the shine, an important part of being a talented pastry chef.

25 CAKES

25 elongated almond mussel cups
17.6 oz (500 g) butterdough, see recipe on p.28

Filling:
14 oz (400 g) vanilla cream, see recipe on p.19
2.6 oz (75 g) potato flour
1.4 oz (40 g) yolk

0.3 oz (10 g) sugar to sprinkle on top

Meringue:
7 oz (200 g) egg white (approx. 7)
1 tsp (5g) lemon juice
3.5 oz (100 g) sugar

8.8 oz (250 g) raspberry jam, see recipe on p.19
3.5 oz (100 g) black currant jelly, see my book *The Jam and Marmalade Bible,* or use your own recipe
7 oz (200 g) fondant, see recipe on p.16
0.9 oz (25 g) dark rum

1. Line the cups with butterdough as described for the Gothenburger, see p.180.
2. Preheat the oven to 370 °F (190 °C).
3. Pass the vanilla cream through a sieve, sift in the potato flour, and add the yolks. Whisk to a smooth cream.
4. Whisk the egg whites and lemon juice with 1 oz (30 g) of the sugar until it begins to stiffen, on medium speed. Add another 1 oz (30 g) sugar during whisking.
5. Add the last 1.4 oz (40 g) of sugar, increase the speed and whisk until the mixture forms stiff peaks.
6. Fold the meringue in the vanilla cream right away. Use a spatula and blend to a light and airy filling.
7. Pipe 0.3 oz (10 g) raspberry jam in each cup. Use a paper cone.
8. Fill the cups three-fourths full with the vanilla filling. Use a decorating bag. Cut a hole in the bottom or use smooth tip no. 12.

9. Bake the cakes until golden brown, for about 25 minutes.
10. Sprinkle sugar on top and turn them out on a piece of parchment paper. Remove the cups.
11. When the cakes are cool, brush them with boiled black currant jelly.
12. Warm the fondant to 95 °F (35 °C) and dilute it with a generous amount of dark rum.
13. Glaze the rum cakes by dipping the baked surface in the fondant and wiping off excess fondant with a straight spatula.
14. Set the pastries in the oven to dry for a couple of minutes with the oven door ajar.

STORAGE:
Eat the rum cakes fresh.

EMPEROR'S CROWNS

This variety of polynéer is hundreds of years old, but still tastes great. The crisp butterdough and crunchy macaroon filling taste amazing, and you should eat them fresh.

24 CROWNS

24 curly mazarin cups
17.6 oz (500 g) butterdough, see recipe on p.28
5.3 oz (150 g) raspberry jam, see recipe on p.19
17.6 oz (500 g) almond paste 50/50
8.8 oz (250 g) sugar
5.3 oz (150 g) egg white (approx. 5)
Egg wash, see p.47

1. Line the cups as described for the Gothenburger, see p.180.
2. Preheat the oven to 320 °F (160 °C).
3. Pipe a top of raspberry jam in each cup with a paper cone.
4. Blend the almond paste (room temperature) with the sugar and one-third of the egg whites. Blend a mass without lumps.
5. Add the remaining egg whites a little at a time and blend into a smooth mass.
6. Fill the cups three-fourths full with the mixture.
7. Roll out some of the leftover dough from the lining, 1/16 inch (2 mm) thick.
8. Cut 3/16 inch (5 mm) wide lengths of the dough. Brush them with egg wash.
9. Make a cross out of the dough on the cups and pinch the leftover dough off.
10. Bake them for 25–30 minutes.
11. Remove the cups right away and let them cool on a cooling rack.

STORAGE:
Eat emperor's crowns fresh.

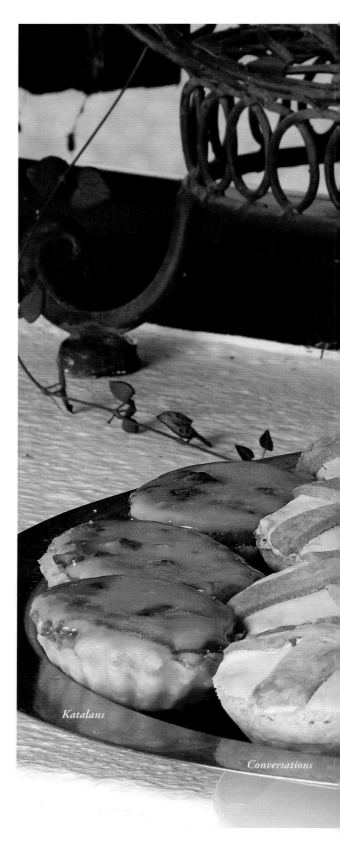

Katalans

Conversations

Emperor's Crowns

Gothenburger

Rum Cakes

179

GOTHENBURGERS

I remember that I tasted this delicious cake for the first time at the prestigious Fahlmans Conditori in Helsingborg. They were very fresh, and I drank a glass of strawberry juice with them. After that I asked frequently for Gothenburger when my mom would buy cakes to go with the coffee.

ABOUT 25 CAKES

25 mazarin cups
17.6 oz (500 g) butterdough, see recipe on p.28
14.1 oz (400 g) almond paste 50/50
3.5 oz (100 g) butter
1.8 oz (50 g) egg (approx. 1)
2.1 oz (60 g) egg yolks (approx. 3)
5.3 oz (150 g) vanilla cream, see p.15
0.9 oz (25 g) wheat flour
Egg wash, see p.47
Sugar for sprinkling

1. Put the molds on the table.
2. Roll out the pastry about 1/8 of an inch (3mm) thick.
3. Roll dough onto rolling pin and unroll it over the molds, see photo on p.36.
4. Flour lightly on top and press the dough into the molds using a small piece of dough.
5. Let them rest for 10 minutes. Flour lightly on top, turn the dough again so that all air is gone from the dough, and shape.
6. Roll off excess from molds using a roller so that the dough is cut away.
7. Release the dough from the mold and crimp the dough slightly above the edge of the mold using your thumb and index finger so that it won't slide down during baking.
8. Place them in the refrigerator to rest for at least 1 hour, or until the dough has shrunk in the molds.
9. Preheat the oven to 370 °F (190 °C).
10. Dissolve the almond paste (room temperature) and the butter into a lump-free mass, then add the egg and egg yolks.
11. Work that mixture gently into the vanilla cream, sift the flour into it, and mix into a smooth mass.
12. Scoop mass into a plastic piping bag, cutting a hole in the bottom, and fill molds three-fourths full.
13. Brush egg wash on top of the filling.
14. Roll out the rest of the dough 1/16 inch (2 mm) thick with a little flour. Cut the lengths so that they are approximately 1/16 inch (2 mm) wide.
15. Make a cross of dough on top of the molds and pinch off any excess dough.
16. Brush gently with egg wash and sprinkle a little sugar on top.
17. Bake for about 25 minutes, or until golden brown.
18. Remove them immediately from the molds and set them to cool on a rack.

STORAGE:
Gothenburgers should preferably be eaten fresh, but they can also be frozen and heated up in the oven.

CONVERSATIONS

Rolf Augustsson was always baking these at Pâtisserie Hollandia in Malmö. When they were finished, Rolf would call and say how beautiful they looked in the shop window, which was Rolf's baby. Unfortunately, Rolf is no longer with us, but he bakes plenty in the sky now, and he did so much good during his lifetime.

25 CAKES

25 mazarin molds, smooth or curly
26.5 oz (750 g) butter pastry, see p.28

Filling:
4.4 oz (125 g) almond paste 50/50
4.4 oz (125 g) butter
7 oz (200 g) eggs (approx. 4)
1.4 oz (40 g) egg yolks (approx. 2)
0.9 oz (25 g) wheat flour
0.8 oz (2.5 cl) dark rum
7.4 oz (210 g) vanilla cream, see p.15

Royal icing:
4.4 oz (125 g) powdered sugar
1 oz (30 g) egg white (approx. 1)
1 tsp (5 g) lemon juice

1. Sift the powdered sugar and beat it with egg white and lemon juice with an electric mixer to a light and fluffy frosting.
2. Line molds in the same manner as in Gothenburg pastries. Let rest for at least 1 hour in refrigerator.
3. Mix the almond paste (room temperature) with one-third of the butter, and cream to a lump-free mass. Work the remaining butter into the mixture to make a smooth paste.
4. Add the eggs (room temperature) and yolks one at a time while stirring.
5. Sift the corn flour and fold it in with a spatula.
6. Add the rum and the vanilla cream and mix to a smooth filling.
7. Fill the molds three-fourths full with the filling and put egg wash all around the edges.
8. Roll out remaining pastry to approximately 1/16 inch (2 mm) thick using wheat flour. Roll it on the rolling pin and roll out across the molds, arranged as closely together as possible.

9. Roll over molds with the rolling pin and set the molds in the fridge for about 1 hour to stiffen.
10. Take them out and apply a thin layer of icing on top with a straight spatula.
11. Roll out a small piece of leftover dough, about 1/16 inch (2 mm) thick, and cut into ¼ inch (5mm) wide strips, then brush with egg wash.
12. Use these strips to make crosses on top of the cakes and set them in the fridge for another 30 minutes before they are baked.
13. Preheat the oven to 338 °F (170 °C).
14. Bake until golden brown, for about 25 minutes.
15. Remove them immediately from the molds and allow to cool on a rack.

TIP!
Lift up a cake from the mold and make sure the pastry is baked through to the bottom before you remove all the cakes from the oven.

STORAGE:
Conversations should be eaten fresh the same day.

LEMON KONGRESSER (CONGRESSES)

Fresh and juicy cake surrounded by crispy puff pastry. My teacher Kurt Lundgren at Blekingsborg's Pâtisserie in Malmö always baked these every day. To my delight, some always stuck in the mold, so you had to try one yourself.

30 CAKES

30 mazarin cups
17.6 oz (500 g) butterdough, see p.28
5.3 oz (150 g) raspberry jam, see p.19

Filling:
1 lemon, yellow and ripe
7 oz (200 g) powdered sugar
7 oz (200 g) vanilla cream, see p.15
7 oz (200 g) sliced almonds
7 oz (200 g) eggs (approx. 4)
1.4 oz (40 g) egg yolks (approx. 2)

Water glaze with lemon:
2.6 oz (75 g) glucose syrup (corn syrup)
5.3 oz (150 g) powdered sugar
2.6 oz (75 g) lemon juice
Preserved strips of lemon peel, see p.20

1. Line pastry molds the same way as in the Gothenburger recipe, see p. 180.

2. Preheat the oven to 356 °F (180 °C).
3. Pipe a dollop of raspberry jam in the bottom of each mold.
4. Zest the washed lemon finely using a grater; only take the outermost skin, otherwise it will be bitter.
5. Sift the powdered sugar.
6. Mix the vanilla cream with almonds and powdered sugar. Stir egg, egg yolk, and lemon zest in little by little.
7. Scoop mass into a pastry bag. Cut a hole in the bottom or use a plain tip no. 12.
8. Fill the molds three-fourths full with the mass.
9. Bake until golden brown, for about 25 minutes.
10. Heat the ingredients for the glaze to about 122–131 °F (50–55 °C).
11. Brush cakes with glaze immediately when they come out of the oven; allow them to cool on a rack.
12. Garnish with a sliver of candied lemon peel.

STORAGE:
Kongressers should be eaten fresh.

HOLLANDERS

These delicious cakes contain crumbs just like vacuum cleaners, but unlike the vacuum cleaners, these have virtually disappeared. Curt Andersson, who was head pastry chef at Residens Schweizeri in Malmö, baked them and glazed them so beautifully that they looked nicer than most other cakes. Curt was one of my favorite pastry chefs when I was a boy, as was Gunnar Svensson, foreman at the prestigious Braun Conditori, beause of their fine caramel desserts displayed in the window of Gustaf's Square in Malmö.

30 CAKES

30 elongated mussel cups
1.8 oz (50 g) butter for the molds
Cornstarch for the molds
7 oz (200 g) powdered sugar
7 oz (200 g) butter
7 oz (100 g) finely ground, unpeeled almonds
0.9 oz (25 g) ground unpeeled bitter almonds
7 oz (200 g) breadcrumbs
3.5 oz (100 g) cornstarch
3.5 oz (100 g) egg (approx. 2)
2 batches apricot glaze, see p.17
10.6 oz (300 g) fondant, see p.16
0.8 oz (2.5 cl) dark rum
30 preserved red cherries

1. Brush the cups with melted butter and powder them with flour; shake off excess flour.
2. Preheat the oven to 370 °F (190 °C).
3. Sift the powdered sugar and mix it with softened butter until it's light and airy.
4. Stir in the almonds, bitter almonds, and the breadcrumb flour, and sift in the wheat flour. Blend the eggs in one at a time and mix carefully with a spatula.
5. Scoop the mass into a decorating bag. Use smooth tip no. 12 or cut a hole in the bottom.
6. Fill the cups three-fourths full with the mass.
7. Bake the cakes until golden brown, about 25 minutes. Take them out and let them rest for 5 minutes.
8. Let them cool on a cooling rack.
9. Boil the apricot icing and brush it over the cakes.
10. Heat the fondant to 95 °F (35 °C), dilute it with the liquor and brush it over the cakes. Place one whole, drained cherry on each cake.
11. Set them back in the oven for 1 minute at 300 °F (150 °C) so that the glaze dries.

STORAGE:
Cakes should preferably be eaten fresh, as the glaze will dull down. In professional jargon, we say that the glaze dies.

COCONUT PATTIES

We used to bake these tasty patties every other day at Konditori Heidi in Limhamn, and they always sold out. The pastry chef was named Philip Liljeqvist, and he also taught me to make perfect Kirch buns.

30 PATTIES

30 almond mussel cups
17.6 oz (500 g) butterdough, see p.28

Filling:
5.3 oz (150 g) almond paste 50/50
7.8 oz (220 g) unsalted butter
6.3 oz (180 g) grated coconut
6.3 oz (180 g) sugar
10.5 oz (300 g) eggs (approx. 6)

5.3 oz (150 g) raspberry jam, see recipe on p.19
1 batch apricot icing, see p.17

1. Line the cups as described for the Gothenburgers, see p.180.
2. Preheat the oven to 340 °F (170 °C).
3. Stir the almond paste (room temperature) in with the softened butter to a mass without lumps.
4. Add coconut and sugar and the eggs one at a time. Stir for a smooth, not overworked, mass.
5. Fill the cups three-fourths full with the mixture with the help of a decorating bag.
6. Pipe 1 tsp (5g) raspberry jam in each cup with a paper cone.
7. Bake the cakes for 25–30 minutes.
8. Take them out of the oven and brush them with apricot icing right away.
9. Remove the cups and let them cool on a cooling rack.

STORAGE:
Eat the coconut patties fresh.

Hollanders

Coconut Patties

Lemon Kongressers

MIRLITON

This cake is easy to make and if you are meticulous with the lining of the cups and the recipe, and it will look beautiful as well—and taste great. The caramelized lid is the signature of this cake, which originated in France. It is most common to garnish with almond.

Because I've always loved gin and tonic, it was a given that I would make a variety of the Mirliton with a wedge of grapefruit at the bottom. I used to bake them at sea for the afternoon tea. The contrast of the sour against the sweet is very refined.

30 CAKES

30 round mazarin cups
17.6 oz (500 g) butterdough, see recipe on p.28

Filling:
1 lemon, yellow and ripe
½ vanilla bean (bourbon)
13 oz (375 g) butter
13 oz (375 g) sugar
8.8 oz (250 g) eggs (approx. 5)
0.9 oz (25 g) wheat flour

30 almonds with the shells for decorating
Powdered sugar for sifting on top

1. Line the cups as described for the Gothenburger, see p.180.
2. Clean and grate the outer zest of the lemon with a grater.
3. Cut the vanilla bean lengthwise and scrape the seeds out with a knife.
4. Boil the butter with the vanilla seeds and the bean.
5. Remove the saucepan from the stove and whisk in the sugar and lemon zest. Continue whisking until the sugar has melted.
6. Add the eggs, one at a time, and lastly sift in the wheat flour. Whisk well.
7. Fill the butterdough-lined cups about three-fourths full with the mass.
8. Place one almond with the shell on top of the filling. Powder a layer of powdered sugar on top and let the sugar melt at room temperature for 30 minutes.
9. Powder a second layer of powdered sugar over the cakes and bake the cakes at 340 °F (180 °C) for about 25 minutes, until they are golden brown.
10. Take the cups out of the oven and increase the temperature to 480 °F (250 °C).
11. Powder another layer of powdered sugar over the cakes and set them back in the oven until they are beautifully caramelized (watch the oven closely so that they don't burn).
12. Remove the cups from the cakes right away and let them cool on a cooling rack.

STORAGE:
Should preferably be eaten fresh but can be frozen before they are baked and baked later.

NUT KONGRESSER

This marvelous cake is always much appreciated when it is served fresh. It is important to place them in the oven right away so that the surface doesn't dry, as they won't turn out as beautifully. My mother loved nut kongresser, as do I.

22 CAKES

22 smooth mazarin cups
17.6 oz (500 g) butterdough, see recipe on p.28
5.3 oz (150 g) raspberry jam, see recipe on p.19
5.3 oz (150 g) vanilla cream, see recipe on p.15

Filling:
0.9 oz (25 g) buter
8.8 oz (250 g) finely grated hazelnuts
8.8 oz (250 g) sugar
6 oz (175 g) eggs (approx. 3 ½)

1 batch apricot icing, see p.17
22 roasted hazelnuts for decorating

Nut Kongresser

Mirliton with Grapefruit

Mirliton

1. Line the cups as described for the Gothenburger, see p.180.
2. Preheat the oven to 340 °F (170 °C).
3. Pipe a ball of raspberry jam in each cup with the help of a paper cone.
4. Pipe a ball of vanilla cream in each cup with the help of a paper cone.
5. Melt the butter and blend it with the nuts and sugar.
6. Stir in the eggs and fill the cups three-fourths full with the butter and sugar mixture.
7. Bake them right away for 25–30 minutes, until they are golden brown.
8. Remove the cups and let them cool on a cooling rack.
9. Brush them with boiling apricot icing until they have a beautiful shine and garnish with a roasted hazelnut.

STORAGE:
Nut Kongresser are eaten fresh.

PUFFS

These excellent pastries have vanished from most of the pâtisseries in Sweden and are almost completely forgotten. They used to be served with warm consommé or a soup at the coffee reception after a funeral.

At Conditori Lundagard they always baked puffs, both for serving and for their store Sigfrid Lunggrens in Lund. Try to bake these puffs and serve them with soup on a cold day.

LINING PUFFS WITH BUTTERDOUGH
Proper puff molds look like muffin cups and are 3 inches (6 cm) tall with a diameter of 2 inches (5 cm).

1. Roll out butterdough, preferably blixt butterdough (p.30), 1/8 of an inch (3 mm) thick. Arrange the cups out on a table with about 1 inch (2 cm) space in between and cover with the dough.
2. Bring the cups together so that the dough may be punched down without stretching, and thus be thinner in certain places. Do this with one piece of dough and press the dough down once, let it rest for 15 minutes, and repeat.
3. Use a rolling pin to roll over the cups then place the cups on a plate. You will get the absolute best result if you line the cups a day in advance. This way the dough won't pull together and shrink, which can happen if it is not allowed to relax properly.

Remember to always heat the puffs in the oven before you serve them with soup or clear consommé.

EGG PUFFS

These tasty puffs are a bit tricky to make. You have to make sure that you slit them at the right time during baking so that they are light and airy and not dense. When I received my journeyman certificate it was very important to be able to bake beautiful butterdough pastries and egg puffs. The pastry chef Algot Svensson noted how egg puffs could be difficult to master.

ABOUT 10 PUFFS

17.6 oz (500 g) butterdough, see recipe on p.28
1.7 oz (50 g) almond paste
5.3 oz (150 g) eggs (approx. 3)
2.8 oz (80 g) yolks (approx. 4)
12.3 oz (350 g) whipping cream (40%)
1 oz (30 g) wheat flour
Approx. 1 tsp (5g) salt, preferably fleur de sel

DAY 1
1. Line the cups with butterdough (see previous recipe), and place in the fridge.
2. Mix the almond paste (room temperature) until smooth with the eggs and yolks, without forming lumps.
3. Whisk in cream and milk. Mix until smooth with a handheld mixer.
4. Add salt, and don't be too sparing with it. Cover and leave in the fridge overnight.
DAY 2
5. Preheat the oven to 430 °F (220 °C).
6. Fill the cups three-fourths full with a measuring cup and place the sheet of each puff using the cups in the oven.
7. After about 5 minutes, when you can see a membrane forming on top of the puffs, remove them from the oven and cut a cross on top with a small sharp knife dipped in warm water.
8. Set them back in the oven and bake until golden brown, about 20 minutes.
9. Make sure that they're baked all the way through at the bottom, then remove them from the oven. Turn them upside down in the cups so that they maintain their height. Let them cool.

Egg Puffs

Rice Puffs

Cheese Puffs

185

RICE PUFFS

ABOUT 12 PUFFS

17.6 oz (500 g) butterdough, see p.28
Egg wash, see p.47

Filling:
3.5 oz (100 g) round-grain rice
1 tsp (5g) salt
10.5 oz (300 g) water
10.5 oz (300 g) milk (2%)
2.6 oz (75 g) butter
3.5 oz (100 g) egg (approx. 2)
0.7 oz (20 g) yolk (approx. 1)
Grated nutmeg

1. Line the cups with butterdough (see p.184) and set them in the fridge.
2. Boil the rice in salted water, covered, for 10 minutes.
3. Add the milk, bring to a boil, and then simmer until the mixture thickens to the consistency of porridge.
4. Stir in the almond paste (room temperature) and the butter; blend well.
5. Add the eggs and yolk and flavor the mixture with grated nutmeg and more salt if needed.
6. Let the porridge cool to room temperature.
7. Fill the cups three-fourths full with the mixture and brush with egg wash.
8. Roll out some leftover dough, about 1/16 (2 mm) thick. Place small strips, about ½ inch (1 cm) thick on the pastry in a cross.
9. Brush the egg wash over once more.
10. Let it rest in a cool place for 30 minutes.
11. Preheat the oven to 430 °F (220 °C).
12. Bake them golden brown and make sure that they are fully baked in the bottom, takes about 25 minutes.
13. Let the patties rest in room temperature for 5 minutes and then turn them upside down in the cups so that they maintain their height and to make the butterodugh crisp.

CHEESE PATTIES

ABOUT 12 PATTIES

17.6 oz (500 g) butterdough, see recipe on p.28
6.3 oz (180 g) milk 3%
4.5 oz (125 g) whipping cream (40%)
3.5 oz (100 g) grated Emmentaler cheese
0.9 oz (25 g) grated Parmesan cheese, matured for at least 24 months
5.3 oz (150 g) eggs (approx. 3)
1.4 oz (40 g) yolks (approx. 2)
Salt and freshly ground white pepper
Grated nutmeg

1. Line the cups with butterdough (see p.184) and set them in the fridge.
2. Warm milk and cream to 113 °F (45 °C), then add the grated cheese, egg, and yolks.
3. Mix until completely smooth with a handheld mixer. Season with the white pepper and grated nutmeg.
4. Preheat the oven to 410 °F (210 °C).
5. Fill the cups three-fourths full with the batter and set them in the oven. Bake them until golden brown for about 20 minutes.
6. Check the bottoms to make sure that they're baked all the way through and turn them upside down in the cups.
7. Let them cool upside down so that they maintain their height.

LARGE VOL-AU-VENT *("windblown," if you translate from French)*

When I baked this in preparation for this book, I served it to my good friends and colleagues: pastry chef Calle Widell with his wife Ulla, pastry chef Hans Eichmuller, my assistant Sabina, and the photographer Ulf. They all thought it tasted great and that it felt nostalgic to eat this delicious appetizer again.

This authentic savory treat is mostly made nowadays in bite-sized pastries called bouchées, or portion-sized vol-au-vent. People would order this lovely appetizer at the pâtisserie for birthdays, parties, and anniversaries, and obviously for restaurants that did not have their own pâtisserie.

In Switzerland, vol-au-vent were served for lunch at pâtisseries, as they were all over the continent. These were filled with various savory ingredients, like creamy chanterelles, stewed shrimp with dill, sweet bread and champignons in supreme sauce, and chicken in curry sauce.

FOR 8 PEOPLE as an appetizer

1 batch butterdough, see p.28
Egg wash, see p.47

1. Roll out ¼ of the dough to about ⅛ of an inch (3 mm) thick with the help of a rolling pin and some wheat flour.
2. Place on a baking sheet lined with parchment paper and prick it with a fork.
3. Cut a bottom out, 9 ½ inches (24 cm) in diameter, or use a dinner plate and cut around it with a knife.
4. Roll out half of the remaining butterdough to about ½ inch (1 cm) thick. Place a ring or a plate on top, 9 ½ inches (24 cm) in diameter, and cut a circle with a sharp knife.
5. Set piece of dough aside.
6. Place a plate at the middle of one of the rounds and make sure that you get a border of about 1 ¼ inches (3 cm) of butterdough around it. Cut out the hole in the middle.
7. Brush the pricked bottom with egg wash and carefully place the ring on top.
8. Brush the surface carefully with egg wash and try to prevent it from running down the sides as it may prevent it from rising.
9. Mark the top side of the ring with a fork so that you get a beautiful pattern (see photo).
10. Slit the ring a little bit with a sharp knife with ½ inch (1 cm) space in between and let it rest in a cold place for 1 hour.

For the lid:

11. Roll out dough to 1/16 inch (2 mm) thick and cut out ½ inch (1 cm) wide strips.
12. Braid this into a lid the same size as the vol-au-vent.
13. Brush egg wash over the lid and let it rest for 1 hour.
14. Preheat the oven to 430 °F (210 °C).

15. Place the vol-au-vent in the oven. If you have a suitable ring to place in the middle of the butterdough, then butter it and set it in the middle to prevent the dough from collapsing.
16. When the dough has risen properly and the pastry has some color, after about 25 minutes, you can lower the heat to 390 °F (200 °C). Bake the butterdough until it is really crisp.
17. Remove from the oven, and if you used a ring, remove it right away.
18. Bake the lid at 370 °F (190 °C) until it is golden brown and crisp, about 10 minutes.

SERVING:
Warm the vol-au-vent in the oven and fill it with the savory filling, which should not be too thick. Cover with the lid and eat right away.

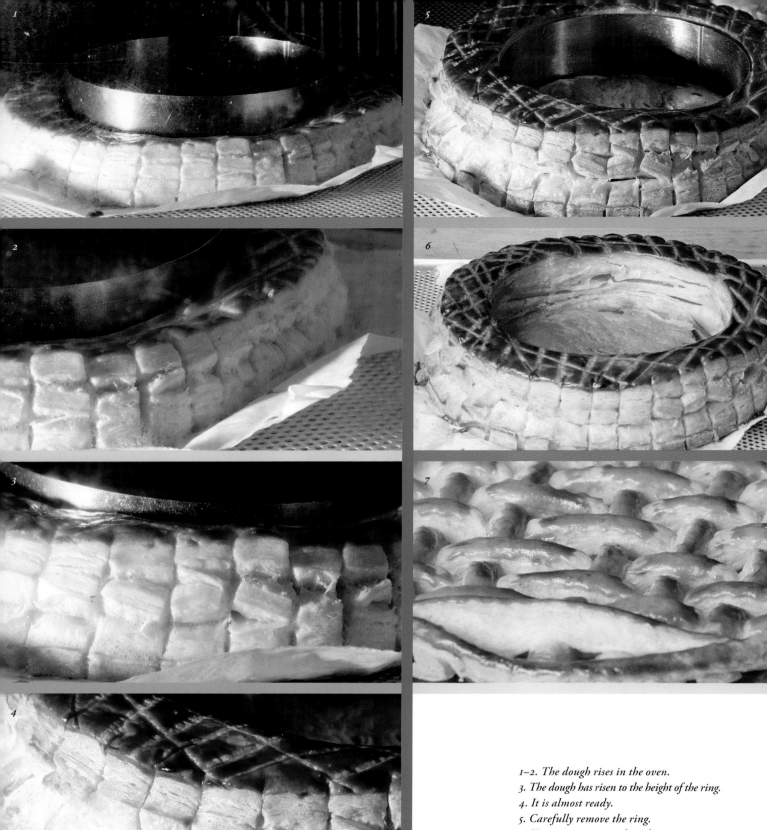

1–2. The dough rises in the oven.
3. The dough has risen to the height of the ring.
4. It is almost ready.
5. Carefully remove the ring.
6. You can now move the vol-au-vent.
7. The braided lid
8. The ready-baked vol-au-vent

PETITS-CHOUX PASTRIES

PETITS-CHOUX DOUGH

The French name of this dough, pâte à choux, means cabbage dough. The French love making pastries with this dough. The eclaire, for instance, is a staple of the French pâtisserie. The Germans call this dough brandteig, since the dough is "boiled" so that the flour swells. Petits-choux should have holes in the middle—spaces for tasty fillings.

GOOD TO KNOW:

When the dough bakes, the starch in the flour will swell up and part of the protein will coagulate, which will prevent the steam from escaping. The steam that is created during baking helps the pastry rise. Make sure that the oven vent is open at the end of the baking time so that the steam can evaporate. Petits-choux dough for Wales bread is also called cold water dough or water mass by pastry chefs.

This is how we used to make petits-choux dough. We also used it for so-called classic Maria Garlands.

5 cups (1 liter) water
0.7 oz (20 g) salt
10.5 oz (300 g) butter
21.2 oz (600 g) wheat flour
20 eggs

If we wanted to bake heavier and tighter petits-choux, we would take 14 oz (400 g) butter instead of 10.5 oz (300 g), and we would increase the amount of flour to 28.2 oz (800 g) instead of 21.2 oz (600 g).

Here is the same recipe but for a smaller batch:

5.3 oz (150 g) wheat flour
8.8 oz (250 g) water
2.6 oz (75 g) unsalted butter
1 tsp (5g) salt, preferably fleur de sel (1 tsp)
8.8 oz (250 g) egg (approx. 5)

1. Sift the flour onto paper.
2. Heat the water with the butter and salt in a roomy saucepan.
3. Bring the blend to a boil while stirring. Remove the saucepan from the stove.
4. Add all of the flour at once.
5. Stir briskly with a wooden spoon.
6. Place the saucepan back on the stove and cook the mixture while constantly stirring until it lets go of the walls of the saucepan and forms a ball.
7. Stir in one egg at a time. Mix after each egg is added. When all of the eggs are added, the dough should be shiny and have a creamy texture.

Maria Garlands

Berliner Garlands

Wales Bread

MARIA GARLANDS

These classic fried petits-choux garlands are rolled in cinnamon sugar, and when served freshly baked they are quite the delicacy.

ABOUT 30 GARLANDS

1 smaller batch petits-choux-dough, see p.190, but increase the amount of butter to 3.5 oz (100 g) and increase the amount of flour to 7 oz (200 g) for a heavier dough
5 cups (1 liter) frying oil

Cinnamon and vanilla sugar:
3.5 oz (100 g) sugar
0.9 oz (25 g) vanilla sugar
0.7 oz (20 g) ground cinnamon

Blend sugar, vanilla sugar, and cinnamon.

1. Cut two pieces of parchment paper into 4 square pieces each.
2. Place petits-choux dough in a decorating bag with curly tip no. 14 and pipe double garlands, two layers, on the square pieces of paper.
3. Heat the oil to 340–355 °F (170–180 °C) in a pot that holds 13 cups (3 liters) or a frying pot. Make sure that it is not too hot.
4. Place a piece of paper in the oil. After 1 ½ minutes the garlands will let go of the paper and you can pull the paper out.
5. When the garlands are starting to brown underneath, turn them with a fork and let them continue to fry until they are golden brown on the other side as well. Keep turning them now and then until they are golden brown all over.
6. Place one garland on a grid and use a knife to check that it is cooked all the way through. Let all the garlands drain on a cooling rack then roll them in cinnamon and vanilla sugar right away. Repeat until all of the rings are cooked.

STORAGE:
Eat these the same day.

BERLINER GARLANDS

We used to bake these for the night-buffet on cruise ships, and at Blekingborgs Pâtisserie in Malmö we baked them every day when we baked Berliner donuts (which is still one of my favorite pastries).

ABOUT 20 GARLANDS

1 smaller batch petit-choux-dough, see p.190
1 double batch apricot icing, see p.17
1 batch water glaze with rum, see p.181. Substitute the lemon juice with 0.3-0.7 oz (1–2 cl) dark rum.

1. Bake the garlands as described for Maria Garlands (see above) and let them drain on a cooling rack.
2. Brush the garlands with heated apricot icing.
3. Warm the glaze to 95 °F (35 °C) and dip the rings in. Let them drain on a cooling rack.
4. Serve with strong coffee as soon as the glaze has hardened.

STORAGE:
Eat fresh.

WALES BREAD

This classic pastry used to be baked in most pâtisseries. In our neighboring country, Norway, they fill Wales bread with a mixture of whipped cream and vanilla cream, a must for birthdays. They are often shaped like kringles instead of cylinders.

½ batch express butterdough, see p.30

Cream filling:
7 oz (200 g) almond paste 50/50
4.5 oz (125 g) vanilla cream, see recipe on p.15.

½ batch vanilla cream, see p.15
1 smaller batch petit-choux-dough, see p.190
1 oz (30 g) almond flakes
0.7 oz (20 g) roasted almond flakes
1 batch apricot icing, see p.17
1 batch water glaze with lemon, see p.181

1. Preheat the oven to 390 °F (200 °C).
2. Roll the butterdough out to about ⅛ of an inch (3 mm) thick and the same length as the baking sheet.
3. Cut 3 ½ inch (9 cm) wide strips, roll them onto the rolling pin, and place two strips on a baking sheet lined with parchment paper. Brush the paper with water before you roll the dough out to prevent them from shrinking in the oven.
4. Prick the bottoms with a fork.
5. Dissolve the almond paste (room temperature) with the vanilla cream a little at a time to prevent lumps. Blend either by hand or in a food processor.
6. Scoop the cream filling into a decorating bag and cut a hole in the bottom.
7. Pipe a line of filling in the middle of each butterdough strip.
8. Scoop the cold vanilla cream into the decorating bag and pipe a thin line on each side of the lines of cream filling.
9. Pipe the petits-choux dough in waves over the strips using star tip no. 12.
10. Sprinkle some almond flakes over the strips and bake them until golden brown, for about 25 minutes. Open the oven vent if you have one.
11. Brush the strips with apricot icing right after taking them out of the oven and glaze them with water glaze. Sprinkle almond flakes on top.
12. Let them cool and cut into pieces that are about 1 ¼ inches wide (3 cm).

TIP!
Serve the Wales bread freshly baked with strong coffee, or as a dessert with whipped cream and raspberries.

SOFT CAKES

BLUEBERRY MUFFINS

I tasted these muffins for the first time on a visit to America, at the Waldorf Astoria Hotel in New York, with bacon and maple syrup on the side. Use Swedish blueberries, and not the large tasteless blueberries.

On the cruiseship Vista/Fjord, where I was Chef Pâtissier, we baked fantastic blueberry muffins every day for our passengers. The bakers George and Nisse were muffin specialists, and they made variations with cranberries, raspberries, apples, and other goodies. Nisse used to live for years in Belem, without speaking Portugese at all, and no real English either, but he still managed. George was German and lived in Dusseldorf, but spoke perfect Swedish because he had worked on the Swedish American line's ships Kungsholm and Gripsholm.

12 MUFFINS

12 large muffin cups
8.8 oz (250 g) wheat flour
2.8 oz (80 g) powdered sugar
0.7 oz (20 g) real vanilla sugar
0.1 oz (4 g) salt, preferably fleur de sel
⅕ oz (7 g) baking soda
⅕ oz (8 g) baking powder
1 tsp (5g) ground cinnamon
½ lemon
3.5 oz (100 g) eggs (approx. 2)
1.7 oz (50 g) brown sugar
6 oz (175 g) milk 3%
¾ cup (150 ml) sunflower oil
5.3 oz (150 g) frozen Swedish blueberries

1. Preheat the oven to 390 °F (200 °C).
2. Sift wheat flour, powdered sugar, vanilla sugar, salt, baking soda, baking powder, and cinnamon onto a piece of waxed or parchment paper.
3. Clean and grate the outer zest of ½ lemon.
4. Wisk the lemon zest with eggs, brown sugar, milk, and oil.
5. Whisk in the flour mixture, just long enough for it to all be mixed together (if you whisk for too long the muffins will be heavy).
6. Fold in the frozen blueberries.
7. Fill the cups about two-thirds full and bake the muffins until golden brown, 20–24 minutes. Let them cool on a cooling rack.

STORAGE:
Muffins should be served the same day, as they are, with coffee or tea, or for breakfast with scrambled eggs, bacon, and maple syrup.

195

RASMUS MUFFINS

Tasty and moist muffins baked in buttered muffins cups sprinkled with almond flakes.

ABOUT 12 MUFFINS

7.9 oz (225 g) raisins
2 oz (6 cl) rum

12 large muffin cups
1.7 oz (50 g) butter for the cups
1 oz (30 g) almond flakes for the cups

7.6 oz (215 g) butter
1.7 oz (50 g) citrus concentrate, see recipe on p.21
6.7 oz (190 g) sugar
3.5 oz (100 g) egg (approx. 2)
0.7 oz (20 g) yolk (approx. 1)
0.1 oz (3 g) ammonium carbonate ("baker's ammonia")
0.3 oz (10 g) real vanilla sugar
2.6 oz (75 g) potato flour
3.8 oz (110 g) wheat flour
1 tsp (5g) baking powder

DAY 1
1. Soak the raisins in rum overnight in a bowl covered with plastic wrap.

DAY 2
2. Preheat the oven to 390 °F (200 °C).
3. Grease the cups with the softened butter with a brush. Sprinkle almond flakes in the cups. Shake out the bits that don't stick.
4. Stir the softened butter until it becomes light and airy with the citrus concentrate and sugar using a whisk. Add eggs and egg yolks (room temperature) one at a time.
5. Sift the dry ingredients together on parchment paper and fold it into the butter blend using a spatula. Lastly, fold in the raisins.
6. Fill the cups three-fourths full with the batter and bake them until golden brown for 20–25 minutes. Remove the cups right away and let the muffins cool down on a cooling rack.

STORAGE:
The muffins will stay fresh at room temperature for 2 days, but you may also freeze them.

OLD-FASHIONED BAKERY SUGARCAKE

This sugarcake is moist, tasty, and cheap to make. The crisp surface makes it especially good.

2 straight loaf pans that hold 5 cups (1 liter)
0.9 oz (25 g) butter for the pans
2 form cake papers to line the pans
  (Alternatively, cut 4 slits from the corners towards the middle of a square piece of parchment paper and fold it)

1 lemon, yellow and ripe
7 oz (200 g) eggs (approx. 4)
13.4 oz (380 g) sugar
0.7 oz (20 g) real vanilla sugar
4.2 oz (120 g) butter
1 cup (2 dl) lukewarm water
14 oz (400 g) wheat flour
0.2 oz (7 g) baking powder

1. Grease the pans with the softened butter with the help of a brush and line them with the paper.
2. Preheat the oven to 410 °F (210 °C).
3. Clean and grate the lemon finely.
4. Whisk eggs, sugar, and vanilla sugar with the lemon zest until it becomes a stiff foam, about 10 minutes.
5. Melt the butter and set it aside. Add the lukewarm water.
6. Sift wheat flour and baking powder on a parchment paper through a sieve.
7. Fold the flour blend into the egg batter with a large spatula until you have a light and airy mixture.
8. Fold two ladles of batter into the water and butter and mix until evenly blended. Fold this into the sugarcake batter.
9. Pour the batter into the two pans.
10. Place the cakes in the oven. When they start to brown, after about 10 minutes, open the oven door and cut a slit in the middle of each cake with a sharp knife. Lower the temperature to 340 °F (170 °C).
11. Bake the cakes until golden brown, for 45–50 minutes total, using a toothpick to make sure that they're ready.
12. Take them out of the oven and let them rest for 5 minutes. Lift them out of the pans and let them cool on a cooling rack.

STORAGE:
The sugarcakes will keep for about 3–4 days at room temperature or you may freeze them.

Old-Fashioned Bakery Sugarcake

Classic Sandcake

Rasmus Muffins

Classic Soft Gingerbread Cake

SOFT GINGERBREAD CAKE

This soft and tasty gingerbread cake is very moist and keeps well. The contrast of the preserved orange peels makes it very refined. Serve it in thick slices with good coffee or tea.

2 ribbed loaf pans that hold 5 cups (1 liter)
0.9 oz (25 g) butter for the cups
1 oz (30 g) almond flakes

8.8 oz (250 g) milk (2%)
2.6 oz (75 g) light syrup
3.5 oz (100 g) butter
7 oz (200 g) granulated sugar
2.6 oz (75 g) brown sugar
1 tsp (5g) ground cinnamon
0.1 oz (4 g) ground ginger
0.1 oz (4 g) ground cloves
3.5 oz (100 g) eggs (approx. 2)
10.5 oz (300 g) wheat flour
0.6 oz (17 g) baking soda
3.5 oz (100 g) chopped, preserved orange peels

1. Brush the two pans with a layer of softened butter.
2. Preheat the oven to 355 °F (180 °C).
3. Pour almond flakes in the pans and shake them so that they stick to the edges.
4. Heat milk, syrup, butter, the sugars, and the spices to 140 °F (40 °C) while stirring.
5. Remove from the stove and whisk until well blended.
6. Add the eggs one at a time.
7. Sift together the wheat flour and baking soda and stir this into the batter.
8. Lastly, add the orange peels.
9. Fill the pans half full with the batter and sprinkle almond flakes on top if you have any leftover.
10. Place the pans in the oven and carefully take them out after about 45–50 minutes. Use a toothpick to make sure that they are baked all the way through in the middle.
11. Let them rest for 5 minutes. Then remove the pans and let the cakes cool on a cooling rack.

STORAGE:
Soft gingerbread cake will keep for about 1 week in the fridge; you can also freeze it.

SANDCAKE THE WAY WE BAKED IT AT THE SAVOY HOTEL IN MALMÖ

We baked this sandcake every week at the Savoy Hotel in Malmö for the guests that wanted afternoon tea. This version is particularly good, and it stands out from other sandcake recipes. In our version, you whip butter, flour, and baking powder first. Then you whisk the eggs with the sugar, vanilla sugar, and cognac on their own; then you blend everything together.

2 ribbed loaf pans that hold 7 cups (1 ½ liter)
0.9 oz (25 g) butter for the pans
Wheat flour for the pans

6.7 oz (190 g) wheat flour
6.7 oz (190 g) potato flour
1 tsp (5g) baking powder
13 oz (375 g) butter
10.5 oz (300 g) egg (approx. 6)
12.3 oz (350 g) sugar
0.9 oz (25 g) real vanilla sugar
1.3 oz (4 cl) cognac

1. Brush the pans with a layer of softened butter. Powder wheat flour over the butter and shake the pans to get rid of excess flour.
2. Preheat the oven to 340 °F (170 °C).
3. Sift potato flour, wheat flour, and baking powder in a bowl and add the softened butter. Stir the mass until light and airy using a stand mixer.
4. Whisk eggs, sugars, and liquor until the mixture becomes a stiff foam, about 10 minutes.
5. Fold the whisked egg batter into the butter mixture with a large spatula. The batter you end up with should be smooth and elastic.
6. Fill the pans three-fourths full and set them in the oven.
7. Bake them for about 45–50 minutes. Make sure that they are baked all the way through using a toothpick.
8. Take the cakes out of the oven and let them rest for 5 minutes. Turn them out on a cooling rack and let them cool.

STORAGE:
Will keep for about 5 days in the fridge, but you can also freeze them.

MARBLED SANDCAKE

I never tire of this tasty marbled sandcake either. The Chinese cleaning experts at M/S Vista/Fjord loved sandcake. Actually, they were the only kind of pastry the Chinese personnel ate, which just confirms its universal appeal.

2 round ribbed loaf pans that hold 5 cups (1 liter)
0.9 oz (25 g) butter for the pans
Wheat flour for the pans

2 oranges
8.8 oz (250 g) butter
8.1 oz (230 g) sugar
0.7 oz (20 g) real vanilla sugar
8.8 oz (250 g) eggs (approx. 5)
8.8 oz (250 g) wheat flour
1/5 oz (8 g) baking powder
0.9 oz (25 g) cocoa, preferably Valrhona
0.7 oz (2 cl) Cointreau or Grand Marnier

1. Brush the pans with a layer of softened butter. Dust the pans with wheat flour, tapping them to remove the excess.
2. Preheat the oven to 340 °F (170 °C).
3. Clean and grate the outer zest of the oranges.
4. Stir the softened butter until light and airy with the orange peel and the sugars.
5. Add the eggs (room temperature) one at a time while stirring.
6. Sift in the wheat flour and the baking powder.
7. Pour one-third of the batter into another bowl. Sift in the cocoa and stir with a spatula. Add the Cointreau or Grand Marnier.
8. Pour one layer of light batter into the bottom of the pans, spread the dark batter on top and cover with the light batter (fill the pans three-fourths full, not more, because the batter will seep over the edges).
9. Bake the cakes for about 45–50 minutes until they are golden brown. Use a toothpick to make sure that they're ready.
10. Take the cakes out of the oven and let them rest for 5 minutes.
11. Turn out on a cooling rack and let them cool.

STORAGE:
Will keep for 1 week in the fridge and may also be frozen.

CLASSIC SANDCAKE

A sandcake looks just like a sugarcake once it's baked. When you exchange half of the wheat flour with potato flour the cake becomes denser and obtains a more sandy texture.

2 straight loaf pans that hold 5 cups (1 liter)
0.9 oz (25 g) butter for the pans
2 sheets form cake paper to line the pans
    (Alternatively, cut 4 slit in the corners and toward the
    middle of a square piece of parchment paper and fold it)

7 oz (200 g) butter
6.3 oz (180 g) powdered sugar
0.7 oz (20 g) real vanilla sugar
7 oz (200 g) egg (approx. 4)
0.2 oz (7 g) baking powder
3.5 oz (100 g) wheat flour
3.5 oz (100 g) potato flour

1. Butter and line the pans as described for sugarcake, see p.196.
2. Preheat the oven to 410 °F (210 °C).
3. Stir the softened butter until light and airy with the sugars.
4. Add the eggs (room temperature) one at a time and mix until smooth.
5. Sift baking powder and flours directly into the batter and mix with a spatula.
6. Pour the batter into the pans and bake as directed for the sugarcake.

CLASSIC SOFT GINGERBREAD CAKE

This classic and tasty gingerbread cake makes me nostalgic when I think of how often I ate it as a child, both at my mother's and grandmother's house. I baked this multiple times a week as an apprentice.

0.9 oz (25 g) butter for the pans
2 sheets of form cake paper to line the pans

7.9 oz (225 g) egg (approx. 5)
5.3 oz (150 g) granulated sugar
5.3 oz (150 g) brown sugar
10.5 oz (300 g) wheat flour
0.4 oz (12 g) baking powder
0.3 oz (10 g) ground cinnamon
1 tsp (5g) ground ginger
1 tsp (5g) ground cloves
2.6 oz (75 g) butter
2.6 oz (75 g) lingonberry jam, see the recipe in my book *The Jam and Marmalade Bible*
5.3 oz (150 g) sour cream

1. Grease the pans with the softened butter and line them with the paper.
2. Preheat the oven to 410 °F (210 °C).
3. Whisk eggs and sugar for 10 minutes.
4. Sift wheat flour, baking powder, and spices though a sieve onto parchment paper.
5. Melt the butter, let it cool, and blend it with the lingonberry jam and sour cream.
6. Fold the flour blend into the egg foam with a spatula until it is blended but still light and airy. Lastly fold in the lingonberry jam, cream, and butter.
7. Fill the cups three-fourths full.
8. Place the cakes in the oven until they have just started to become solid and acquire some color, for about 10 minutes. Then cut a slit lengthwise with a sharp knife and lower the temperature to 340 °F (170 °C).
9. Bake them until golden brown, for 40–45 minutes total. Use a toothpick to make sure that they're baked all the way through.
10. Take the cakes out of the pans and let them cool on a cooling rack.

STORAGE:
Gingerbread cake will keep for 1 week in the fridge. You can also freeze it.

CHOCOLATE GLAZED ALMOND CAKE WITH WALNUTS

I used to always bake this cake at the M/S Vista/Fjord for our famous afternoon tea. We had different themes every day and prepared the most amazing pastries from all over the world. If you garnish the cake with gold leaf it becomes even more luxurious—it will be just as good without but not as pretty. Enjoy it with fresh berries, vanilla ice cream, and a glass of good sweet wine.

2 round, ribbed pans that hold 5 cups (1 liter)
0.9 oz (25 g) butter for the pans
1 oz (30 g) almond flakes for the pans

14.8 oz (420 g) almond paste 50/50
5.3 oz (150 g) eggs (approx. 3)
5.3 oz (150 g) yolks (approx. 8)
0.7 oz (20 g) butter
2.8 oz (80 g) walnuts
1 oz (30 g) wheat flour
0.2 oz (6 g) baking powder
3 oz (90 g) sugar

1 batch glazing ganache, see p.15
Gold leaf
0.9 oz (25 g) roughly chopped pistachio nuts

1. Brush the pans with the softened butter. Sprinkle almond flakes in the pans and shake out the excess.
2. Preheat the oven to 320 °F (160 °C).
3. Stir the almond paste until smooth, adding one egg at a time until you have an even batter with no lumps.
4. Add the yolks and whisk the batter until light and airy, for about 10 minutes.
5. Melt the butter and set it aside.
6. Crush the walnuts roughly using a rolling pin.
7. Sift the wheat flour and the baking powder together. Fold into the almond mixture using a spatula.
8. Add the walnuts and the butter and fold all of the ingredients together until you have a light and airy mixture.
9. Fill the pans three-fourths full and bake them for about 45–50 minutes, until they are golden brown. Make sure that they are ready using a toothpick.
10. Turn the cakes out on a cooling rack to cool.
11. Place them in the freezer for 1 hour.
12. Make sure that the temperature on the glazing ganache is between 95 and 113 °F (35–40 °C). Place the cakes on a grid and pour the glaze over them.
13. Garnish with some gold leaf from a sheet. Sprinkle chopped pistachio nuts on top.

STORAGE:
The cake will keep in the fridge for 1 week. You can also freeze it.

PLUMCAKE

I learned how to bake this moist and tasty cake when I was twenty years old, and it has accompanied me to every workplace since then. It is moist and it keeps for weeks. My old friend Rolf Augustsson at the Konditori Hollandia in Malmö was so proud of his plumcakes that he often showcased them in his windows. I hope he is served a plumcake in pastry chef heaven—where there has to be room reserved for him. We always baked them in large wooden frames and the next day we would cut 24 cakes per frame so that the fruit would show when they were packed in plastic wrap. This cake is especially nice for Christmas, but tastes great all year round.

2 straight loaf pans that hold 7 cups (1 ½ liter)
0.9 oz (25 g) butter for the pans
Wheat flour for the pans

8.8 oz (250 g) raisins
5.3 oz (150 g) chopped preserved orange peel
7 oz (200 g) candied fruit/fruit peel
3.5 oz (100 g) red preserved cherries
3.5 oz (100 g) preserved pineapple, see p.20

3.5 oz (100 g) dark rum

2 lemons, yellow and ripe
13.4 oz (380 g) butter
10.5 oz (300 g) sugar
4.2 oz (120 g) yolks (approx. 6)
7 oz (200 g) eggs (approx. 4)
1 tsp (5g) baking powder
8.8 oz (250 g) wheat flour

8.8 oz (250 g) wheat flour for the fruit
Shelled almonds

DAY 1
1. Marinate raisins, orange peels, candied peel, cherries, and pineapple in the rum overnight. Keep at room temperature covered with plastic wrap.

DAY 2
2. Brush the pans with softened butter and sprinkle wheat flour inside the pans. Shake out the excess flour.
3. Preheat the oven to 340 °F (170 °C).
4. Clean and grate the outer zest of the lemons.
5. Lightly stir the softened butter and sugar with the lemon zest.
6. Add the eggs and yolks (room temperature) one at a time.
7. Sift baking powder and 8.8 oz (250 g) wheat flour into the batter and mix it with a spatula.
8. Blend the fruit with 8.8 oz (250 g) wheat flour so that the fruit is evenly coated.
9. Fill the pans three-fourths full and garnish with shelled almonds on top.
10. Place the pans in the oven and bake them until golden brown, for about 60 minutes. Use a toothpick to make sure that they're ready.
11. Turn them out onto a cooling rack to cool.

STORAGE:
The cakes will keep for weeks, and you can also freeze them.

ROLLCAKES—SWISS ROLLS

Very few cakes have been as mistreated as the roll cake. Swiss Roll is the international name of this pastry, and legend has it that the Swiss created the cake as a mistake.

Our grocery stores are full of Swiss Rolls that will keep for months and are packed with additives and jam of mediocre quality. Try baking real, old-fashioned Swiss Rolls the way I baked them as an apprentice at Blekingborgs Pâtisserie in Malmö. Every morning I made Swiss Rolls using 40 eggs, which became 8 pastries. From every pastry we cut 3 Swiss Roll slices. The filling was mostly raspberry jam and gooseberry jam. A thin layer of good, natural buttercream, with butter, and not margarine, was spread on top so that the pastry wouldn't go soft. They were sold out every single afternoon, and we sold them unpackaged directly to the customer.

The difference between Swiss Rolls and regular tart bottoms is that you do not need as much flour for the Swiss Roll as you usually need for tart bottoms. However, the whisking method is the same. Swiss Rolls are moister and tastier when they are warm-whipped instead of cold-whipped. The little added work this requires is well worth it.

I have featured many Swiss Roll bottoms in by books. Nowadays I mostly fill my Swiss Rolls with rhubarb, strawberry jam, and apple jam with cinnamon. See the jam recipes in my book *The Jam and Marmalade Bible*.

Swiss Roll dough:
4.9 oz (140 g) wheat flour
1.2 oz (35 g) cornstarch
0.3 oz (10 g) baking powder
1 lemon, yellow and ripe
8.8 oz (250 g) egg (approx. 5)
5.8 oz (165) sugar
0.3 oz (10 g) real vanilla sugar

Granulated sugar for sprinkling on the Swiss Rolls

5.3 oz (150 g) vanilla buttercream, see recipe on p.152
5.3 oz (150 g) raspberry jam, see recipe on p.19

1. Preheat the oven to 445 °F (230 °C).
2. Sift wheat flour, cornstarch, and baking powder through a sieve onto parchment paper.
3. Boil a saucepan of water.
4. Clean and grate the zest of the lemon.
5. Whisk eggs, sugar, and lemon zest in a 20 cup (4 liter) metal bowl. Place it in the waterbath and warm-whip until it reaches 113 °F (40 °C) degrees.
6. Whisk the eggs until light and airy, for about 10 minutes, using an electric beater.
7. Fold the flour mixture into the egg foam with a large spatula until you have a light and airy batter.
8. Spread the batter as evenly as possible on a baking sheet lined with parchment paper (alternatively, a Silpat baking mat). Use a straight spatula.
9. Bake the roll until light brown, for 7–8 minutes.
10. Sprinkle granulated sugar on top and cover with parchment paper. Place the Swiss Roll on a cooling rack with the smooth side facing downward. Let cool.
11. Brush the section of the parchment paper the bottom is lying on with a brush dipped in water and let stand for 10 minutes. Carefully pull the paper off. (If you are using a Silpat baking mat, this is not necessary.)
12. Spread 5.3 oz (150 g) vanilla cream on the bottom as soon as it's cooled down and later a layer of raspberry jam or another good jam. It can't be too wet because that will make the cake squishy, and it will lose its texture.
13. Roll together to a tight roll. Let it chill and set in the fridge.

STORAGE:
Swiss Rolls will keep for 1 week in the fridge.

Plumcake

Chocolate Swiss Roll

CHOCOLATE SWISS ROLL *(Dream Tart)*

People would travel far to buy these cakes at Blekingborgs pâtisserie in Malmö. The contrast of the orange marmalade and fine vanilla buttercream in a chocolate swiss roll is as far as you get from the terrifying mass-produced swiss rolls you can buy at the grocery store, which should be known as nightmare tarts instead.

My mother used to make a fantastically good nut swiss roll with whipped cream, chocolate, and banana that she sometimes served with Sunday coffee.

Eat it in pieces directly from the fridge with a nice cup of coffee. I have baked this with plumcake for Christmas. I think a good dream tart works well for the holidays because it keeps for so long. Not to mention the fact that you can freeze it.

8.8 oz (250 g) egg (approx. 5)
0.9 oz (25 g) vanilla sugar
5.3 oz (150 g) sugar
1 oz (30 g) cocoa, preferably Valrhona
0.3 oz (10 g) baking powder
1.2 oz (35 g) cornstarch
3.8 oz (110 g) wheat flour

3.5 oz (100 g) orange marmalade, preferably English Bitter.
See my book *The Jam and Marmalade Bible.*
10.5 oz (300 g) vanilla buttercream, see p.52

Bake the chocolate swiss roll by following the instructions for the classic swiss roll, see p.204.
Spread a thin layer of orange marmalade on the bottom, followed by a layer of buttercream on top.
Roll the swiss roll together and keep it in the fridge.

STORAGE:
Will keep for 1 week in the fridge.

LEMON ROLLS

I baked these light, tart miniature rolls every morning when I was sixteen and an apprentice. Nowadays I sometimes use passionfruit purée instead of the lemon, which is also delicious.

In Switzerland, at the Honold Confiserie in Zurich, you can always find fresh lemon rolls. We made hundreds every day, and it's the same at Georg Maushagen in Düsseldorf, one of Germany's most renowned confectioners.

ABOUT 30 ROLLS

Swiss roll bottom special (for 2 normal baking sheets):
2 pieces of parchment paper, enough to cover the baking sheet
2.1 oz (60 g) unsalted butter
2.6 oz (75 g) wheat flour
2.6 oz (75 g) cornstarch
1/5 oz (7 g) baking powder
8 oz (235 g) eggs (approx. 5)
2.6 oz (75 g) yolks (approx. 4)
6 oz (175 g) sugar
1.7 oz (50 g) granulated sugar to sprinkle on the paper

1 batch passionfruit curd or lemon curd, see p.26
½ batch French buttercream, see p.17
3.5 oz (100 g) powdered sugar to sift on top

1. Preheat the oven to 445 °F (230 °C).
2. Melt the butter in a small saucepan and set it aside.
3. Sift wheat flour, cornstarch, and baking powder through a sieve onto a piece of parchment paper.
4. Whisk eggs, yolk, and sugar in a 20 cup (4 liter) metal bowl.
5. Place the bowl in a water bath with boiling water and warm-whip to 130 °F (55 °C).
6. Remove the bowl from the saucepan and whisk the egg foam until light and airy, about about 10 minutes, using an electric beater or hand mixer.
7. Fold the flour blend into the foam using a large spatula so that you have a light and airy batter.
8. Stir a ladle of the mass into the butter, blend well, and then carefully fold the butter mixture into the egg foam, sugar, and flour mixture.
9. Divide this batter between the two baking sheets lined with parchment paper.
10. Bake the roll bottoms until light brown, for 7–8 minutes.
11. Sprinkle sugar on two pieces of parchment paper on the table. Turn the bottom out onto the parchment paper right out of the oven (use a generous amount of sugar so that the bottoms don't stick to the paper). Let cool for about 30 minutes.
12. Blend the lemon curd or passionfruit curd with the buttercream so that you have a light and airy cream.
13. Brush the underside of the parchment paper with water and let sit for 10 minutes. Carefully peel the paper off. (If you're baking with a Silpat baking mat, this is not necessary.)
14. Spread the curd and buttercream mixture over the bottoms with a straight spatula.
15. Measure with a ruler and divide the bottoms lengthwise with a sharp knife, three strips per bottom.
16. Take 3 new sheets of parchment paper and roll

one strip in each. Roll each one into a tight roll with the help of a ruler. Repeat the procedure until they are all rolled. Wrap tightly in plastic wrap and place them in the freezer to stiffen properly.

17. Take a roll out of the freezer and cut it into 3 ½ inch (9 cm) wide slices, then place a ruler on top and powder powdered sugar over them to create stripes

(see photo). Serve with coffee or tea, or as a side with another dessert.

STORAGE:
These rolls will be fine for weeks in the freezer. Thaw them at room temperature for 15 minutes.

ARRACK GARLAND

When I was a young pastry chef, this pastry could be found at every pâtisserie, and it was great with a cup of coffee. Most gentlemen fell for the punch flavor that the arrack provides. We baked it in Switzerland as well, and there we called it Parisian ring, but there it hasn't disappeared. At Hanold Confiserie in Zurich I still see them in the window every time I pass. In Germany it's called the Frankfurter Garland and at the Konditorei Heinemann in Düsseldorf it shines in the window as well. I hope this book aids the comeback of this lovely pastry.

FOR 12 PEOPLE

TIP!

It's important to blend the melted butter with some of the egg mixture before you fold it into the batter. That way the batter keeps its volume better than if you just add the butter directly. If you add butter to the nougat it will not be as moist as it should be.

Do not heat the butter so long that it becomes too dark either, as the nougat will taste bitter and be moister.

The baking soda makes the nougat lighter and airier, and makes it easier to crush.

2 ring pans that hold 5 cups (1 liter) or 1 pan that holds
  10 cups (2 liter)
0.9 oz (25 g) butter for the pans
Wheat flour for the pans

3.5 oz (100 g) butter
2.6 oz (75 g) wheat flour
2.6 oz (75 g) potato flour
5.3 oz (150 g) eggs (approx. 5)
0.5 oz (15 g) real vanilla sugar
3.8 oz (110 g) sugar

Nougat:
7 oz (200 g) hazelnuts
5.6 oz (160 g) sugar
2.1 oz (60 g) water
0.9 oz (25 g) unsalted butter
¾ tsp (3 g) baking soda

1 cup (2 dl) punch (alternatively dark rum or arrack)
½ batch French buttercream, see p.17

1. Preheat the oven to 355 °F (180 °C).
2. Brush the pans with softened butter. Powder flour in the pan and shake out the flour that doesn't stick.
3. Melt the butter and set it aside.
4. Sift wheat flour and potato flour onto a piece of parchment paper through a sieve.
5. Heat water in a large saucepan. Lightly whisk eggs, yolk, vanilla sugar, and sugar. Place the bowl in a waterbath and whisk until the mixture reaches a temperature of 113 °F (40 °C).
6. Continue mixing until the batter has cooled down and the foam is stiff, preferably using an electric mixer (do not mix at full speed, however, because the batter will lose volume).
7. Fold the wheat flour and potato flour into the batter with a spatula, carefully, so that the batter doesn't lose volume.
8. Stir a ladle of the mixture into the butter, carefully folding it in.

9. Pour the batter into the pans and place them in the oven. Bake for about 25–30 minutes, until they are golden brown. Check with a tip of a knife to make sure that the cakes are ready.
10. Take them out of the oven and let them rest for 5 minutes.
11. Turn out onto a cooling rack and cool.
12. Preheat the oven to 390 °F (200 °C).
13. Roast the hazelnuts. Stir often so that they don't burn. Place the nuts in a kitchen towel and rub the shells off.
14. Heat sugar and water to 245 °F (118 °C), or do a marble test, see p.40.
15. Add the nuts and let them boil with the water and sugar until they start snapping. Stir now and then.
16. Increase the stirring when the sugar starts to whiten and crystalize. Stir quickly until the sugar has turned into a golden-brown caramel.
17. Stir in butter and baking soda.
18. Remove from the stove and put the nougat on a piece of parchment paper to cool down.
19. Crush with a rolling pin.
20. Cut the cake into three equally sized pieces with a bread knife. Brush these pieces with the punch so that they are a little wet.
21. Flavor the buttercream with the remaining punch; the flavor should be pretty intense.
22. Spread a 1 inch (2 cm) thick layer of buttercream on one piece. Place another piece on top and repeat with another layer of cream. Place the last piece on top.
23. Cover the entire pastry with a layer of cream, about ³⁄₁₆ inch (5 mm), with the help of a straight spatula. Chill the cake for 1 hour in the fridge.
24. Take the cake out and let it sit at room temperature for 30 minutes. Sprinkle nougat all around the cake. Sprinkle with one hand and hold the other hand under the cake. The ring should be coated in a generous amount of nougat.

Eat the cake fresh.

SWEDISH COOKIES

When I first started the process of choosing recipes for cookies based on which ones I liked the best, I had a lot of trouble deciding. How many should I include? Or should I write an entire book about cookies? There is so much material that I thought, it that would be no problem at all.

I didn't write a cookie book; instead I decided to include here my absolute favorites. And I'm sure I'll sneak a few cookie recipes into future books as well.

Swedish cookies are really variations on short-crust dough cakes with different flavors and shapes. The quality of the recipe depends on the combination of ingredients: butter, sugar, and flour. Eggs, nuts, and almonds are also important, and there is no basic recipe, even if many use the short-crust dough known as 1-2-3 short-crust dough. This consists of 1 part sugar, 2 parts butter, and 3 parts flour, and it is common to add 1 egg if the dough is to be rolled out. Naturally, there is butter in these cookies, and absolutely no margarine.

Ingredients for cookies:

Butter
Butter should be as fresh as possible and should be unsalted. You may add salt to the recipe for balance. The butter should be room temperature (with very few exceptions) when you mix the dough so that it mixes well with the other ingredients.

Sugar
Most of the recipes use sugar; this results in crispy cookies. Powdered sugar is mostly used for stirred cookie dough, like Strassburgare, which gives it a sandier texture and helps it to bake evenly. The vanilla sugar should be real and not contain vanillin. Brown sugar is also good in cookies and provides a bit of chewiness as well as more character than the granulated sugar. You may, of course, use raw cane sugar for baking cookies.

Flour
For cookies you should use regular all-purpose wheat flour with a low protein content. If, for instance, you wish to substitute some of the wheat flour with potato flour or cornstarch the cookies will be more fragile and crumbly because of the lack of gluten.

Egg
Eggs make the dough easier to roll out; the yolk makes the dough a bit crumblier, while the egg white provides chewiness.

Baking powder
Baking powder mostly consists of 25–30% baking soda, plus tartar and starch. A good baking powder helps the dough rise evenly and doesn't leave an aftertaste.

Baking soda
Baking soda gives a light brown color, and it develops a soda during baking that gives cookies their character. The soda leaves a slight taste that limits its use.

Ammonium carbonate
Also known as "baker's ammonia," it is used for dry pastries, as it produces cookies with large holes inside and large volume. You can smell the ammonia scent during baking.

MIXING COOKIE DOUGHS
Mix the doughs as little as possible when the butter is added so that the dough doesn't get gluey or oily. The ingredients should simply be distributed evenly throughout the dough.

BAKING
Most cookies are baked at 355–390 °F (180– 200 °C), but there are exceptions. For instance, dreams demand a lower temperature so that they don't collapse.

STORAGE
Store them in an airtight container and they will keep for about 6 weeks before they start losing flavor. Well-packaged in the freezer, they can keep for 6 months. Take them out 15 minutes before serving and allow them to thaw.

CLASSIC VANILLA DREAMS

This classic Swedish cookie is a delicacy, if properly baked, light and airy. I have never seen a similar pastry anywhere in the world.

ABOUT 60 COOKIES

10.5 oz (300 g) wheat flour
1 tsp (4 g) ammonium carbonate, or "baker's ammonia"
7.9 oz (225 g) butter
7 oz (200 g) sugar
0.9 oz (25 g) vanilla sugar

Coconut Dreams: Add 2.8 oz (80 g) grated coconut
Nut Dreams: Add (70 g) finely ground roasted hazelnuts
Chocolate Dreams: Take away 1 oz (30 g) wheat flour and substitute with cocoa
For Christmas I usually bake saffron dreams; they are very good as well.

1. Preheat the oven to 300 °F (150 °C).
2. Sift flour with ammonium carbonate onto parchment paper.
3. Blend the softened butter with the sugars and carefully work the flour into a dough.
4. Roll out sticks, about 1 inch (2 cm) wide, with the help of a little wheat flour. Cut pieces of 0.4 oz (11 g) and roll them into round marbles in your hand. Space them out on a baking sheet lined with parchment paper.
5. Bake them until golden brown for 20–25 minutes. If the oven is too hot, the dreams will collapse.

FINNISH STICKS

ABOUT 55 COOKIES

8.8 oz (250 g) butter
2.6 oz (75 g) sugar
10.5 oz (300 g) wheat flour
2.6 oz (75 g) grated almond with shell
Egg wash, see p.47

3.5 oz (100 g) shelled chopped almonds for sprinkling
1.7 oz (50 g) granulated sugar to sprinkle on top

1. Blend the softened butter with sugar, wheat flour, and almonds to a smooth dough.
2. Chill the dough for 1 hour wrapped in plastic wrap.
3. Preheat the oven to 390 °F (200 °C).
4. Weigh the dough in bites of 4.2 oz (120 g). Roll out each piece to finger-thick lengths and place them next to one another.
5. Brush them with egg wash and sprinkle almonds and sugar on top.
6. Cut pieces of 0.4 oz (12 g), 2 inches (55 mm) long. Place them on a baking sheet lined with parchment paper with even spaces in between.
7. Bake them until golden brown for 10–12 minutes.

CINNAMON STICKS

The same dough as for Finnish sticks is rolled out the same way, but sprinkle with cinnamon sugar instead of almond and sugar.

1 batch Finnish sticks, but exchange almond and sugar for cinnamon sugar
3.5 oz (100 g) sugar
0.3 oz (10 g) ground cinnamon

Bake as Finnish Sticks, but blend sugar and cinnamon and sprinkle on top.

COGNAC WREATHS

These tasty cookies are rarely seen today, they are a good fit with the Christmas cookies when you want something extra for the coffee table.

ABOUT 50 WREATHS

7.8 oz (220 g) butter
1.7 oz (50 g) powdered sugar
0.7 oz (2 cl) cognac
15 oz (425 g) wheat flour

1. Blend the softened butter with the sifted powdered sugar, cognac, and wheat flour into a dough. Do not overwork.
2. Wrap it in plastic wrap and leave it in the fridge for 2 hours.
3. Work the dough smooth by hand and weigh out pieces of 4.2 oz (120 g). Roll them as logs with a little wheat flour.
4. Cut each log in 10 pieces. Keep them in the fridge and take them out to divide them by hand so that they don't become warm.
5. Roll out each piece into an 8 inch (20 cm) long rope.
6. Fold it over the middle, twist, and fold it together as a garland.
7. Place the wreaths on baking sheets lined with parchment paper.
8. Continue to pick them from the fridge when you shape the wreaths, and it will go much quicker.
9. Preheat the oven to 390 °F (200 °C).
10. Bake the wreaths until golden brown for about 12 minutes.

OATMEAL COOKIES WITH RAISINS

I used to love these chewy cookies as a child. I had a worse time with the oatmeal.

ABOUT 50 COOKIES

5.6 oz (160 g) butter
5.3 oz (150 g) sugar
3 oz (90 g) oats
3.5 oz (100 g) wheat flour
3.5 oz (100 g) raisins
A pinch (2 g) baking soda

1. Blend the softened butter with the other ingredients into a dough.
2. Weigh dough pieces of 4.2 oz (120 g) and refrigerate them for 30 minutes.
3. Preheat the oven to 355 °F (180 °C).
4. Roll out logs of the dough and cut each length in 10 pieces.
5. Roll the pieces round and space them out on baking sheets lined with parchment paper.
6. Press the cakes down with a fork.
7. Bake them until golden brown for about 12 minutes.

SAND RULADE

These cookies have a strange name, but they taste great. We always baked these at the pastry chef trade school in Uppsala.

ABOUT 50 COOKIES

7.9 oz (225 g butter)
2.1 oz (60 g) powdered sugar
0.9 oz (25 g) cocoa, preferably Valrhona
10.5 oz (300 g) wheat flour
1.7 oz (50 g) almond flakes to roll the logs

1. Blend the softened butter with the sifted powdered sugar and cocoa.
2. Carefully work the wheat flour in the dough. Do not overwork it.
3. Refrigerate the dough for at least 1 hour wrapped in plastic wrap.
4. Work the dough smooth by hand.
5. Divide the dough in the middle and roll out two logs, 1 1/3 inches (35 mm) in diameter.
6. Roll the logs in the almond flakes and place them in the freezer.
7. Preheat the oven to 370 °F (190 °C).
8. Cut slices of 0.4 oz (12 g) with a sharp knife.
9. Place the cakes on the parchment paper and bake them golden brown for about 10 minutes.

DESERT SAND

The king of cookies, in my opinion. This recipe is originally from Tage Hakansson's pâtisserie in Lund. There, Willy Boy was a pastry chef. The cooking of the butter makes a water shortage in the dough that provides a sandy texture. There are many recipes for Desert Sand and most of them contain ammonium carbonate, but these are baked with baking powder instead and not as much sugar as most of the other recipes.

10.5 oz (300 g) butter
7 oz (200 g) sugar
0.3 oz (10 g) real vanilla sugar
13.4 oz (380 g) wheat flour
1 tsp (5g) baking powder

1. Boil the butter in a saucepan until it starts to brown and rise in the pan.
2. Pour it into a metal bowl right away to cool. Place it in the fridge for a couple of hours when it has cooled.
3. Loosen the butter from the bowl by dipping it in warm water, and weigh it. There should be 9 oz (260 g) left.
4. Blend the cold butter with the other ingredients for an even dough without lumps of butter.
5. Refrigerate the dough for 1 hour.
6. Preheat the oven to 355 °F (180 °C).
7. Work the dough smooth by hand and weigh pieces of 4.2 oz (120 g).
8. Roll the pieces out with a little wheat flour and divide each rope in 10 pieces.
9. Space them out standing straight on a baking sheet lined with parchment paper and give them a waist by squeezing with your thumb and index finger.
10. Bake them golden until brown for about 10–12 minutes.

STORAGE:
Store these fragile cookies on their own, and eat as many as you can while they are still fresh.

BORAS GARLANDS

These tasty cookies may be found in the far back of the sugar baking literature. They have a nice and clean flavor, but they should be well-baked so that the almond tastes really roasted.

ABOUT 60 COOKIES

8.8 oz (250 g) butter
2.6 oz (75 g) sugar
0.7 oz (20 g) yolk (approx. 1)
1.7 oz (5 cl) cognac
A pinch (2 g) ammonium carbonate, "baker's ammonia"
13 oz (375 g) wheat flour
Egg wash, see p.47
3.5 oz (100 g) sugar to sprinkle on top
3.5 oz (100 g) almond flakes to sprinkle on top

1. Blend the softened butter with sugar, yolk, and cognac.
2. Sift the wheat flour with the ammonium carbonate into the butter blend and work into dough.
3. Roll the dough in plastic wrap and leave it in the fridge for 2 hours.
4. Preheat the oven to 390 °F (200 °C).
5. Work the dough smooth by hand and roll it out 1/8 inch (3 mm) thick.
6. Cut out bottoms with a smooth cookie cutter, 2 1/3 inches (60 mm) in diameter. Cut a hole in the middle with a smaller cookie cutter, 1 inch (25 mm) in diameter.
7. Place the cookies on a baking sheet lined with parchment paper and brush them with egg wash.
8. Bake the garlands until golden brown for 8–10 minutes.

FRENCH GINGERTHINS

It is with the French gingerthins as with the Finnish sticks—I've never seen any French gingerthins in France (or Finnish sticks in Finland). These are delicious with a piquant contrast of orange peel in the dough that makes them a delicacy on the coffee table or for the glögg party.

ABOUT 60 COOKIES

7.9 oz (225 g) butter
2.6 oz (75 g) powdered sugar
2.6 oz (75 g) brown sugar
1 tsp (5 g) ground cinnamon
½ tsp (3 g) ground ginger
½ tsp (3 g) ground cloves
8.8 oz (250 g) wheat flour
Pinch (1 g) of baking soda
3.5 oz (100 g) whole almonds with shells
1.7 oz (50 g) chopped preserved orange peels

1. Empty the softened butter in a bowl and sift in the powdered sugar. Add the brown sugar and spices.
2. Sift in the flour with the bicarbonate and work together into a smooth dough.
3. Lastly, work in the almonds and orange peels.
4. Shape lengths 1 ¼ inches (3 cm) wide and 2 ½ inches (6 cm) tall.
5. Freeze the lengths for 2 hours.
6. Preheat the oven to 390 °F (200 °C).
7. Cut the gingerthins with a sharp knife, slices of about 0.4 oz (12 g) each, and place them on a baking sheet lined with parchment paper.
8. Bake the until golden brown for about 10 minutes.

Cinnamon Leaves

French Gingerthins

Chateau Cookies

Chocolate Cuts

Vanilla Dreams

Hinterland Bread

Rye Cookies

Oatmeal Cookies with Raisins

Brussel Kex

Butter Stars

Marbled Brussel Kex

Checkers

Piped Wreaths

Finnish Sticks

Desert Sand

Vanilla Arches

Boras Garlands

Strasburgare

Farmer's Cookies

Vanilla Diamonds

Gingerthins

Nut Crusts

Sand Rulade

Currant Cookies

Regents

Kurt Lundgren's
Lemon-Brussel Kex

Checkers

Glass Garlands

Caramel
Bread

Uppakra Cookies

Vanilla Kringles

Cognac Wreaths

Vanilla Hooks

VANILLA DIAMONDS

These fantastically good cookies are almost a vice—once you start baking them you can't stop. I remember an American lady on the cruise ship Saga/Fjord who was absolutely dependent on these cookies, as she called them, which are nothing like American cookies. I remember that she also could eat our chocolate chip cookies in endless amounts, but then she was a sturdy lady.

ABOUT 45 COOKIES

7 oz (200 g) butter
2.5 oz (70 g) powdered sugar
0.3 oz (10 g) real vanilla sugar
0.7 oz (20 g) yolk (approx. 1)
7.9 oz (225 g) wheat flour

1.4 oz (40 g) yolks (approx. 2) to brush the logs
Granulated sugar to roll the yolks in

1. Blend the softened butter with the sifted powdered sugar and vanilla sugar and work the egg yolk in as well.
2. Carefully work in the wheat flour to make a dough, but be careful not to overwork the dough.
3. Weigh pieces of 4.2 oz (120 g) and roll them out with a little wheat flour to 6 inch (15 cm) long logs. Place them in the freezer right away and leave them there for 30 minutes.
4. Whisk the yolks and brush the logs with it. Then roll them in the sugar and place them in the freezer again for 10 more minutes.
5. Preheat the oven to 355 °F (180 °C).
6. Divide each log in 10 pieces and space them out on a baking sheet lined with parchment paper.
7. Make an indent with your thumb in the middle of the cake.
8. Bake them until golden brown for 8–10 minutes.

CURRANT COOKIES

For these nice and tender cookies it is important to use currants and not raisins, as raisins are too large and will burn during baking. If the currants are dry, soak them in a little water and they will turn soft again.

ABOUT 55 COOKIES

10.5 oz (300 g) butter
5.3 oz (150 g) sugar
8.8 oz (250 g) wheat flour
1.7 oz (50 g) potato flour
1 tsp (5 g) baking soda
1.7 oz (50 g) currants

1. Cook the butter as described for Dessert Sand, see p.214.
2. Weigh 8.8 oz (250 g) cooked butter.
3. Add the remaining ingredients and work together into a smooth dough.
4. Refrigerate the dough for 1 hour.
5. Preheat the oven to 370 °F (190 °C).
6. Weigh pieces of 4.2 oz (120 g) and roll them out with the help of a little wheat flour. Divide each length in 10 pieces.
7. Space out on a baking sheet lined with parchment paper and gently press down with a fork.
8. Bake them until golden brown for 8–10 minutes.

CUT CHOCOLATE BREAD

We used to bake mounds of these tasty and easily baked cookies at Olof Viktor's bakery in Glemminge.

ABOUT 45 SLICES

5.3 oz (150 g) butter
2.8 oz (80 g) sugar
0.7 oz (20 g) real vanilla sugar
1/2 lb (240 g) wheat flour
0.7 oz (20 g) cocoa
1 tsp (5 g) baking powder
Egg wash, see p.47

1.7 oz (50 g) almond flakes to sprinkle on top
1.7 oz (50 g) granulated sugar to sprinkle on top

1. Preheat the oven to 355 °F (180 °C).
2. Blend a dough out of all the ingredients.
3. Weigh pieces of 7 oz (200 g) and roll them out to the length of a baking sheet.
4. Place them on baking sheets lined with parchment paper, two on each sheet.
5. Brush the strips with egg wash and sprinkle almonds and sugar on top.
6. Bake the strips until golden brown for about 15 minutes.
7. Cut them in pieces of 0.4 oz (12 g) while they are still warm.

CARAMEL BREAD

This delicious cookie is easy to bake and tastes everything but simple.

ABOUT 60 COOKIES

5.6 oz (160 g) butter
4.6 oz (130 g) sugar
0.3 oz (10 g) real vanilla sugar
2.5 oz (70 g) yellow syrup (1/4 cup)
1 tsp (5 g) baking powder
11 oz (320 g) wheat flour

1. Preheat the oven to 355 °F (180 °C).
2. Blend the softened butter with the other ingredients into a dough. Be careful not to overwork it.
3. Weigh pieces of 7 oz (200 g) and roll them out to the length of a baking sheet.
4. Place the strips on baking sheets lined with parchment paper, two on each sheet.
5. Bake them until golden brown for about 15 minutes.
6. Cut them in pieces of (12 g) right away after taking them out of the oven.

VANILLA HOOKS

These tasty cookies are reminiscent of the Austrian pastry vanilj-kipferli that's eaten for Christmas, but they often contain a little almond flour as well. Sandy texture and wonderfully butter-flavored with real vanilla—is there anything more delicious?

ABOUT 50 COOKIES

8.5 oz (240 g) butter
1.4 oz (40 g) real vanilla sugar
1.3 oz (36 g) wheat flour

Vanilla sugar to roll them in:
5.3 oz (150 g) granulated sugar
0.9 oz (25 g) real vanilla sugar

1. Blend the softened butter with vanilla sugar and flour to form a dough.
2. Refrigerate it for at least 1 hour wrapped in plastic wrap.
3. Preheat the oven to 370 °F (190 °C).
4. Work the dough smooth by hand.
5. Weigh pieces of 4.2 oz (120 g) and roll them out with the help of wheat flour to pen-thick lengths.
6. Divide the lengths in 2 inch (55 mm) long pieces with a sharp knife.
7. Bake them until golden brown for 8–10 minutes.
8. Blend the granulated sugar and vanilla sugar by hand and roll the warm cakes in the vanilla sugar. Be careful so that they don't break.

UPPAKRA COOKIES

These cookies have a sandy and wonderful texture, and the contrast of the good raspberry jam makes them something special. Uppakra is a small community right outside of Lund.

ABOUT 50 COOKIES

7.9 oz (225 g) butter
2.6 oz (75 g) powdered sugar
7.9 oz (225 g) wheat flour
1.9 oz (55 g) potato flour
Egg wash, see p.47
3.5 oz (100 g) raspberry jam, see p.19

3.5 oz (100 g) almond flakes for decorating
Granulated sugar

1. Work the softened butter with sifted powdered sugar, wheat flour, and potato flour into a dough.
2. Wrap the dough in plastic wrap and leave it in the fridge for at least 2 hours.
3. Work the dough smooth and roll it out 1/8 of an inch (3 mm) thick.
4. Cut out circles, 2 1/3 inches (60 mm) in diameter, with a smooth cookie cutter.
5. Place them next to each other and brush the lower half with egg wash.
6. Pipe a small dot of raspberry jam with a papercone, fold the dough over the jam, and pinch the edges together.
7. Brush the top of the cakes with egg wash and sprinkle almonds and sugar on top.
8. Space them out on a baking sheet lined with parchment paper.
9. Bake the cookies golden brown, for about 7–8 minutes.

CINNAMON LEAVES

A wonderful pastry to serve with desserts, especially with apples. These very good cookies are light and crispy thanks to the cinnamon sugar on top and the light dough. Don't make the tips of the leaves too long, as they will only fall apart.

ABOUT 55 COOKIES

7 oz (200 g) butter
5.3 oz (150 g) sugar
1.7 oz (50 g) egg (approx. 1)
10.5 oz (300 g) wheat flour
A pinch (2 g) ammonium carbonate, "baker's ammonia"
Egg wash, see p.47
Cinnamon sugar, see p.62

1. Blend the softened butter with the sugar and stir in the egg.
2. Sift in the wheat flour mixed with the ammonium carbonate. Blend to form a dough, but do not overwork it.
3. Wrap the dough in plastic wrap and leave it in the fridge for 2 hours.
4. Preheat the oven to 370 °F (190 °C).
5. Roll half of the dough out about 1/8 inch (4 mm) thick. Cut the leaves out right away and move them onto baking sheets lines with parchment paper.
6. Continue with the remaining dough until you have all the leaves.
7. Brush the cakes with a thin layer of egg wash.
8. Lift one leaf at a time and dip the brushed side in the cinnamon sugar. Place them back on the sheet.
9. Bake the cookies until golden brown for 8–10 minutes.

PIPED WREATHS

These fantastic tasting cookies are among the finest and best-tasting cookies Sweden has to offer in my opinion. They are made from first-rate ingredients and nothing more. Bake them well so that they are not too light.

ABOUT 45 COOKIES

7 oz (200 g) butter
3.5 oz (100 g) sugar
0.7 oz (20 g) yolk (approx. 1)
8.8 oz (250 g) wheat flour

1. Blend the softened butter with the sugar and the yolk and carefully work the flour into the dough.
2. Refrigerate the dough for 1 hour.
3. Preheat the oven to 370 °F (190 °C).
4. Work the dough smooth by hand and scoop it into a dough piping bag with curly tip 1/3 inch (10 mm) plate.
5. Pipe the dough in strips on a baking table lightly powdered with flour. Carefully bring them together.
6. Divide the strips in 3 inch (8 cm) long pieces and twist them around a finger. Place on a baking sheet lined with parchment paper.
7. Bake the wreaths until golden brown for 8–10 minutes.

RYE CAKES

Personally I enjoy these good, classic Swedish cookies very much, and they also feel healthy.

ABOUT 60 COOKIES

3.5 oz (100 g) butter
4.5 oz (125 g) sugar
0.7 oz (20 g) egg yolk (approx. 1)
6.7 oz (190 g) wheat flour
6.7 oz (190 g) fine rye flour
A pinch (2 g) baking powder

1. Blend the softened butter with sugar and yolk. Sift in the flour varieties blended with the baking powder. Work into a dough.
2. Wrap in plastic wrap and set in the fridge for 2 hours.
3. Preheat the oven to 430 °F (220 °C).
4. Roll the dough out about 1/8 of an inch (3 mm) thick with the help of fine rye flour. Poke the dough with a fork.
5. Cut out round cookies with a cookie cutter, 2 inches (50 mm) in diameter.
6. Space them out on a baking sheet lined with parchment paper and cut out a small hole on one side with a small cookie cutter, ½ inch (15 mm) in diameter.
7. Bake them golden brown for 6–7 minutes.

CLASSIC BRUSSEL KEX

Professionals call this dough 1-3-4 dough because it consists of 1 part powdered sugar, 3 parts butter, and 4 parts wheat flour. The pastries are easy to vary; it is traditional to roll the logs in red sugar, even though you should be careful with coloring in baking. The flavor should be vanilla sugar. Since the dough is very stable it is especially suitable for checkers.

ABOUT 60 COOKIES

2.8 oz (80 g) powdered sugar
0.7 oz (20 g) real vanilla sugar
10.5 oz (300 g) butter
14 oz (400 g) wheat flour

3.5 oz (100 g) granulated sugar
1 drop red food coloring, preferably natural

1. Sift powdered sugar and vanilla sugar and blend with the softened butter.
2. Work the flour into a dough.
3. Wrap in plastic wrap and leave in the fridge for 1 hour.
4. Blend the sugar and color carefully by hand.
5. Work the dough smooth by hand and roll out to form logs, 1 1/3 inch (35 mm) in diameter.
6. Roll the logs in red granulated sugar.
7. Set them in the freezer for about 30 minutes.
8. Preheat the oven to 370 °F (190 F)
9. Cut the lengths in slices of 0.4 oz (12 g) with a sharp knife, and space them out on a baking sheet lined with parchment paper.
10. Bake the cakes until golden brown for about 10 minutes.

CHECKERS

1 batch classic Brussel Kex, see p.223
0.7 oz (20 g) cocoa, preferably Valrhona
Egg wash, see p.47

1. Blend 10 oz (280 g) of the white dough with cocoa.
2. Roll out the chocolate dough to a square, ½ inch (15 mm) thick, and brush it with egg wash.
3. Roll out 10.5 oz (300 g) white dough to an equal square and layer it on top of the chocolate. Leave the plate in the freezer for 10 minutes.
4. Cut out ½ inch (15 mm) wide strips and stick together, light dough against dark.
5. Roll out the remaining light dough, 1/8 of an inch (3 mm) thick, and brush it with egg wash. Cover the layered strips in the dough.
6. Preheat the oven to 370 °F (190 °C).
7. Cut pieces of 0.4 oz (12 g) and space them out on a baking sheet lined with parchment paper.
8. Bake the cakes until golden brown for about 10 minutes.

KURT LUNDGREN'S LEMON BRUSSEL KEX

Kurt was the supervisor at Blekingborgs Konditori when I was an apprentice, and he was a real professional. He had his own ideas about recipes and methods and was very meticulous about our pastries.

ABOUT 65 COOKIES

1 large lemon, yellow and ripe
4.5 oz (125 g) almond paste 50/50
4.2 oz (115 g) butter
7.9 oz (225 g) powdered sugar
0.4 oz (12 g) real vanilla sugar
14 oz (400 g) wheat flour

3.5 oz (100 g) sugar for rolling the logs

1. Clean and grate the outer zest of the lemon.
2. Blend the zest with the almond paste (room temperature) and half of the butter to a smooth batter.
3. Sift in the powdered sugar and vanilla sugar.
4. Add the remaining butter and the wheat flour and work to form a dough. Be careful not to overwork it.
5. Wrap the dough in plastic wrap and refrigerate for about 1 hour.
6. Work the dough smooth by hand and divide it at the middle. Roll it out to form two logs, 1 1/3 inches (35 mm) in diameter, with the help of a little wheat flour.
7. Roll the logs in the granulated sugar and place them in the freezer.
8. Preheat the oven to 370 °F (190 °C)
9. Cut pieces of 0.4 oz (12 g) with a sharp knife.
10. Space out on a baking sheet lined with parchment paper and bake them until golden brown for 10–12 minutes.

STRASSBURGERS

The classic Strassburger dough is called pipe short-crust dough in Germany and Switzerland, and that is precisely what this is. Since you whip the butter light and airy, the dough will get a pipeable and sandy texture. Many piped out rings of the dough were stuck together with nougat or truffle. Or they were baked as shells that were stuck in pairs with raspberry jam, and then dipped in chocolate. Yes, the varieties of this tasty dough are many. If you want to make a chocolate Strassburger, then exchange 1.7 oz (50 g) of the wheat flour for cocoa.

3.8 oz (110 g) powdered sugar
0.5 oz (15 g) real vanilla sugar
8.8 oz (250 g) butter
1.7 oz (50 g) egg (approx. 1)
0.7 oz (20 g) yolk (approx. 1)
13 oz (375 g) wheat flour

1. Sift powdered sugar and vanilla sugar and stir it until light and airy with the softened butter.
2. Add eggs and yolk while stirring and sift in the wheat flour. Blend to a smooth, but not chewy, dough.
3. Pipe the dough as a curvy S of 0.4 oz (12 g) with curly tip no. 12.
4. Preheat the oven to 390 °F (200 °C).
5. Bake the cakes until golden brown for 8 minutes.

KURT LUNDGREN'S STRASSBURGERS

Kurt Lundgren preferred his Strassburgers without the eggs, and they obtain a sandier texture for sure. We piped them as rosettes with a curly tip and piped raspberry jam in the middle.

ABOUT 65 COOKIES

3.5 oz (100 g) powdered sugar
0.5 oz (15 g) real vanilla sugar
10.5 oz (300 g) butter
13 oz (375 g) real wheat flour

3.5 oz (100 g) raspberry jam, see p.19

1. Preheat the oven to 390 °F (200 °C).
2. Sift powdered sugar and vanilla sugar and stir it until light and airy with the softened butter.
3. Carefully fold in the sifted wheat flour to make a dough that is not overworked.
4. Scoop the dough into a decorating bag with curly tip no. 12.
5. Pipe rosettes of 0.4 oz (12 g) on baking sheets lined with parchment paper and push a small indent in the middle with the index finger.
6. Pipe a small spot of raspberry jam with the help of a papercone.
7. Bake the cakes until golden brown for 8–10 minutes.

CHATEAU COOKIES

We baked these delicious cookies at Conditori Lundagard in Lund.

ABOUT 50 COOKIES

6 oz (175 g) almond paste 50/50
6 oz (175 g) butter
8.8 oz (250 g) wheat flour
0.7 oz (20 g) yolk (approx. 1)
½ tsp (2.5 g) ground ginger
0.3 oz (7.5 g) ground cinnamon
0.3 oz (7.5 g) cocoa

3.5 oz (100 g) grated almonds with shells to roll the
    lengths in

1. Preheat the oven to 390 °F (200 °C)
2. Dissolve the almond paste (room temperature) with
   the cold butter to form a batter without lumps.
3. Add the remaining ingredients and work to form a
   dough. Be careful not to overwork it.
4. Divide the dough in half and roll out two logs, 1 inch
   (25 mm) in diameter, with the help of wheat flour.
5. Roll the logs in the grated almonds and place them in
   the freezer.
6. Cut cookies of 0.4 oz (12 g) and space them out on a
   baking sheet lined with parchment paper.
7. Bake until golden brown for 8–10 minutes.

FARMER'S COOKIES

It won't be easy to let these tasty cookies sit in the
cookie jar. Well baked farmer's cookies are always
good. If you add 3.5 oz (100 g) chopped dark chocolate to the dough, they will be like American chocolate
chip cookies; but now we're baking Swedish cookies,
not American.

ABOUT 80 COOKIES

7 oz (200 g) butter
7 oz (200 g) sugar
3.7 oz (105 g) light syrup
12.3 oz (350 g) wheat flour
1 tsp (5g) baking soda
5.3 oz (150 g) chopped almonds in shells

1. Blend the softened butter with sugar and syrup.
2. Sift in the wheat flour mixed with the baking soda and
   blend everything to a smooth dough.
3. Lastly, add the almonds.
4. Wrap in plastic wrap and leave it in the fridge for
   1 hour.
5. Work the dough smooth by hand and divide it in
   4 equal parts.
6. Roll the parts out to logs, 1 1/3 inch (35 mm) diameter,
   with the help of wheat flour.
7. Leave them in the freezer for 1 hour to stiffen.
8. Preheat the oven to 370 °F (190 °C).
9. Cut slices of 0.4 oz (12 g) with a sharp knife and space
   them out on a baking sheet lined with parchment
   paper.
10. Bake until golden brown for about 10–12 minutes.

VANILLA KRINGLES

These vanilla flavored kringles are good old-fashioned cookies—fragile and lovely.

Parfait-dough for vanilla kringles
6 oz (175 g) butter
1.7 oz (50 g) powdered sugar
0.5 oz (15 g) real vanilla sugar
8.8 oz (250 g) wheat flour

Vanilla glaze:
3.5 oz (100 g) water
7 oz (200 g) powdered sugar
0.9 oz (25 g) vanilla sugar

1. Blend the softened butter with 1.7 oz (50 g) powdered sugar and 0.5 oz (15 g) vanilla sugar.
2. Carefully work in the wheat flour to form a dough.
3. Wrap the dough in plastic wrap and refrigerate it for 1 hour.
4. Weigh pieces of 4.2 oz (120 g) and roll them out as lengths. Cut each length in 10 pieces and leave them in the fridge for another 30 minutes.
5. Preheat the oven to 370 °F (190 °C)
6. Shape the dough as kringles (see p.217) and space them out on a baking sheet lined with parchment paper.
7. Bake them until golden brown for 8 minutes.
8. Stir powdered sugar and vanilla sugar together with the warm water to make a smooth glaze.
9. Dip the kringles directly in the glaze and let them drain off on a cooling rack.
10. Lift the cakes onto parchment paper to cool.

HINTERLAND BREAD

Delicious cookies that should be sufficiently baked so that the nut flavors are apparent.

6.7 oz (190 g) butter
4.8 oz (135 g) sugar
0.3 oz (10 g) real vanilla sugar
0.5 oz (15 g) egg white (approx. ½)
0.9 oz (25 g) cornstarch
10 oz (280 g) wheat flour
5.3 oz (150 g) roasted hazelnuts

1. Blend the softened butter with the sugars and add the egg white.
2. Carefully work in the wheat flour and the cornstarch to make a dough.
3. Lastly, work in the whole hazelnuts.
4. Divide the dough in pieces of 7.8 oz (220 g) and roll them out to 1/8 of an inch (3 mm) thick logs. Flatten them with a ruler.
5. Leave them in the freezer to stiffen.
6. Preheat the oven to 370 °F (190 °C).
7. Cut each length in 20 pieces and space them out on a baking sheet lined with parchment paper.
8. Bake them until golden brown for 10–12 minutes.

REGENTS

This is an old classic that requires a really good almond paste and a good raspberry jam.

ABOUT 50 COOKIES

7 oz (200 g) almond paste 50/50
7 oz (200 g) butter
7 oz (200 g) wheat flour
1.7 oz (50 g) almond flakes to roll the logs in

3.5 oz (100 g) raspberry jam, see p.19

1. Blend the almond paste (room temperature) and softened butter, a little at a time, to form a mass without lumps.
2. Carefully add the flour and blend to form short-crust dough.
3. Refrigerate the dough for at least 2 hours wrapped in plastic wrap.
4. Divide the dough in 3 pieces of 7 oz (200 g) that you roll out as logs, 1 inch (30 mm) in diameter.
5. Roll the logs in crushed almond flakes.
6. Freeze the logs for 1 hour.
7. Preheat the oven to 370 °F (190 °C).
8. Cut cookies of 0.4 oz (11 g) with a sharp knife. Space them out on a baking sheet lined with parchment paper.
9. Make an indent in the middle and pipe a small dot of raspberry jam in it, ½ tsp (2–3 g).
10. Bake the cookies until golden brown, 8–10 minutes.

LITTLE STARS

I have baked these as rounds instead—the stars break so easily.

ABOUT 50 COOKIES

1.7 oz (50 g) powdered sugar
8.8 oz (250 g) butter
8.8 oz (250 g) wheat flour
1.7 oz (50 g) whipping cream, 40 % (¼ cup)
Egg wash, see p.47
1.7 oz (50 g) chopped shelled almonds for decorating
1.7 oz (50 g) granulated sugar for decorating.

1. Sift the powdered sugar and carefully blend with the softened butter and wheat flour.
2. Work the cream in the batter to form a dough. Be careful not to overwork it.
3. Wrap in plastic wrap and refrigerate for 2 hours.
4. Roll the dough out 1/8 of an inch (3 mm) thick with the help of a little wheat flour.
5. Cut out stars with a cookie cutter and brush them with egg wash.
6. Sprinkle almonds and sugar on top.
7. Let the cakes rest for 1 hour on a baking sheet.
8. Preheat the oven to 390 °F (200 °C).
9. Bake the cakes until golden brown for 12 minutes.

GLASS KRINGLES

These delicious kringles are so crisp and tasty that it's hard not to eat them all at once. The recipe is quite large, but they are good enough that it's not really a good idea to make less, even if you can easily make half a batch.

ABOUT 80 COOKIES

11.5 oz (325 g) butter
15 oz (425 g) wheat flour
1 tsp (5g) ammonium carbonate, "baker's ammonia"
12.3 oz (350 g) whipping cream, 40% (approx. 1 ¾ cup)
Egg wash, see p.47
Granulated sugar for decorating

1. Sift wheat flour and ammonium carbonate, and blend it with the softened butter to a batter without lumps.
2. Quickly work the heavy cream into the batter for a smooth dough. Be careful not to overwork it.
3. Wrap in plastic wrap and leave it in the fridge for 2 hours.
4. Roll the dough out 1/8 of an inch (4 mm) thick and 5 inches (12 cm) wide.
5. Cut out strips that weigh 0.4 oz (12 g) and twist them as a kringle.

6. Set them close to each other on baking sheets lined with parchment paper. Continue until all the kringles are ready.
7. Carefully brush them with egg wash and sprinkle some sugar on top of each kringle.
8. Preheat the oven to 430 °F (220 °C)
9. Bake the kringles golden brown for 7–8 minutes (watch the cookies closely, they burn easily).

BUTTER COOKIES

Awfully delicious cookies. The dough is the same as for glass kringles, but the cakes are sprinkled with almond flakes and pearl sugar instead of granulated sugar.

1. Roll the dough out 3/16 inch (5 mm) thick and cut out round rings, 2 inches (50 mm) in diameter. Cut a hole in the middle, ¾ of an inch (20 mm) in diameter.
2. Brush the garlands with egg wash and sprinkle almond flakes and pearl sugar on top.
3. Bake them golden brown in 390 °F (200 °C), about 10 minutes.

BAKING POWDER CRUSTS

These classic crusts that my mother and grandmother served with rose hip soup and fruit cream may either be baked naturally or flavored with cardamom. They are also sometimes called yeast powder crusts.

Baking powder crusts were baked in large batches each week and packaged in bags of 3.5 oz (100 g), while most other cookies were sold by weight.

ABOUT 120 HALVES

4.5 oz (125 g) butter
6 oz (175 g) sugar
3.5 oz (100 g) eggs (approx. 2)
4.5 oz (125 g) milk 3%
17.6 oz (500 g) wheat flour
0.9 oz (25 g) baking powder
0.7 oz (20 g) roughly ground cardamom

1. Preheat the oven to 390 °F (200 °C).
2. Stir the softened butter in with the sugar.
3. Add the eggs (room temperature) one at the time while stirring.
4. Carefully stir in the milk (room temperature) so that the batter doesn't separate (if eggs and milk are cold, the dough will separate right away and become impossible to bake).
5. Sift in the wheat flour with the baking powder and add the cardamom. Work to form a dough.
6. Divide the dough in pieces of 5.3 oz (150 g) and roll out lengths with the help of a little wheat flour on the baking table.
7. Divide each length in 10 pieces.
8. Brush the rolls with egg wash.
9. Bake them golden brown for 10–12 minutes.
10. Take them out and divide them in half with a fork. Place the halves with the cut side facing upwards.
11. Lower the temperature to 300 °F (150 °C).
12. Dry the crusts until golden brown.

Store the crusts dry in a jar.

NUT CRUSTS

These tasty crusts were among the first cakes I ever baked, and they are just as good today as they were back then. I used to take the edge bits home with me.

Try to get a hold of Italian hazelnuts from Piedmont, or Spanish hazelnuts. They taste so much better than the Turkish hazelnuts, in my opinion.

ABOUT 120 CRUSTS

7 oz (200 g) butter
7 oz (200 g) sugar
0.3 oz (10 g) real vanilla sugar
3.5 oz (100 g) eggs (approx. 2)
3.5 oz (100 g) milk 3 % (approx. ½ cup)
17.6 oz (500 g) wheat flour
0.2 oz (7 g) ammonium carbonate
7 oz (200 g) hazelnuts
Egg wash, see p.47

1. Preheat the oven to 390 °F (200 °C).
2. Stir the softened butter in with the sugar.
3. Add the eggs (room temperature) one at a time while stirring.
4. Add the milk (room temperature) and stir.
5. Sift the wheat flour and ammonium carbonate into the butter mass. Blend to form a dough.
6. Lastly, mix in the hazelnuts without overworking it.
7. Weigh pieces of 7 oz (200 g) and roll them to the length of a baking sheet.
8. Place two lengths on each baking sheet lined with parchment paper and brush with egg wash.
9. Bake the lengths for 18–20 minutes.
10. Cut them in slanted pieces of 0.5 oz (15 g) with a sharp knife while they are still warm.
11. Lower the temperature to 300 °F (150 °C).
12. Set them on the sheet standing up and roast them golden brown in the oven for 2 minutes.

Store the crusts dry so that they stay crisp longer.

GINGERTHINS

These tasty gingerthins are easy to bake and to roll, and they taste like real gingerthins should taste. The dough is also suitable for making gingerbread houses, since it maintains its shape during baking.

The gingerbread house on page 231 is in Swiss style, but I won't leave a drawing for it, because you should always make gingerbread houses using your own creativity. I vary the design every year, as it is more fun that way.

38.8 oz (1100g) wheat flour
0.4 oz (12 g) ground ginger
0.4 oz (12 g) ground cloves
0.7 oz (20 g) ground cinnamon
Pinch (2 g) ground allspice
0.5 oz (15 g) bicarbonate
10.5 oz (300 g) butter
14.8 oz (420 g) light syrup
7 oz (200 g) granulated sugar
7 oz (200 g) brown sugar
10.5 oz (300 g) whipping cream 40%

1. Sift the wheat flour with all of the spices and the bicarbonate in a bowl.
2. Add the softened butter and the other ingredients. Work to form a dough.
3. Wrap the dough in plastic wrap and leave it in the fridge overnight.
4. Preheat the oven to 390 °F (200 °C).
5. Roll the dough out thinly with the help of a little wheat flour and a rolling pin, and cut out various shapes.
6. Space them out on baking sheets lined with parchment paper and brush them with milk.
7. Bake the gingerthins until golden brown, about 8–10 minutes depending on size.

Almond Mussels

ALMOND MUSSELS

These fantastic tasting almond mussels are almost impossible to stop eating. The
recipe is from a vicarage in Tomelilla, where my mother worked when she was young.

ABOUT 60 COOKIES

60 almond mussel cups

15 oz (425 g) butter
15 oz (425 g) sugar
3.5 oz (100 g) eggs (approx. 2)
5.3 oz (150 g) finely chopped, shelled almonds
1.7 oz (50 g) finely ground bitter almonds
1 tsp (5g) salt
15 oz (425 g) wheat flour

DAY 1
1. Leave the butter out so that it reaches room temperature. Blend all of the ingredients to form a dough. Be
   careful not to overwork it.
2. Wrap it in plastic wrap. Leave it in the fridge overnight.

DAY 2
3. Preheat the oven to 355 °F (180 °C).
4. Roll the dough out 1/8 of an inch (3 mm) thick and line
   the cups by rolling the dough onto the rolling pin and
   later rolling it over the closely gathered mussel cups.
5. Powder flour on top and press the dough in the cups
   with a piece of dough.

Klenäter

6. Roll over the dough with a rolling pin and squeeze the dough upward along the walls of the cups. Place them on a baking sheet lined with parchment paper.
7. Bake them until golden brown, 12–15 minutes.
8. Knock them out of the cups and continue baking until you've used the entire dough.

KLENATER—FRIED PASTRY

The people from Skane call these Klenor, and the variations of the dough are many, from thin and crisp to thick. This recipe is for the best klenater I've ever tasted, and I hope you agree. They are airy and light with a clear lemon flavor.

ABOUT 45 KLENATER OF 1.4 OZ (40 G)

1 large lemon, yellow and ripe
5.3 oz (150 g) butter
1.7 oz (50 g) whipping cream 40 % (approx. ¼ cup)
0.8 oz (2.5 cl) cognac
1.7 oz (50 g) egg (approx. 1)
2.8 oz (80 g) yolks (approx. 4)
5.3 oz (150 g) powdered sugar
1 tsp (5 g) salt
16 oz (450 g) wheat flour
0.5 oz (15 g) baking powder

5 cups (1 liter) frying oil
Sugar

DAY 1
1. Clean the lemon and grate the outer zest very fine.
2. Melt the butter in a saucepan and set aside. Add cream and cognac.
3. Whisk eggs, yolks, zest, sugar, and salt to stiff peaks, for 5 minutes.
4. Sift wheat flour and baking powder into the egg foam and stir. Add the butter blend and work to form a dough. Be careful not to overwork it.
5. Wrap the dough in plastic wrap and refrigerate overnight.
DAY 2
6. Roll the dough out 1/8 of an inch (3 mm) thick and cut out lengths the width of a ruler with a pastry cutter. Cut out klenater a little slanted and make an incision in the middle of each one. They should weigh about 1.4 oz (40 g)
7. Fold one of the tips through the holes in the middle and drag it through to shape a klenat. Place them on parchment dusted with wheat flour and let them stiffen in the fridge.
8. Warm oil to 355 °F (180 °C) and fry the klenater golden brown in batches. Let them drain on a cooling rack and roll them in the granulated sugar.

STORAGE:
Feel free to freeze these after they've cooled down. Take them out of the freezer 30 minutes before serving and they are good as new.

INDEX

CANAPÉS AND BUTTERFLIES

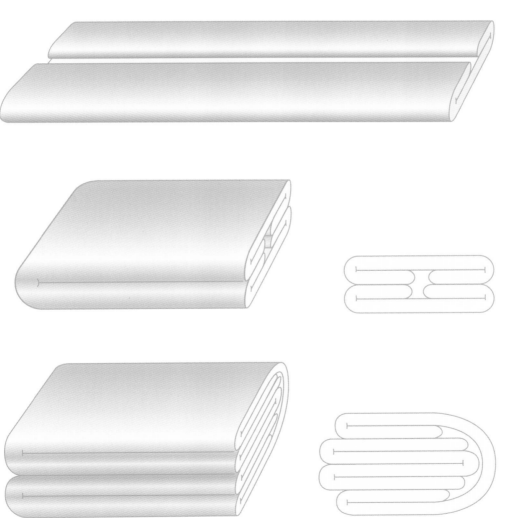

CLASSIC SWEDISH BAKERY